THE

NeXT

DISTRIBUTING INDEPENDENT
FILMS AND VIDEOS

STeP

Morrie Warshawski

EDITOR

FIVF

FOUNDATION
FOR INDEPENDENT
VIDEO AND FILM

A PUBLICATION OF THE FOUNDATION FOR INDEPENDENT VIDEO AND FILM, INC.

The Foundation for Independent Video and Film (FIVF) is supported in part through the generous contributions of the Center for Arts Criticism, Con Edison, The John D. and Catherine T. MacArthur Foundation, National Endowment for the Arts, National Video Resources, New York City Department of Cultural Affairs, The New York Community Trust, New York State Council on the Arts, the Rockefeller Foundation, The Andy Warhol Foundation for the Visual Arts, Inc., and the members and friends of the Association of Independent Video and Filmmakers.

Special thanks to the Florian Loan Fund of the Funding Exchange and the National Endowment for the Arts Challenge Grant Program.

The publishers, authors, and copyright owners do not assume liability to any party for loss or damage caused by possible errors or omissions in this book, whether such errors or omissions result from accident or any other cause. Neither do they endorse any organization or individual listed in this book nor assume any liability for loss or damage resulting from dealing with the organizations and individuals listed herein.

The Foundation for Independent Video and Film, Inc. (FIVF) is a nonprofit, tax-exempt educational foundation dedicated to the promotion of video and film. FIVF publishes *The Independent*, the leading monthly magazine on issues of concern to the field. It is affiliated with the Association of Independent Video and Filmmakers (AIVF), the largest association of independent media makers in the country. AIVF provides a range of programs and services to the field including access to health and production insurance; trade and publication discounts; informational and educational programs and seminars; and national legislative advocacy.

For AIVF membership information:
Association of Independent Video and Filmmakers
304 Hudson Street, 6th Floor
New York, NY 10013
(212) 807-1400 tel
(212) 463-8519 fax
aivffivf@aol.com

AIVF/FIVF staff: Ruby Lerner, executive director; Pamela Calvert, director of programs and services; Susan Kennedy, resource/development director; Leslie Singer, director of administration; Patricia Thomson, editor, *The Independent*; Sue Young Wilson, managing editor, *The Independent*; Laura D. Davis, advertising director, *The Independent*; Johnny McNair, information services coordinator; Leslie Fields, membership coordinator; Judah Friedlander, membership associate; Cleo Cacoulidis, advocacy associate; Lisa Smith, resource/development assistant; Adam Knee, editorial assistant, *The Independent*.

RUBY LERNER
Executive Director

PAMELA CALVERT
Project Coordinator

DANIEL CHRISTMAS
Design

ISBN 0-9622448-1-3

I t is with great pride that the Foundation for Independent Video and Film (FIVF) and the Association of Independent Video and Filmmakers (AIVF) present the second edition of *The Next Step: Distributing Independent Films and Videos*. We felt it was critical to publish this new guide, given how dramatically the media landscape has altered since it was first published in 1989. Since that time, *The Next Step* has been widely utilized by independent makers throughout the country. The book is of value to makers interested in self-distribution as well as those interested in obtaining a distributor.

AIVF/FIVF has a commitment to collect, organize, and disseminate information that helps to create opportunities for independent media producers. We do this in a number of ways: through our ongoing advocacy efforts, our popular magazine, *The Independent Film and Video Monthly*, our resource library, workshops and seminars, and through our book publication program. In addition to *The Next Step*, this fall we are also pleased to publish new editions of *The AIVF/FIVF Guide to International Film and Video Festivals* and *The AIVF/FIVF Guide to Film and Video Distributors*. Taken together, these three volumes create a comprehensive library of distribution resources.

We would like to thank Morrie Warshawski, the editor of *The Next Step*, for his diligent work on this important publication. We would also like to extend our gratitude to all of the writers, who did a terrific job in communicating their personal wealth of experience and information in a clear, engaging fashion.

I want to especially thank Pamela Calvert, Director of Programs and Services, for her tireless efforts to ensure the most accurate and complete information possible, and our designer, Daniel Christmas, for his inventiveness and vision.

We hope you find this volume helpful, and would appreciate hearing from you as we plan both for its next edition, and for other future AIVF/FIVF publications.

— Ruby Lerner
Executive Director, AIVF/FIVF
Fall 1995

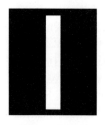magine, if you can, a world where computers are not omnipresent; a world where programs are shot on 16mm film and distributed almost exclusively in 16mm to a limited number of markets providing a high margin of profit for filmmakers with each sale. This is the universe that was already disappearing when the first edition of *The Next Step* was originally commissioned, in 1988—a simpler, slower, and more profitable place.

Many of the chapters in that first edition were submitted in hard copy format by writers still working on electric (or correcting Selectric) typewriters. The words "Internet," "multimedia," "CD-ROM" and "e-mail" were nowhere to be found either in my dictionary, or in my conversations with filmmakers. With this edition, *every* chapter in the book was created using word-processing software on a computer and then submitted in digital form, either on a disk or via e-mail.

In just seven short years a profound revolution has taken place in the ways we gather, create, disseminate, and view information. No one can know what the next seven years will bring, but I can say the following with a great deal of certainty: filmmakers will continue to experience constant, exponentially increasing change that propels them toward an ever more unpredictable future.

For interdependent independent filmmakers the art of distribution has morphed into a blurry moving target approaching the speed of light. That is why as you read this new edition of *The Next Step* you will notice that it has been greatly expanded, that only four chapters have reappeared (completely re-written), and that there are twelve new chapters and authors. That also explains why I have worked with all the authors to create chapters chock-full of both practical and philosophical advice—advice for today and for a chaotic tomorrow.

I hope you will be surprised and pleased by what awaits you in the following chapters. All the authors have brought their years of experience to bear on shaping words into sentences and paragraphs that will speak directly to filmmakers in the field who struggle valiantly to create important new works—features, documentaries, video art—that will actually get seen by their intended audience and make a difference in the world.

The book is structured to cover all the most important aspects of distribution—methods, markets, and formats. Any one chapter could easily become a whole book on its own, so the authors and I have attempted to strike a balance of information that is more than just introductory, but not exhaustive. Because my experience shows that filmmakers cannot hear these maxims too frequently, I have let stand a number of threads that appear over and over again in many chapters, including the following:

- think about distribution early and often, and talk to distributors during pre-production,
- have a professional photographer take good production stills,
- never underestimate the power and importance of press coverage, and
- set aside adequate financial resources for distribution and include these funds in your budget.

The other new theme in these chapters concerns the advent of new technologies and the looming emergence of technologies not yet known. Today a filmmaker might shoot in 16mm, then edit in video, and distribute in 16mm, 35mm, any number of video formats, on laser disk, and/or on CD-ROM. Tomorrow that same filmmaker might be shooting digitally, editing digitally in a non-linear format, and then distributing over telephone lines through the Internet throughout the world. This means rethinking potential markets, reconsidering production plans, and, sometimes, rewriting distribution contracts.

Quite often a filmmaker will begin a project infused by a compulsive commitment and with the following phrase as a mantra: "This is a story that must be told!" From a filmmaker's perspective, this is absolutely true. However, from a distributor's point of view, there exists a more salient consideration: "Is this a story that must be heard or seen?" This edition of *The Next Step* has been designed to help you answer that question and create a healthy, vibrant, and long life for your projects that will ensure that once your story is told it will actually get seen and heard.

Many, many thanks to the filmmakers whose work compelled the creation of this book; to the wonderfully generous authors who toiled under my many revision requests to create the following chapters; to Pam Calvert, who added this book to an already heavy workload and gave it the kind of heartfelt energy and meticulous attention every publication should get; to our proofreader, Graham Leggat; and to AIVF/FIVF, an organization that took a great risk to create this new edition, and which daily puts the well-being of interdependent independent filmmakers at the top of its agenda.

— Morrie Warshawski, Editor

HOW TO CHOOSE A DISTRIBUTOR (AND NOT CRY YOURSELF TO SLEEP AFTER THE FIRST YEAR)

Debra Zimmerman

ost independent producers think of distribution as the step following the end of production. Once they have finished the arduous task of raising the money, gone in and out of production, struck a couple of prints, and/or dubbed their first batch of tapes, they are delighted to look around a bit and then hand their programs over to (hopefully) reputable distributors and be done with it. Well, that is one way of working. However, if you are really interested in the best distribution for your independent production, there is a better way.

My suggestions are geared primarily to producers of social issue documentaries—media that aim to educate others about a certain topic—and to theatrical film producers. For experimental filmmakers and video artists the options are much more limited, so the process is different. For those producers, I have included a short section, "How to Make a Distributor Find You," at the end of this chapter.

DO I NEED A DISTRIBUTOR?

The first question to seriously consider is whether you need a distributor. In the last five to seven years, the market for independent films and videotapes has dramatically changed. The primary difference is that traditional markets have greatly expanded and fragmented. Although the extensive use of videotape and the entry of multimedia formats have brought new audiences to independent film, this also means that it is much more expensive and difficult to reach those markets. Most nontheatrical distributors are still firmly rooted in the university market, which still has the largest numbers of proven media users with the budget to purchase at institutional prices.

Although every film has a potential audience—even if it is made up of your family—not every film has a market. Remember that it is the cost of marketing a film to its audience that makes it difficult to distribute. The reality is that unless you can think of a college class that is going to use your film/tape, utilizing an educational distributor may not be the best route for you. And unless your film has true box office potential, theatrical distributors will not be interested in acquiring your film. At Women Make Movies, we often get submissions that we know we would not be able to effectively market at institutional prices. Some documentaries may be best suited to home video distribution through placement in a number of catalogs that reach individuals interested in a particular subject area. For short dramas—and in particular the calling-card films that film students are encouraged to make—festival exposure is probably the most appropriate distribution. That type of distribution is best done by the filmmaker.

LEARNING ABOUT MARKET POTENTIAL AND WHEN TO START LOOKING FOR A DISTRIBUTOR

Relationships with distributors and the process of finding a good distributor should begin when the film is but a concept in a maker's mind. There are many important advantages to beginning the process early, not least of which is that the task of finding a distributor later will be much easier. First, it is critical to get a realistic idea of the market potential for your proposed project. Distributors are an excellent source of this information. It is important to find out if there have been other films or tapes made on the same subject and if your proposed project is really needed. For example, if the market is completely glutted with films and tapes on abortion rights, then most new productions are almost undistributable, unless they have an original perspective or cover an area that has not been explored previously. You should also find out whether your proposed treatment (length, format of production, etc.) is appropriate for the market you will be trying to reach. There is little need to worry that distributors will steal your idea. Few distributors have production divisions and those that do usually have separate staff dealing with acquisitions.

Another reason to contact distributors early in the project's life is that it will assist you in the fundraising process. Foundations have come to understand that there is no purpose in funding a production that will not reach its intended audience. Fundraising proposals should include a distribution plan and letters of support from interested distributors. Another financial reason to contact a distributor while in production is that some distributors will be able to advance post-production costs (e.g., financing an internegative or a film-to-tape transfer). Developing a relationship early with a distributor will increase your chances of finding this source of financing. Distributors are also excellent people to use for looking at rough cuts, especially if you want a fairly candid opinion of the changes you may have to make for more successful distribution.

Finally, it is important to know distributors' release schedules. Contacting distributors early means that they can plan for space in their next catalog or tell you deadlines for key festivals and important media reviewers. Most educational distributors print their catalogs for release in September, which means that they are at the printer in August. There's nothing more frustrating that receiving a really good submission in August or September!

WHY DISTRIBUTE, OR, WHAT AM I GOING TO GET OUT OF THIS?

I always tell filmmakers that there are three things they can get out of distribution— fame, fortune, and a good conscience (making sure the work reaches its intended audience). Few, if any, producers are going to get really famous or rich, but it is possible to attain some income and exposure from distribution. You may not have to choose one over the other, but it is important for you to have a sense of your priorities. For many independent producers the key factor is how much money they are going to make. It would make sense that the more money you make, the more your production will be seen. That may be true, if the people who buy your program are primarily universities, which generally pay the most for purchasing media. However, this may mean that the small folk, like grassroots activists and community groups, may never get to see your program. Often, large distributors with the best connections to traditional educational markets do not do the type of marketing that will assure the use of your production on a grassroots level.

On the other hand, the amount of money some films/tapes will make in educational distribution may be small compared to the impact good exposure can have on an independent producer's ability to get the next grant or find a television buyer for their next film. In that case, you may want a distributor who is actively engaged in 16mm distribution, who will enter the film in festivals, preview it for free to media centers and museums, and send it to critics and reviewers. Whichever way you order your priorities, the first criteria for selecting a distributor should be how well they meet those priorities.

HOW TO FIND A DISTRIBUTOR

After you have given your priorities some thought, the time is ripe for making a decision about which distributor is right for you. If you have taken my advice already and begun talking to distributors throughout production, you will already have a list. If not, there are a number of resources you can use—AIVF/FIVF's *Guide to Film & Video Distributors*, and the Bay Area Video Coalition's annual list of video distributors (included in their newsletter, *Video Networks*). The National Educational Media Network (formerly the National Educational Film and Video Festival) is publishing a guide to distributors as well. Their media market, which takes place in May each year in Oakland, provides good exposure and contacts for titles appropriate for the educational market. Other good sources are festival catalogs, and other producers of films/tapes similar to your own.

HOW TO CHOOSE THE RIGHT DISTRIBUTOR

In many ways, signing a contract with a distributor is like getting married or hiring a baby-sitter. Trust is the most important element for a good relationship. But there are other important criteria by which you can judge prospective distributors:

Track Record and Reputation. Talk to a variety of users about the distributor: programmers, theater bookers, festival directors, university faculty, librarians, or local media art center staff. Ask what they know about various distributors. Do they send films/tapes out on time? Do they send publicity materials? Is their staff professional? Find out from the distributors themselves how long they have been in business. Contact other producers who are represented by the distributor. Do not get a list from the distributor unless you want to speak only to the producers that are the happiest. Look at the distributor's catalog and pick out the producers who have films most similar to yours. Questions you should ask include: Are their royalty statements detailed? How often do they communicate with their producers? Do they send copies of reviews? Are they open to suggestions from producers? And most important: Do they pay royalties regularly and on time? You can find out lots of information from this source. No one likes to complain or rave about distributors more than other producers!

Catalog and Promotion. I cannot count the number of producers I have spoken to who have signed a contract without asking to see a copy of the distributor's catalog. A distributor's catalog is its calling card and its importance cannot be overestimated. Does the catalog have titles on subjects similar to yours? When was it issued? When is the next one planned? In what quantity? Do they send catalogs to the kind of markets you are interested in reaching? Read the copy on different kinds of films. Is it well written? If they do not have a catalog, ask why. Do they print targeted direct-mail pieces? Once again, ask how many copies they printed and to whom they were sent. Do not be fooled by very fancy promotional bro-chures—some markets do not need four-color glossy flyers to have an impact. Rather, look for the creativity of a distributor's approach to marketing different kinds of films. Ask for some ideas on promotional strategies. Who do they see as primary and secondary markets for the film? How would they market it? Are they willing to print a one-sheet flyer or a poster? What are their upcoming promotional campaigns? Will your title be included in a group mailing? It really does not make sense to ask for expected income because every film/tape is different. It is almost impossible to project income, but you can ask for an estimate based on a similar title.

Contracts, Rights, and Percentages. There is an entire chapter on contracts in this book because contracts are so important. However, the key things you should look at include length, exclusivity versus non-exclusivity, whether the contract is net or gross, geographic and market limitations, and who pays for print and promotional costs. Here are a couple of tips. Net contracts are very tricky business and should be reviewed very carefully. Unscrupulous distributors can use net deals to deduct so many costs you will never see a dime. Do some math in terms of print costs. Sometimes fifty percent of the net is less than thirty-five percent of the gross. Exclusive versus nonexclusive contracts is another important area. Given that the industry for educational distribution is exclusive contracts, I would be cautious about signing with an educational distributor who does not require exclusivity. On the other hand, the standard for video art distributors and home video catalog distributors is non-exclusive.

Few distributors can actually reach all of the markets that may be appropriate for your work, so you should carefully review what markets are covered in the contract. If a distributor handles theatrical distribution, it is appropriate for them to want to control the television and home video release. However, if they specialize in educational distribution and do not even distribute in 16mm or 35mm formats, you may be better off getting other distributors to handle those markets. Multimedia rights are a new area of concern. Unless a distributor has plans to utilize new technologies in marketing strategies or is distributing in laser disc or CD-ROM, you may want to exclude those rights. In addition, few educational distributors can market outside North America, so you should be careful about signing a contract that asks for world rights in any market. The exceptions to this rule are television distributors and sales agents, like Jane Balfour Films in London. With these types of distributors it may be possible to negotiate the contract to exclude certain territories and markets where you may have your own contacts.

Another area to review is pricing strategies. With the fragmented marketplace of the 90s, tiered pricing has become the norm. Public libraries and high schools, for instance, will not pay more than $99 for a title. Consider whether the distributor has flexible pricing policies.

Small Distributors versus Large Distributors. This is a very important subject. The first question you should ask is how many titles they distribute. There are many small, fly-by-night theatrical distributors who handle one or two films and should not even be in business. Yet, they talk a great deal, have a beautiful card, and promise the world. Remember, contracts are for five or seven years, and are ordinarily written in such a way that they are extremely difficult for producers to break. However, there are advantages and disadvantages to both large and small companies. Larger companies have more capital, which enables them to offer advances. They also may utilize sales reps in the field and have good relationships with large media buyers. However, just because a distributor has a large catalog does not mean your film/tape will get the attention it deserves, and may very well need in order to be successful. Distributors need to concentrate on promoting those titles that do well. Sometimes a small, less well-known distributor who concentrates in the best markets for your film will be a better choice. This is particularly true if your film/tape is not destined to be a major seller.

Location. The distribution process works best if the producer is involved in developing distribution strategies and working with the distributor. If you know a local distributor who is willing to work closely with you, this might be a better option than a larger distributor farther away.

HOW TO MAKE A DISTRIBUTOR FIND YOU, OR, WHAT TO DO WITH EXPERIMENTAL FILMS AND VIDEO ART

Frankly, the situation for short narrative and experimental media is pretty bleak. There are very few distributors that handle this type of work, and those that do must be willing to spend a great deal of time marketing. In fact, the number of distributors that have continued to make 16mm film available to the educational market is quite limited. Let us say yours is not the kind of film or video that is going to be in great demand by a variety of distributors. What do you do? In this case, you need to market your work to distributors by making it as appealing as possible. Here are some ways to do that:

Enter as many festivals as appropriate. Many distributors attend festivals looking for product, or read festival catalogs looking for new product. Getting your work in festivals may mean there will be some name recognition when you contact distributors. Festivals do increase the prestige of a work. And an award or two never hurt anyone! To find out which festivals are most appropriate, read *The Independent* or refer to AIVF/FIVF's *Guide to International Film and Video Festivals*.

Send out your own press releases. If the film wins an award or is screening in a museum or festival, write your own press release. You do not need to send it to a huge list of people. But do be sure to send your release to the distributors you are trying to interest in your work. For help on marketing strategies and writing press releases, Media Alliance in New York publishes an excellent reference guide, *Something Pressing: A Guide to Public Relations for the Video and Filmmaker*.

Create a press kit and send it along with your tape to the distributor. A good press packet should have a description of the work, biographies of key personnel, production stills, list of screening sites, and press clippings. It is almost always possible to get press on a film—even if it is from small local papers.

Get recommendations and endorsements. If a prestigious programmer likes your work, ask for a quote you can use in promotion. Type some of the quotes on a sheet of paper titled, "WHAT PEOPLE ARE SAYING ABOUT...," and include it in the press packet. If you know someone who knows the distributor, ask your friend to call and recommend that the distributor look at your film or tape.

The more promotional material you have on your film, the easier it will be to find a distributor. All distributors have limited promotion budgets so it helps them to know that there is a designed flyer.

In conclusion, choosing the right distributor is as important to the life of your film or tape as choosing the right cameraperson. The decision should not be made quickly or without a great deal of thought. Don't just select the first distributor who contacts you. Be sure to contact at least three to five different distributors. Even if you end up signing with the first, you will probably have gotten a much better idea of the marketability of your work and have more realistic expectations of the distribution process. Good luck!

CHAPTER 2

SELF-DISTRIBUTION:
IF YOU DON'T DO IT, WHO WILL?

Christina Craton and Tim Schwab

If you possess the chutzpah and energy to actually complete an independent film or video[1] in this climate, in this country, under the worst conditions in decades, you probably have the right temperament and tenacity to self-distribute. You no doubt have spent years immersed in the world of your subject matter. You already know the players, have the contacts, and understand the market for your work better than anyone else. So why not self-distribute?

Ralph Arlyck[2] a filmmaker who lives in Poughkeepsie, New York, has been self-distributing for years. His early films were distributed by Canyon Cinema and by Filmmakers Co-op, both established in the early 1960s by experimental filmmakers. Since his days at Berkeley in the 60s, Arlyck has been an important figure as a filmmaker and an advocate for independent media. His film *An Acquired Taste* is a wry look at success and the media influences in his life (and all our lives). He says, "If you are an independent producer, any one of the four or five things you do can be considered a full-time job. You are a fundraiser, a producer, a distributor, and often an advocate. The important thing is to strike a balance."

Self-distribution does require balance, and the same talents and determination that independent production requires. In many ways it is a natural outgrowth of production work. Distribution completes the circle. One of its most rewarding aspects is the opportunity to interact with the groups and individuals who are using your work, the ones you hoped would see your work when you decided to start the project in the first place.

In this chapter we will outline some of the practical steps you can take in self-distributing independently made media, focusing on documentaries because that is what we know. By the time you read this, there may be several wonderful and scary new ways of getting independently produced media to audiences throughout the world. But the basic principles should remain the same. Self-distribution requires a realistic evaluation of the film or video's market, access to money to prepare work for distribution, a professional approach, an understanding that self-distribution is also self-promotion, strategic thinking, busy work, and, above all, a sincere commitment to the process.

Before you make that commitment ask yourself these questions: Can you face spending more time and energy on the project? Can you afford to? Do you think there is a group of individuals and organizations who will be interested in your film or video? Will they pay money for it? Do you have access to $2,000 to $5,000 to pay for the start-up costs of self-distribution—things like getting a master and videocassettes duplicated, printing thousands of brochures, and purchasing mailing lists? Do you want to get involved in designing brochures and stuffing bubble packs? Do you want to send your program off to reviewers and festivals? At the very least, do you want to supervise someone else who will do all these things for you? If yes, then please continue. If not, then skip to the chapter on contracts because you will want to sign one with a distributor.

We are veteran independent filmmakers (meaning on our way to old and tired) who have made a living making films since 1979. We pursued production grants and fellowships during the 1980s when such things were easier to obtain, and during the 1990s we have had luck with cable and satellite deals, and self-distribution. Every year as the market gets tighter, and the prospects grow dimmer, we have had to explore new strategies to get our films into the world.

In 1984, when we were offered our first distribution deal with a small, friendly distributor, we were so excited by their offer we didn't even ask what the terms were. As it happened, the terms didn't matter. Twenty-five percent of almost nothing is almost nothing. Within a few years, a big, unfriendly distributor absorbed the small one and our royalty checks went from small to non-existent. They didn't even return our phone calls. In 1991, we tried a friendly, non-profit distributor. The last check we got from them was for $19.75. In all three cases, the film titles were simply added to an already crowded catalog that was mailed out to the same list of names once a year, or twice a year. Most distributors simply can't afford the time or money required to give individual attention and publicity to a film or tape unless they are quite certain that it will be a big money maker. We have had much better luck with self-distribution.

In 1989, we completed *Letters From America*, a half-hour film biography of author Ole Rolvaag. Rolvaag, a Norwegian immigrant, explored the tragedies of empire-building, and was critical of the materialism he encountered in America.

While making the film, we got to know the thriving and proud Norwegian-American community in the Midwest. We knew that this affluent, well-organized, and active group with a host of academic connections would make an ideal audience—and a likely market—for the film. And so we opted to distribute it ourselves. We were also lucky enough to catch the tail end of the days when libraries were still paying $500 for 16mm film prints and $400 for videocassettes. In one year, we sent out several batches of brochures, generated lots of publicity in Scandinavian-American publications, made dozens of presentations at Sons of Norway Lodges, and made a profit of about $15,000 from video sales and 16mm film rentals. The whole experience was rewarding, financially and professionally.

In 1990, we completed *Ghost Dance*, a short film commemorating the one-hundredth anniversary of the Wounded Knee Massacre. The film received strong reviews and won several awards, but because of the ten-minute length and subject matter, we were not sure how to market it beyond festivals and the obvious regional institutions. We decided to submit the piece to New Day Films, a self-distribution cooperative formed in 1971 and run by independent media producers. In New Day, members share the expense of annual catalogs and running a central office, but individual members are in charge of their own distribution. New members benefit from the training and advice more experienced members can offer. When we were accepted into the co-op, we were cautioned that our film might have only a marginal market. We decided to join anyway, primarily because we wanted to interact with other filmmakers—it gets lonely living in the rural Midwest.

As it turns out, the film did better than anyone expected. Using New Day's mailing lists, we did several bulk mailings to organizations that had previously purchased tapes related to Native American issues. Our timing helped, too. We launched the film in 1992, the year of the Columbus Quincentenary, when interest in Native American subjects was very high. Our efforts promoting the film paid off with a lucrative satellite deal. In total, *Ghost Dance* has grossed between $30,000 and $40,000, and netted about half that. But the most rewarding part of joining New Day has been our association with the remarkable people in the independent media field who taught us to see self-distribution as part of a much larger picture.

While we were busy promoting the films we were distributing, we discovered that every time the production's title got exposure, we got exposure, and when our film received recognition, we did too. Self-distribution is an excellent way to help you raise your profile and build networks with the people who are interested in seeing and promoting independent media. Self-distribution is also an excellent way to learn what the independent market looks like and how it works, or doesn't work, as the case may be. And if you are lucky, and work hard, self-distribution can help pay the rent.

To get started self-distributing, we suggest that you do the following—with or without the help of paid professionals:

Evaluate the market for your production. Debra Zimmerman, executive director of Women Make Movies, defined the difference between market and audience at a National Alliance of Media Arts and Culture (NAMAC) Conference in Chicago in 1993. To paraphrase her, every film and video has an audience—a group of people who would like to see the work. A market can be quite different from an audience, and not all films have markets. A market is a group of people and organizations who will pay money to purchase or rent your program.

Ellen Bruno, a San Francisco media artist, had been doing refugee work for eight years when she decided to make *Samsara*, a documentary about the Cambodian genocide and its aftermath. "I was working on the ground, doing the actual bandage work, and I kept thinking that if people knew what I knew, if only they could see what I see, then there would be policy changes, and money for these efforts." A few years later, she was basking in the glow of receiving three awards at the American Film and Video Festival, when, as she said, "The distributors came at me like sharks. I thought, if these people think there is a market for my film, I should check it out myself. I know the network, and I know how to tap into the market." As it turned out, she has been able to support herself and her work with the income from self-distribution of *Samsara*, and her more recent *Satya*, a work about the Buddhist nuns in Tibet.

Evaluate your costs. Once you decide that there is a market for your work (and once you have read over the rest of this chapter), complete a budget estimating the actual costs you will incur. Find out from designers and printers how much design and printing costs will be. Talk to the post office about actual costs of bulk mailing. Determine how much cash you can spend. You can adjust the size of your mailing, apply for grants to cover the costs of distribution, or refer to the chapter on finding a distributor.

Get quotable reviews. In all the publicity materials you send out, whether they are video covers, one-sheet brochures, or three-page news releases, it will be helpful to have quotes from well-known individuals or people with impressive titles. If you are working on a health piece, a prominent physician or scholar would help. If you are working on an art piece, then a quote from a museum director, art critic, etc., would work. You probably already know reviewers who might be sympathetic to your work and what you have accomplished. When you can, develop career-long relationships with good reviewers. Ask them to review your work. Once you have these quotes, you can select just the right phrase, and use it in all your materials. Do pursue quotes from *Library Journal*, *Booklist*, and *Video Librarian*— three publications that media librarians pay attention to. Also, pursue getting reviews or articles in publications that are subject-specific and curriculum related. Ellen Bruno had good luck with a review in a publication directly related to her subject matter, *Cultural Survival Quarterly*.

You might be surprised how willing people are to provide quotes. We once requested a quote from Meridel LeSueur, a marvelous writer with roots in the Depression era. She watched the film, and sent us a long, passionate letter scolding us for not attacking the capitalists more thoroughly, and closed with the words, "As far as a quote goes, you can say I said..." and then she gave us a lovely, usable, and complimentary quote. She made us bold, and we have not been turned down for a quote since then.

Get awards and screenings. There is one "must do" festival for the educational market—the National Educational Film and Video Festival. As for other festivals, be selective. Festivals can be expensive. Some like the CINE charge an $85 entry fee for a half-hour work. Some are free. Festivals are a good way to reach a sophisticated audience and generate attention for your work. But once you have won two or three awards, especially if they are recognizable, one more award or festival showing may not make any difference, even to your parents.

Be professional. Have some professional-looking stationery made up. You can also get a logo made up, but at the very least, include your name, address, etc., in clear type that is easy to read after it has been faxed and photocopied. Also, work on your phone manners. Use your company name to answer the phone, and be pleasant, alert, and professional when speaking with anyone, especially those interested in your films. It can't hurt you in the United States, and it certainly will help with the Canadian and European markets where politeness is encouraged and admired.

Develop a synopsis for the work. In three or four sentences, describe what the program is about and why someone should be interested. Don't hesitate to use descriptive words, but do hesitate to use silly ones, like "brilliantly directed" (leave that to your reviewers). Remember that often publications will print what you send them verbatim. Read the entries in other festival and distribution catalogs. What would you like someone to read about your work, and who would you like to read it?

Get photographs. Select one memorable or provocative image that you want to be associated with your title. Sometimes it is an image that has become obvious during production. Sometimes you have to pick from several by asking friends, family, or designers for their opinions. Get 50-100 photographs made up at a bulk house (the cost should be under $2 each). They can put on the bottom of the photos the production's title, credits, and name and address of the distributor—whatever information you would like. This photo can then be sent to festivals, reviewers, journalists, etc. Very often, including a photograph with your publicity materials is the best way to get coverage.

Make a video master and 50-100 VHS copies. You will use up twenty-five *justlikethat* sending preview copies off to reviewers, etc. Remember the old business adage, "Don't advertise if you don't have the stock." If you have 16mm film prints available, they will come in handy for large public showings, the occasional rental, and festivals, but do not spend large amounts of money having multiple 16mm prints made up. They are expensive, and only a handful of venues prefer 16mm film prints.

Create a cover for the videocassettes. You can do it yourself by cutting, pasting, photocopying, and cutting to size, or you can design one on a computer, or hire a fabulous designer—just do it. Don't send a cassette with a blank cover to anyone. Use the photo that you have selected as the identifying photo, and use the quotes and festival awards you have been gathering. Let people know where they can get a copy of the video. Don't forget the spine of the video cover. It should include the film's name and an interesting visual.

Set a realistic price for your work. VHS cassette is the most popular format for public consumption in the mid-1990s. It doesn't matter what your work's original format was, and it doesn't matter that you want audiences to see your beautiful 16mm film on film, or your sharp 3/4" on 3/4". The reality is that VHS cassette tapes are what sell the most. If you have 16mm film prints available, do include a price for sale and rental. Given the mid-90s market, a well-made, well-reviewed, award-winning ten- to sixty-minute film or video can sell to college libraries, media centers, and university departments for about $100 to $250 per VHS cassette. If you work hard, and send out brochures to well-targeted mailings, you might sell three hundred to five hundred VHS copies over the life of the work. Selling one thousand would be good, very good.

Les Blank's *In Heaven There is No Beer* has sold over one thousand copies. Blank is a San Francisco-based filmmaker who has been self-distributing since 1969. He prefers self-distribution in part because "you don't have to live in fear and loathing of a distributor who lives someplace else." Unlike many independents, Blank's main market is home video, and his approach to pricing basically boils down to "charge what the market can bear" ($19.95 to $49.95). "It is all bread and butter...and mayonnaise and mustard." If you price your video at $300 or more, your sales will go down. And of course you can opt to price it at $19.95 and try to sell thousands for home video use—just make sure your titles are as crowd-pleasing as Blank's meditations on food, music, and gap-toothed women.

There are persistent rumors of people making gazillions of dollars marketing the *How To Keep Your Teenagers from Doing What You Did When You Were Growing Up* video at home video prices. (For an excellent discussion about home video vs. the institutional video market, see Debra Franco's book, *Alternative Visions: Distributing Independent Media in a Home Video World*.) If you do the math, it becomes clear that to make any money with video sales, you must charge more than $19.95, or sell thousands. If you plan on selling thousands, set aside plenty of time to stuff envelopes and take orders. As Blank says, "The deadliness is in the details. Someone gets sleepy and they send out *Garlic Is Better Than Ten Mothers* instead of *Gap-Toothed Women* because both start with 'G'." Be prepared to pay attention to the details.

Have a brochure for bulk mailings made up and test it. If you have moral qualms about adding to the oceans of bulk mail in the country, then overcome them, or self-distribution might not be for you. Using the quotes, photographs, synopsis, pricing, and list of awards and impressive screenings you have been gathering, have a captivating brochure made up for bulk mailings. Be visual, and be brief. Be clear, and be specific. Be frugal. Walk through the process. In other words, fill out the information you have requested. Make sure you have left enough room, asked for all pertinent information, included elements like prices, return addresses, and bulk rate indices on the appropriate panel. Check with your local post office about sizes, prices, and specific requirements you should follow for sorting (they have handouts). If you are involved with a non-profit organization, you can save about forty percent on postage using the non-profit bulk rate. Oversize brochures can add to your postage costs. Take a draft brochure to the local college or school and ask faculty members for feedback. Remember, the entire world is awash in bulk mail, and it must be distinctive to float to the surface. Also, check around for the best printing prices. We have had great luck working with a printer in the small town near where we live. With fax, or a modem, it is not that difficult to work with printers at a distance. Above all, do not get carried away with costs. Les Blank put it succinctly: "You can kill yourself mailing out ten thousand fancy color brochures."

Obtain suitable mailing lists. Consider all those people who helped you complete the project—the organizations, schools, individuals who helped fund the work, who provided space, equipment, whatever. These might be your best customers. Ask if you can insert a one-page brochure in their next newsletter mailing, or if you can at the very least obtain a copy of their mailing list. There are two well-known companies where you can purchase slick, sorted, specifically directed mailing lists, printed on the labels of your choice: CMG Informational Services, and

Market Data Retrieval. (Addresses in the resource list.) You can order lists sorted by college departments, subject interest, zip codes, size of media collections, etc. Be realistic about mailing lists. A one percent return on a commercial bulk mailing list is considered average. That means if you mail out two thousand brochures you could hope for at least twenty responses. Some New Day returns have been as high as four percent.

Mail out the brochures. For now, the reality is that bulk mail is the most-used way to reach buyers. J Clements, a New Day Films Coop member, is becoming legendary for her ability to tap the bulk-mail market. J's films, *Man Oh Man* and *Dear Lisa: A Letter to My Sister*, are both personal works, and both deal with gender. Both have sold well. In 1994, J sold a total of 126 copies at an average price of $250. "The key to self-distribution is individual mailings. For the university market, time your mailings so they hit by Labor Day, or arrive right after New Year's." J spends lots of time perusing mailing lists, and she follows her sales instinct, which she didn't know she had until she started marketing her films. She also adapts her brochures to suit different targeted groups. She freely admits that there is not too much glory in selling VHS tapes to colleges, but "I really like the idea of my films being seen and maybe inspiring students in classrooms all over the country." J is also experimenting with online services that will reach a world-wide market. Follow your own hunches in figuring out new ways to reach new markets. In the meantime, with your bulk mailings, if you don't want to spend the time putting labels on the brochures, check with your printer. For a small fee, they can often attach labels to brochures directly as a part of the printing process, and even sort and deliver the mailing to the post office.

Have a system in place to receive and process orders. Be prepared for orders to come in. You will have to set up a system to receive the orders, package the tapes, and send out and receive invoices and payment. You can do it yourself. Or, for a fee of about $4-$7 per transaction plus shipping charges, you can have a fulfillment company such as Transit Media take over the tasks of packaging and invoicing. (Be sure you mail VHS cassettes in bubble packs. Do not use fiber-filled envelopes. They can harm tapes.)

Remain optimistic and innovative. As Les Blank says, "Good luck. You will need a lot of it. A lot of it is luck, and a lot of it is being present. You gotta get out there and be seen." Ultimately, remember that every time you do send out your mailings, and every time you enter a festival, you are getting your work and your name into the world. The professionalism and organization that you refine while self-distributing will help pave the way for other income-generating deals with cable, satellite, and foreign distributors. It is all part of the independent media production process.

Now go forth and self-distribute!

NOTES:

[1]The distinction between formats has blurred in recent years with media artists recording, editing, and releasing productions on a combination of formats, including 16mm, 8mm, VHS, BETA, 3/4", Hi8, High Definition, and CD-ROM. For the purpose of this discussion, we will use the word "film" to refer to 16mm film prints, and "video" to refer to VHS cassette tapes, largely because these are the formats most often purchased or rented.

[2]Distributors/filmmakers mentioned in chapter:

Ralph Arlyck, New Day Films (listed below)

Les Blank/Flower Films, 10341 San Pablo Avenue, El Cerrito, CA 94530/(510) 525-0942.

Ellen Bruno, Transit Media (listed below)

Canyon Cinema, 2325 Third St., Suite 338, San Francisco, CA 94107 /(415) 626-2255.

J Clements, New Day Films (listed below)

Filmmaker's Cooperative/New American Cinema Group, 175 Lexington Ave., New York, NY 10016/(212) 889-3820.

New Day Films

Orders: 22-D Hollywood Ave., Hohokus, NJ 07423/(201) 652-6590 tel/ (201) 652-1973 fax

Membership/submissions: c/o Ralph Arlyck, 79 Raymond Ave., Poughkeepsie, NY 12601/(914) 485-8489

Transit Media, 22-D Hollywood Avenue, Hohokus, NJ 07423/(201) 652-1989

CHAPTER 3

STEPPING OUT:
THE ART OF PUBLICITY

Karen Larsen

oes publicity really matter? Is it really necessary to seek out the media in order to get attention for your project? I would suggest that it is, and the reasons go far beyond simply attracting crowds to a particular screening. Publicity can also help you attract funders, distributors, festival programmers, and exhibitors; it can further your career as a filmmaker; and it can help to facilitate future projects. Publicity also can effect change or raise consciousness, as in the case of a film like Debra Chasnoff's Oscar-winning *Deadly Deception*.

Whether your film is made for theatrical release, television, home video, or for educational purposes, there is little point if no one sees it. And, no one will see your film if they do not know about it. Publicity generates business. I do the publicity for a number of film festivals. Every time I work on a film that achieves a good amount of publicity and attention, Landmark Theaters calls me with an offer to show the film.

In order to achieve your goals, planning for publicity should begin at the outset of the project when you are raising funds and writing grants. Start before you get caught up in script writing, shooting, editing and all their attendant problems and details. Funds should be set aside early to ensure that there will be enough in the budget for publicity. Sometimes an advance story in the newspaper can even assist in fundraising efforts. Potential investors, reps, and distributors, who are always looking for product, notice media coverage. They can help you most if they find out about your project before it is finished. Since editorial coverage in the media is free, you might as well take advantage of it.

Filmmakers should avoid the scenario where the film is finished and ready to show to the public, and they suddenly realize there are no stills and no press packet. With the screening date fast approaching, filmmakers usually do one of three things: desperately try to manage the publicity themselves, hire a publicist, or call everyone they know for advice on how to get some notice for the film.

At this late date, it is often a minor miracle that the filmmaker or even an accomplished publicist can get any attention at all. Even if one does attract attention, the coverage is not nearly as effective or thorough as it might have been had the publicity been started earlier.

A filmmaker once told me that no one had attended the opening of her film. "Was there anything in the paper?" I asked. "Nothing," she replied, "Not one mention." "Which papers did you send info to?" I asked. "None of them," she replied. I asked the filmmaker how she expected her film to receive coverage if she did not inform the press. She gave a telling if somewhat naive response. "I assumed that reporters are well-informed and make it their business to find out what's happening."

Unfortunately, this attitude is more prevalent than one might think. While it is true that reporters do go after a good "news" story, this is not as likely in the entertainment section. Reviewers and feature writers depend on releases and phone calls from publicists for many of their ideas. Reaching these people requires a carefully worked-out strategy that should begin *before* the first day of shooting.

PLANNING AHEAD

The first thing you need to do is define your goals. What audience are you trying to reach? Is your production for television, cable, home video, or the theatrical market? Should it play the film festival circuit? Do you want publicity now or later? Consider what is unique about your project. Keep in mind the fact that you will not get a long interview in your local paper both while in production and again later when the film is completed, unless there is another angle for the writer to pursue. Too much coverage in a festival can compromise your film's future, since newspapers will not run a review twice. These are just a few of the reasons for planning your coverage carefully throughout the production period. Asking these questions will aid the publicity process even if you do not know all of the answers.

During production you will need the following:
* a working title that sums up the spirit of the film;
* a written synopsis;
* biographies of crew and actors; and
* background information about the project.

A graphic image to identify your project is helpful but not absolutely necessary.

Press materials early in your project will be simple. You will add to them as you go along. Get biographies and head shots from personnel as you hire them. Begin keeping files of funding information, credits, and notes about the shooting. Learn how to write a press release that imparts the necessary information of who, what, why, where, and when. Make a time-line with realistic deadlines and above all, TAKE PHOTOGRAPHS!

GOOD PHOTOS BEGET GOOD COVERAGE

The single most important thing you must do is to have a good photographer on the set. So many filmmakers forget about stills until the film is set to open. Then they have to use frame blow-ups or scurry around to come up with something suitable. In some cases, as happened with *Visions of the Spirit*, a documentary about Alice Walker, or the several films about Jack Kerouac, we were able to overcome the lack of production stills by using photos of the subjects of the documentaries. Most of the time this simply will not work. Competition for space in the print media is fierce and you need to have at least as good a shot as everyone else. If you have great photos, you are almost guaranteed calendar listings, providing you make deadlines.

Your photographer should take color slides and black-and-white photographs. Color slides are for "slick" magazines, posters, postcards, brochures, and some newspapers. More and more newspapers are using color. While color is more expensive, it attracts more attention and may get your story or review on the cover, or the image above the masthead on the front page. Black-and-whites are for most newspapers and all other print media. There is no point in taking color prints except for your scrapbook—print sources will not use them. Do not expect to get usable black-and-whites from color slides. It may seem like a way to save money, but all too often the result is a muddy print.

Your stills should be shots of actual scenes from the film taken during production. Budget for a good photographer who knows how to shoot well-composed production stills. Ideally, the photographer would be on the set all the time in case something wonderful happens. In the interest of economy, save the photographer for the important days when there is a big scene scheduled with the principals, a well-known person is visiting the set, or a visually gripping shot is likely to occur. Photos of the director and crew working are useful to have for trade publications, but otherwise are not that important. One last piece of advice: DO NOT SHOOT YOUR OWN STILLS. Even if you are a proficient still photographer, you will not have the time to concentrate on getting the right kind of shots.

To successfully promote your film, you will need at the very least: VHS videotapes, stills, and press kits. One-sheets, postcards, and flyers are optional, although I would encourage all of them for more coverage in venues like coffee shops, bookstores, theaters, etc. An asset for television stations is to have a 3/4" or Betacam clip-reel to accompany interviews or reviews. Without clips, television coverage is unlikely. Producer's rep Peter Moore says, "Don't economize on materials, especially stills. After all, you wouldn't build a half-million dollar house and then give it a crummy paint job."

GETTING ADVANCE PRESS

There are things the filmmaker can do while the production is under way that will help attract coverage. If you can interest a national magazine like *Entertainment Weekly* in doing a feature on the making of your film or running an advance in a *What's New* column, this would greatly increase public awareness and create enthusiasm on a national level.

Keep production notes and assign yourself or someone else the task of getting a few local stories during shooting. These types of "local boy makes good" or "guess what's happening on Main Street" stories are especially easy to generate in a small town where news is scarce. When the stories appear, xerox and add them to your growing press packet. Major pieces may end up in the final press packet.

While in production keep making media contacts that will prove useful later on. Remember who you talked with and keep them informed with releases and phone calls. Stay in touch with your local *Variety* correspondent and with other trade publications. The trades are always interested in stories about who got a grant to make this or that project.

Design an overall look for your film while you are in production. If you do not have a bold graphic or logo, make something simple with the title of the film at the top of the page. Work on developing a style in presenting yourself and the film. This will help to identify you to the press person who gets tons of mail each day.

PRESENTING YOUR FILM TO THE PRESS

If you have followed the instructions above, when the film is completed you will have the makings of a good press packet. You will have a selection of stills from which you can choose three or four to make multiple copies, and you will have other stills to give to papers and magazines that want an exclusive photo. You will also have a synopsis of the film, production notes, a full credit list of cast and crew, biographies of key actors and personnel, special credits such as music, and, if your film is a documentary, information about the person or event portrayed. You will make a few 1/2" videotapes for those who cannot attend a press screening, and 3/4" or Betacam clips for television coverage.

Stills should be labeled with the name of the film, the names of those shown, the photographer's credit, and a "please return to" with an address. Tapes should be labeled with the name of the film on the cassette and the box, as well as a "please return to." With clips, identify each briefly and give the length in minutes and seconds.

Whoever publicizes your film is your liaison to the press. This person must be at a telephone or have a machine where messages are picked up regularly—no less than twice a day. Often a newspaper writer calls in the middle of his story and needs a quick answer or needs stills for a deadline. Writers for the dailies, in particular, are used to a quick response. A delay could cost you the piece, which is one of the cases for hiring a real publicist whose job is to be available to the press at all times.

If you are doing your own publicity, prepare a short spiel about your project. Be able to define quickly how your film is different from all others. Media people have a short attention span. Because they are overworked and busy, if you cannot make your point succinctly they are less likely to be interested. It is not uncommon to have a film reviewer or editor say something like, "You have exactly thirty seconds to convince me that I should cover this."

OPENING A FILM

When your film is about to open theatrically, you must decide whether to screen it for the press. If the print is ready and looks much better on a screen than a VCR, you will want to press-screen. A screening two weeks before the opening will allow the reviewer to make the deadlines of weekly newspapers. In order to get some earlier pieces in magazines or papers with long lead times, such as the Sunday entertainment sections of most city newspapers, you will either have an earlier screening or show the film on 1/2" videocassette to those writers. You can also show your VHS screener copy to reviewers who cannot make the press screening.

If your piece is shot on video and intended for television, you might decide to play it theatrically to garner interest and publicity. If your goal is to attract PBS and/or video sales, then show the work on a large screen at a local theater. This might generate a Sunday piece in the newspaper and reviews in the dailies and weeklies. With these tearsheets in hand, you can try to convince PBS to air your tape. When the video later plays on PBS, it will be reviewed in the same papers, this time by the television reviewers. George Csicsery opened *Where the Heart Roams* to a lot of attention from the media and used that coverage to get a distributor. Your goals might be different; the important thing is to define them, then strategize from there.

The more available a filmmaker and/or actors can make themselves for promotion of a film, the better. It is relatively easy to arrange radio interviews with directors, screenwriters, actors, etc., and it is free publicity. The same applies to print media. Be sure to have a photograph of anyone being interviewed because quite often newspapers ask for one. Photos can be hard to find at the last minute. It is always a plus for coverage if the filmmakers can be present on opening night, adding that special touch to the festivities.

Another option is to hold a press conference. If you have a film like *Houses Full of Smoke* and former spy Philip Agee is in town, holding a press conference will attract more attention to the film. You should only hold a press conference if it is news. Rama Wiener of Tara Releasing timed the New York opening of Connie Field and Marilyn Mulford's *Freedom On My Mind* during the reunion of the summer volunteers in Mississippi exactly thirty years after the murders of Goodman, Schwerner, and Chaney. This helped Weiner secure feature news stories in addition to reviews and interviews with the filmmakers.

TO HIRE OR NOT TO HIRE

What are the pros and cons of actually hiring a publicist for your project? What a publicist can do, how you work with one, and how much it costs are some of the areas to explore. A publicist can advise you at the strategy stage and work with you on your publicity plan. A publicist knows deadlines and has media contacts you do not have. You can discuss with your publicist whether to play in a festival or open theatrically, whether to try for a PBS airing or the educational market. The publicist can also discuss strategy for promotional tie-ins such as T-shirts, postcards, stickers, buttons, flyers, and radio ticket giveaways. A publicist can help point out that special cost-effective item that can attract attention. For example, Tara Releasing's *The Secret Adventures of Tom Thumb* made glow-in-the-dark spider rings for audience giveaways. The rings cost only a penny each!

Doing publicity means wading through an enormous number of functionaries—editors, producers, public affairs directors, calendar editors, feature writers, television and film critics, radio disc jockeys, reporters, and freelancers. The publicist can answer questions concerning who should be contacted and when, who is on vacation, who just did a similar story, what materials should be sent, when screenings should be scheduled and releases sent out.

Publicists talk to other publicists and often this leads to new ideas. For instance, I was opening Daniel Bergman's *Sunday's Children* in San Francisco. He was not available for interviews so I called Kahn and Jacobs who had handled the film in New York. They suggested several writers who had conducted interviews with Mr. Bergman but had not placed them. One of these worked out and resulted in a Sunday interview piece.

A publicist can talk about a film in ways the filmmaker might find difficult. Often it is hard for a filmmaker to sing his or her praises, but the publicist can get away with it. Facts must be accurate and well-documented, phone calls must be returned promptly, and one must have a pleasant manner. The publicist works with this in mind.

Coverage usually depends on newsworthiness, interest, timeliness, and human interest. It is the publicist's job to convince the proper person, without belaboring the point, that his story fulfills some of these requirements. Publicists are not necessarily treated gently by the press, but if materials are presented well and have something pertinent to say, and the publicist is polite, punctual, and tenacious, publicity will result. If you decide to hire one, do so in enough time that they will be able to make deadlines. Ideally, a publicist would be on board *four months before the first showing*, thereby leaving enough time to get a story into the national magazines. Hiring the publicist at the beginning of the production would be even better. The publicist could function as a consultant during production and be hired later to open the film.

How do you know whom to hire? Ask other filmmakers who they recommend. Look in the papers, notice campaigns that seem to be working and find out who is doing the publicity. Ask local film organizations such as Film Arts Foundation and the Independent Feature Project. Ask reviewers who they like to work with. Interview all of those recommended and find out their rates. Ask publicists what they would do for you and determine their interest and availability. It would be better to hire a person with experience who cares about your project even though he/she charges a bit more, than to hire an inexperienced person who would work for less money and probably get less coverage.

One solution for those on tighter budgets is to hire an experienced publicist as a consultant and have a less experienced person act as an assistant making press kits, stuffing envelopes, and even calling press people. Recently Lynn Hershmann-Leeson paid me a consulting fee to meet with her assistant and walk him through the writing and placing of a press release about an award she won. I went over the release, made some suggestions, and basically told him who to send it to and how to follow up. Several weeks later I was delighted to see a news story about the award in our daily paper. Filmmakers can save money by writing their own press materials, putting together the press packet, labeling stills and tapes, stuffing press releases, and buying supplies. Then you can hire the publicist to set up screenings and interviews and get major stories.

All publicists have their own styles. The bottom line is that you must like the person you choose and feel that he/she is the best person for the job. Remember that the publicist is working for you. If you are unhappy with some aspect of the publicist's work, do not go along with it. Lizzie Borden told me that one of the regional publicists working on *Working Girls* used stills that Borden did not like. I told her that she didn't have to accept that, and when I worked on the film in San Francisco we used the stills Borden picked herself.

Even if your film has a distributor who hires a publicist, call that person and discuss your ideas about how to present the film. You will both feel better afterwards. In the event your film is in a festival, I recommend calling the festival's publicist, introducing yourself and making sure they know your goals and also that they have all the stills and written materials they need. If the film is scheduled for television, I would not leave anything to chance. Again, call the publicist and ask if there is anything you can do to help. Naturally, if you are polite and helpful you will get more attention from that publicist, who is likely handling a lot of other projects at the same time. If you do decide to hire someone, you need to be aware of what they are doing and how they are doing it. The relationship between you and your publicist is extremely important.

If you decide not to use a publicist, you must build your own contacts with the press. Start by going to the library or to film organizations. Many of them have lists of media people, their areas of interest and their deadlines. In San Francisco, KNBR Radio publishes a list of radio and TV stations with names of personnel at each station and information such as what length PSAs they air. Carefully scan every publication you find. If it covers film and video put it on your press list. Listen to the radio, watch TV, and notice who is doing what. Ask people you know who they think might cover your story. Out of all this you will begin to have a personalized list for your project. Remember to include reviewers, editors, calendar people, feature writers, freelancers, television and radio personnel.

To ensure a successful opening you must do outreach to the communities that have an interest in your project. Marc Huestis's *Sex Is* and Arthur Dong's *Coming Out Under Fire* must be reviewed in the gay papers. *Saviors Of The Forest* by Santa Cruz's Camera Guys should be written up in the *Sierra Club Bulletin*; Yale Strom's *The Last Klezmer* must be reviewed in *The Jewish Bulletin*; information about Barry Minott's *Harry Bridges* should be sent to labor journals. You must be creative if you want the widest possible audience to see your film.

When I worked on *Black To The Promised Land*, I enlisted the help of the

Education Coordinator for the San Francisco Film Society, Robert Dunn. He worked with me on reaching teachers and students. We set up a special screening for several classrooms, invited the press to participate, and from that garnered additional news coverage on radio and television and a feature story in *The Jewish Bulletin*. If you see a story about a topic similar to yours, call the writer. Be prepared to explain how your project is different and how it is alike. Be consistent, make deadlines, be succinct, and be available to the press by phone or message machine. Don't take anything for granted even if the reviewer is your best friend. Keep in mind that the reviewer has an editor who must also be convinced to run the story.

BUDGETING FOR PUBLICITY

Money for publicity should be included in the budget at the fundraising stage. By the time the project is completed often there is no money left for publicity. I encourage you to put a certain amount of money under lock and key until the right moment. Early planning can also save costs. Anticipating needs for packets and stills means that money can be saved by copying large quantities of these materials as well as posters, postcards, stationery, and envelopes. Other expenses to consider are: flyers, postage, phone calls, messenger services, and tape duplication.

In 1993 and 1994 Irving Saraf and Allie Light's very successful *Dialogues With Madwomen* played in forty cities, thirty-five festivals and on PBS-TV (*P.O.V.*). They spent $16,583 for the national publicity effort. Here is a breakdown of the expenses:

POSTERS (full size & color, design, separations and printing)	$4,489
PRESS KITS	339
PUBLICITY PHOTOS	782
FLYERS (4 different kinds)	438
VHS VIEWING CASSETTES	818
ADS (design and litho reproduction)	295
35-MM THEATRICAL TRAILER (including 15 copies)	3,702
PREVIEW ROOM RENTAL	175
TV SPOTS	90
PUBLICIST'S SERVICES	5,455
TOTAL	$16,583

Saraf told me that all of the expenses were important. He and Light used 550 posters and were greeted by them in festivals all over the world. They still have an occasional use for them. In Saraf's opinion, 35mm theatrical trailers are the cheapest form of advertising and filmmakers should definitely make them. Saraf adds that you should order at least a hundred viewing cassettes to start with, maybe even two hundred, and that you should not expect to get them back. (I disagree; if you label cassettes as I suggested, you should get some of them back.)

Irving's figures do not include advertising costs that were deducted by theaters from the producer's share, telephone calls, shipping, festival expenses, and cost of film prints. Telephone and shipping expenses were buried in the costs of distribution. Also, they saved money by editing their own theatrical trailer and TV spots, and designing and producing the press kits.

I handled the publicity for *Dialogues With Madwomen* in San Francisco, beginning with a sold-out benefit at the 1,500 seat Castro Theater for the San Francisco Women's Building, late theatrical engagements at the Castro and UC Theaters, and at the Nuart Theater in Los Angeles. The film was a huge success partly because of the very careful strategy on the part of the filmmakers all the way along. After the openings in San Francisco and Los Angeles, Sande Zeig booked the film across the country and Lawrence Helman and Marc Huestis of Outsider Productions handled publicity duties.

Rama Wiener echoes the need for the materials that Saraf lists above. In the interest of keeping costs down, she feels it is important to invest the money for a lot of materials early to avoid costly reorders later. Tara always prints full-size posters. For *Freedom On My Mind*, where a four-color poster seemed unnecessary, they printed two thousand posters in black-and-white with red for $2,000. Another poster option is to make blueprints from a full-sized film positive. The film costs about $50 and the blueprints are about $3 each (there is no minimum order, and our office gets a price break by doing the labor). As 8" X 10" black-and-white stills cost approximately one dollar apiece, Tara orders lithos of their publicity stills (with the captions, company name, and other pertinent information) from a lab in the Midwest in lots of 500 for $70 including tax and shipping.

Rama believes that it also helps to create ad slicks. There is a high minimum order—200 for $85—but ad slicks can also be used to generate flyers and postcards. Postcards are inexpensive and effective advertising, especially if there is a nice image for the front. The back can have all the pertinent information and a four-star quote (if available). Cards can be customized by labels with specific theaters and playdates (hand highlighting the dates always helps). Rama also thinks that 3/4" clip reels are very important, even though they cost $40 apiece. Usually five clip reels will suffice, and you will keep the price down if you keep the time under ten minutes. Shop around; there are bargains to be found.

The cost of a publicist varies from city to city, with New York being the highest, Los Angeles in the middle, and San Francisco and Seattle at the low end. In San Francisco, you should expect to pay about $2,500 for publicist fees and other expenses to open a film. In Los Angeles the amount doubles and in New York it triples. The cost of screening rooms in San Francisco varies from $75 to $95 an hour. In New York, rooms start at $100 per hour. Every cost is greater in New York, so if you are opening there you have to take that into consideration.

Unit publicists, who garner press for the film while it is in production, are usually paid by the week, while publicists hired to open a film are usually paid by the project—$800 to $1,200 in San Francisco. You could consider hiring a publicist as a consultant for an hourly fee of $50 to $100 per hour in San Francisco. Given an hour, a competent publicist can look over your materials and give advice as to how to target the right audience and who in the press might be interested.

THE FUTURE IS COMING

Any current discussion of publicity would be incomplete without a brief discussion on how the information superhighway and other new technologies are impacting media and the publicist's job. The ability to transfer or access information instantly on the Internet has enormous potential to make everyone's lives a lot easier, and coverage a great deal more efficient. Just as faxing became commonplace in the late 1980s, being online may well be the publicity standard as we enter the twenty-first century.

Imagine the following scenario. The editor of the largest daily newspaper calls you on deadline for tomorrow's paper and cannot find stills you sent the previous week. You frantically search your cluttered desk for one of your production stills. You cannot find the one that would be perfect, so you send your second, or maybe even your third choice by messenger and hope for the best. Ten minutes later the paper calls to fact check the playdates of your film. They cannot find your release, so you answer the questions and fax another release.

The time is coming when this scenario might be replaced by the following: The editor calls to discuss coverage and images. You mention that you can provide eight images in a digital (TIFF) file format sent via e-mail, in either color or black-and-white. As for those fact checkers, they will have gone to the local indie film bulletin board on the Internet where you have posted your release and presskit for the media's convenience. Your main press list will already have received the materials and any specific requests in their individual e-mail boxes.

As ideal as this all sounds, with modems and CD-ROMs replacing photos, slides, and presskits—saving dollars and trees—this reality is still several years away. According to *San Francisco Examiner* film critic Scott Rosenberg, "There's an incredible logic to the online approach. It's the older editors that are holding up progress." Rosenberg prefers e-mail to voice mail, and now receives some of his press releases electronically.

Although the new computer online technology has become a factor in conventional print media, with more and more dailies and weeklies on the Internet, it is still essential for the independent filmmaker to provide press materials in the current conventional standards. According to San Francisco publicist Jeff Diamond, some publicists are now posting releases in various news groups and running ticket giveaways on bulletin boards with no appreciable response as yet.

Larger studios and some independents have provided publicists with Electronic Press Kits (EPKs) for the past several years. These kits usually include: 3/4" clips of scenes from the film; a trailer; B-roll footage of director, crew, etc.; and a music video if there is a hit song in the film with potential MTV airplay.

The time is not far off when the learning curve will disappear. As the price of equipment falls, scanners could be commonplace, modems are already a necessity, CD-ROMs will be cheaper to produce than photos, and filmmakers who are currently editing digitally will find it even easier to develop electronic press materials. Be prepared and the new technology will make your life easier. For now, make sure you make all of your snail-mail deadlines with the appropriate photos for calendar listings, and don't forget those follow-up calls!

49ers pull off trade to draft defensive star

Page B-1

Lineup switch helps Giants beat the Mets

Page B-1

Allie Light aims new play at women

CUE-1

WEATHER: Partly cloudy. High 57, low 47. Details, A-16.

MONDAY: April 25, 1994

The Oakland Tribune.

THIRTY-FIVE CENTS

FRIEND OF THE PEOPLE IT SERVES

★★ LATE SPORTS FINAL

"The first reason I made it was to reach other women," says Allie Light of her film "Dialogues with Madwomen."

Enlightening 'Dialogue'

Bay Area filmmaker Allie Light explains
how her 'Dialogues with Madwomen' came to be

By Barry Caine

San Francisco Sentinel

CALIFORNIA'S GAY & LESBIAN NEWSWEEKLY

20 April 1994 • volume 22, number 16

The *Sentinel's* Arts, Entertainment & Classifieds Section

by GARY MORRIS

We're All Mad Here

CHAPTER 4

STEP BY STEP:
SEQUENCING YOUR RELEASE

Marc Mauceri

hen Andrew Young and Susan Todd won the Best Documentary Award at the 1993 Sundance Film Festival for their searing documentary *Children of Fate*, they were flush with the kind of excitement that only a major award can bring. With the film hailed in the press as "breathtakingly poetic" and "an extraordinary, powerful work," Susan and Andy were suddenly confronted with an intriguing thought: if people loved *Children of Fate* this much, maybe it shouldn't go on public television right away. Maybe it should have a theatrical release.

Another situation faced John Valadez and Peter Miller, the director and producer of *Passin' It On*. Their stirring documentary about the rise, fall, and resurrection of a Black Panther leader had garnered praise and had people talking. Now they and their distributor were thinking that perhaps a significant consumer market for a home video of *Passin' It On* existed. A nationwide public television broadcast was imminent, and some decisions had to be made quickly: how should they coordinate the home video release with the broadcast? And how could they try to protect the potentially lucrative educational market from the much cheaper home video price?

These decisions have to do with something called *sequencing*, which is simply determining the order in which a film is sold or offered to various markets. Before we jump into what constitutes the normal sequence and some of the possible permutations, it is important to understand not only what the potential markets are, but why you must think about a possible sequence before you jump into bed with a distributor.

MARKETS AND AVENUES OF DISTRIBUTION

There are several markets and avenues of distribution for independent film: the festival circuit, theatrical, semi-theatrical, non-theatrical/educational, international, free television, basic cable, premium cable, rental-priced home video, sell-through-priced home video, and laser disc. The first thing you must do as a filmmaker is know these markets, and decide which are most appropriate for your film. I will briefly go over them:

The *festival circuit* includes all festivals, large and small, in the United States and international, that exhibit new films. Some are more important than others, some are difficult to get into, and some simply require you to pay an entry fee. If you are trying to find a distributor, then those that attract large numbers of buyers are the best: Berlin, Toronto, Cannes, and Sundance are the ones most companies attend.

The *theatrical market* encompasses movie theaters, or, in legalese, locations designed primarily for the commercial viewing of motion picture entertainment that are open to general admission. Whether it is a sixteen-plex, a calendared art house, or your local single screen movie palace, they all fall under this designation.

Semi-theatrical sounds a bit odd, and the way I usually describe it is by saying what it is not. I include in semi-theatrical any place that rents films but is not a commercial movie theater or an educational, classroom situation. Practically speaking, this usually means film societies, museum film series, university film clubs, art centers, community organizations, and anyplace else that is nonprofit but open to the public. Contractually, semi-theatrical is almost always a part of non-theatrical; however, many distributors have separate sales people to handle semi-theatrical sales.

Non-theatrical/educational can more easily be defined: films and videos that are sold or rented to institutions for classroom, instructional use.

International, or foreign sales, is of course to any place outside of the United States. Most countries where agents and distributors sell have approximately the same set of markets that are listed here. Some U.S. companies acquire (or try to acquire) not only domestic rights but also North American rights, which includes Canada.

Free television covers the networks, the wanna-be networks, local affiliates, and any public television entities. Within this market, independent films are rarely sold to any place other than public television.

Basic cable comprises those cable networks that do not have a premium charge attached to them for viewers. It includes Bravo, A & E, the Sci-Fi Channel, MTV, and Lifetime.

Premium cable encompasses those cable networks that do have a premium, like HBO, Cinemax, The Movie Channel, and Showtime.

The *home video market* is considered by many distributors to be the most lucrative market for their titles. There are two possible phases in home video, *rental* and *sell-through*. Rental means that the video is intended to be sold primarily to stores that rent out the video. Prices range anywhere from about $59.95 to $99.95. Sell-through means that the video is being offered at a lower price to entice consumers to purchase it. The sell-through price will range from $9.95 to $29.95. Normally, a video is offered at a rental price first, and then dropped to sell-through after at least six months. Since each phase has its own set of potential buyers, rental and sell-through are sometimes regarded as separate markets, with separate contractual terms.

Laser disc is usually treated as a variant of the home video market. Generally, the holder of the home video rights will try to sell the laser disc rights to a specialized distributor of laser disks. Sometimes a producer who knows the laser disc market will retain the laser rights and try to make that sale himself.

WHY THINK ABOUT SEQUENCES?

It is easy to say, "Well, I'll let my distributor worry about which markets and which sequence are best for my film. After all, they're the experts." But the producer who says this is making a mistake and may be endangering the successful exploitation of his or her film.

The truth is, some distributors are better in certain markets than others. If you can figure what the most exploitable markets are for your film, then you can find the distributor (or distributors) who best handle those markets. An obvious mistake would be to give an educational documentary to a company that does not have a strong educational division, or to give a fiction feature to a company with no theatrical or home video division. A more subtle mistake might be in giving a film with a strong catalog potential to a distributor who does not like to drop the home video to sell-through (thereby eliminating most catalog and consumer interest in the film; consumers do not like to buy, nor catalogs like to list, home videos that cost $70 or $80).

If you have decided to split up the rights to your film among more than one company, then it is even more important to think about the possible sequence your film will have. Because each of the companies will have its own interests at heart, it will be up to you to coordinate when each company offers the film to its particular market. You would not want your theatrical distributor, for instance, to delay the release of the film so that it ran into the television airdate. Similarly, you do not want your television/cable distributor to commit the film to an airdate that does not leave time for a theatrical release. Or, in a more subtle scenario, if your television or cable airdate is with a television or cable company that makes lucrative sell-through home video sales off a card at the tail-end of the broadcast, you want to make sure that your home video is available to be sold at a sell-through price when that broadcast airs.

Once you have intelligently chosen a distributor, then it is time to sit down together and determine—for real, this time—to which markets, and in what sequence, your film will be offered. It will probably come as a surprise to some producers that once the distributor has a signed a contract, s/he will then assume that the producer's participation in the distribution of the film has ended. It is up to you to make sure this does not happen. As a distributor, I have found that when a producer works closely with me on the distribution of the film, usually it is to the benefit of the film.

DETERMINING THE SEQUENCE

There are some obvious—and not-so-obvious—factors that go into determining the sequence that your film will follow in its distribution strategy. The most obvious factor is the kind of film you've made.

Different kinds of films do better in certain markets than others. A forty-five-minute documentary about the tribal conflict in Rwanda may appeal to educational and public television buyers, while a sexy, Generation X comedy will appeal to theatrical, home video, and cable buyers. The appeal of your film to the various markets will largely determine the sequential arc of your film.

Another fairly obvious factor is the success of your film. If your Generation X comedy finds no theatrical buyer, then it will be tougher to sell it to the home video and cable companies. Or if your Rwandan documentary wins some awards and rave reviews, and is selected to appear in the New York Film Festival, then perhaps it may find a semi-theatrical, or even a limited theatrical life. Success opens the doors to other markets; this is why a successful theatrical release is deemed so important for most fiction features, and why many companies are willing to take a loss in the theatrical marketplace trying to ensure success.

Another factor in determining the release sequence is who funded your film. If it was funded in large part by a public television entity, then your funders are going to want to see the film on public television sooner rather than later. They may or may not allow a theatrical window. Or perhaps you were involved with a made-for-television/cable film, like John Dahl's hugely successful *The Last Seduction*. Once in a blue moon, a film that was originally shown on cable may make its way into theaters, as did Dahl's film or the superb documentary *Hearts of Darkness*. Another example is direct-to-video release, which is often funded by a home video distributor who may deem a theatrical release unnecessary. The bottom line: if the company that provided your budget is itself a player in any of the markets, then there is a chance your film will not be following the normal sequence.

And there is one more factor we should not forget about: distributor preference. Distributors do not always like to do things the normal way. Some do not believe in wasting time with educational sales. Others do not believe in endangering educational sales with a home video release. Some do not want to "cheapen" their home video by dropping its retail price to sell-through. Still others pursue television and cable sales at the cost of a potential theatrical release. I am always saddened when a filmmaker says to me, "So-and-so picked up my film, but they didn't even pursue a (fill in the blank) release." I usually ask, "Did you talk about this before you signed a contract? Did you agree on the distribution strategy?"

THE NORMAL SEQUENCE

Let us consider the normal sequence of feature fiction films or high-profile documentaries.

The first step in sequencing is usually taken at least in part by the producer: the *festival circuit*. Once you have finished your film (and hopefully gone to the Caribbean for a couple of weeks) the first order of business is to find a distributor. One way to do this is to enter your film in film festivals and markets. With luck (or simply because you have made a great film) you will soon find a distributor. That distributor may continue to have the film play the festival circuit, because it is good for publicity. A smart producer or distributor will work to withhold any local reviews—you do not want to be told six months from now on the eve of your theatrical release that a major newspaper will not re-review or reprint your festival review.

The next step is the most expensive, the most risky, and the most important: the *theatrical release*. Starting with exclusive runs in the major cities, your distributor will turn years' worth of blood, sweat and tears into a product that can be seen by consumers for a small fee, usually about seven or eight bucks. Your initial opening weekend is the foundation for this vital market: strong numbers will lead to more weeks, which will lead to more cities, and to more theaters. You are not only selling a product, you are creating an awareness: this awareness will benefit every other market you approach.

Now consider those theatrical documentaries that can also be seen as educational: with a little coordination and common sense, the educational buyers and programmers can be approached from the outset of a film's distribution. The distributor should not allow any sales or rentals that might interfere with a theatrical opening—those angry calls from a theater owner who has discovered his neighboring university just had a big symposium featuring the film he is about to open are quite unpleasant.

The same applies to semi-theatrical rentals. Since some cities have few or no theaters that cater to independent films, your film will often have to open in a semi-theatrical location if it is going to play at all. In this sense you want to treat these customers as you treat any of the other theatrical venues: approach them from the beginning, and try to set up playdates that follow the openings in any nearby larger cities. Just be careful again not to step on anybody's toes.

Once you have finished your major theatrical runs—which can take anywhere from a few months to more than a year—your distributor will set a release date for the *home video*. Usually the video will be offered at the rental price first, and targeted at chains, stores, and the sub-distributors who handle both. About six to nine months after the video release date your distributor may choose to pursue the consumer home video market. In this case, the distributor will drop the price to sell-through (which will have its own release, or availability, date) and target the chains, stores, and sub-distributors for the second time around, as well as now pursuing the catalog market. The distributor may even take out advertisements in magazines or newspapers to sell to consumers directly.

In the meantime, your *television* or *cable* date should be coming up soon. It is more common for the initial home video release to precede any cable or television broadcasts than for those airdates to precede the home video. After all, why is the person who wants to see your film going to rent it for three dollars if it has already been on television for free? But many exceptions exist to this rule, especially for smaller independent films: the television/cable entity may need it for a certain slot; it may offer more money, or exert more pressure, to premiere it before any home video date; or your home video release may have been delayed or is not planned to happen at all.

What about free television versus the different levels of cable? Hollywood films and a very few high-profile independent films will usually play first on premium cable, and then be sold to free television and basic cable. The typical independent film is more or less offered to everyone at once, and whoever comes up with the most money gets it. Unless you have made a particularly successful or relevant film, you will not have too many subsequent sales.

Your *international* distributor or sales agent will probably try to start selling your film as soon as you have signed the contract. This will have little effect on anything happening domestically. Often a film's success in the United States makes it easier to sell to foreign markets. Unfortunately the reverse is not always true.

The final piece of the puzzle—*laser disc*—is usually sold and released well after the home video date. Laser disc distributors can afford to be choosy: there are a lot more films than the existing companies can handle. So do not be heartbroken if no offers are made. I suspect that if the laser disc catches on with more consumers, more companies will form and a broader range of titles will be purchased for the laser disc market.

It is important to understand that sometimes all these markets are approached from the outset. A distributor who has laid out a serious advance will often start the legwork leading to a successful cable or home video sale before the contract is even signed. This will not necessarily change the sequence of distribution, but it might allow the company president to sleep at night. And sometimes the opposite is true: a distributor will wait for theatrical success before approaching anyone; after all, a hit is easier to sell than an unknown.

EDUCATIONAL FILMS

Educational films and videos appeal to fewer markets than features. The markets they appeal to are less dependent on being in a particular sequence. Universities, schools, libraries, and other institutions should be approached over the life of the contract. A new class whose subject is the same as your film may begin anytime. When a new Department of Asian Studies is created by a school, they may want to acquire a dozen of the best films about Asia that have been made in the last ten years. If your film is good, it may not matter if it is a few years old.

Television or cable sales of educational films or videos are welcome at any point. While a broadcast may have a slight negative effect on the higher-priced sales, the awareness that is created by the broadcast may lead to other sales.

A serious issue for documentaries that straddle the line between education and entertainment is home video. Many distributors believe that a cheaply priced home video will undercut non-theatrical sales of the same title. Since the non-theatrical price for a video can be as much as $500, there is usually a big price difference. Educational buyers looking to stretch their purchasing dollars may be tempted to buy the cheaper tape, even though non-theatrical rights do not come with a home video (which is intended for home use only). This issue leads to some documentaries never being offered to the home video market, because the educational market is deemed more lucrative.

SUMMING UP

So, what happened to *Children of Fate* and *Passin' It On*?

The directors and producers of *Children of Fate*, along with their distributor, decided to forgo the early public television date. The film opened theatrically in calendared art houses in the major cities. Despite mostly favorable reviews, the film did not draw large enough audiences to make it a hit. A sale was made to HBO for approximately the same amount as the PBS sale, due in large part to the quality of the film, and also to the fact that it had a theatrical release and received good press. Home video was avoided for fear the sales would not be strong enough to justify jeopardizing the educational market.

For *Passin' It On*, the distributor went into high gear and released the home video at a sell-though price ($29.95) a couple of weeks before the airdate. A card offering the home video was placed at the tail-end of the broadcast. All in all, for a serious documentary with no theatrical exposure, it sold well in home video, grossing almost $15,000. The distributor tried to minimize the harm done to the non-theatrical market by being flexible with the non-theatrical pricing, at times offering as much as twenty-five to fifty percent off the $390 list price.

Sequencing is something that is rarely thought about by anyone other than distributors. But in this brave new world of media, with its myriad of market options and the labyrinths in which they might co-exist, it is time for the producer to think about sequencing as well. After all, you've worked hard to make your film. Don't you want it to have the best release possible?

CHAPTER 5

NAVIGATING THE PBS LABYRINTH

Julie Mackaman

"The puzzle palace."
—*Neil Seiling, Alive TV*

"It's a maze."
—*Janice Sakamoto, National Asian American Telecommunications Association*

"It's not like anything else."
—*Tsui Ling Toomer, PBS Program Management*

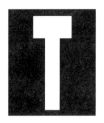 he roads leading to a broadcast on PBS (Public Broadcasting Service) are many and complex. To give you an idea, think of PBS not as a monolithic network but a confederation of some 350 member stations who pay for programs and services provided by national headquarters and a constellation of independent organizations. To navigate any of the hundreds of roads to reach your destination of a public television air date, you will need the same ingenuity, resourcefulness, and persistence that have seen you through as an independent producer.

It is never too soon to think about all the different audiences for your program and the distribution mechanisms—described in other chapters of this book—that will help you reach those audiences. For independent producers who want to reach mass audiences, national television is the grand prize. Independents have always had an uneasy relationship with the market-driven world of commercial television. Public television, unlike its commercial counterpart, has a Congressional mandate to offer a broad range of programs to serve a public that is as diverse as the taxpayers who fund it. PBS, the country's only non-commercial national television system, claims that it is available for free to ninety-nine percent of all U.S. television households, that its audience reflects the demographic makeup of the entire United States, that more than eighty percent of all households tune in each month, and that it has "…more than twice the weekly reach of cable stations like A&E, CNN and Discovery."

The history between independent producers and PBS has been rocky, but do not think of PBS as your enemy. Yes, PBS is a bureaucracy grown fatigued by Congressional battles, competition from cable channels that are putting the squeeze on traditional PBS markets, audiences who often resist adventurous programming, and a financial structure that leaves member stations at the economic mercy of crowd-pleasing pledge nights and cautious corporate underwriters. These conditions have drained the pluck and vitality from many PBS staffers, station programmers, and other gatekeepers. Take heart. Your chances of appearing on PBS depend directly on the quality of your program, your professionalism in presenting it, and your show's real potential to interest and serve an identifiable part of the public television viewership.

A BUDGET AND TOOL KIT FOR GETTING STARTED

You have finished your film or video project. It has cost you everything you've got and a piece of your future, as well. Just when you thought your fundraising hell was over, here comes the news you have been dreading. There is little or no money paid for broadcast rights, and it may cost you $1,000-$5,000 to pursue even a modest strategy to arrange "carriage" on public television. That's not all. Down the line, if you score with PBS at the national level, brace yourself for a "buffer" budget of $5,000-$10,000 for re-editing the piece for television (PBS packaging decisions will affect your final cut), correcting technical problems, paying for the transfer to the final digital broadcast format (currently D3 or D5), and providing the promotional "deliverables" required by PBS. Finally, visualize success and start thinking about a publicity budget of another $5,000-$10,000 to cover the costs of telephone calls, press kits, videocassette duplication, mailings, first class postage, and express mail. Some producers peg a more realistic national publicity campaign at $30,000-$50,000, a range possible only with corporate or foundation underwriting.

The good news is that an upcoming public TV broadcast can breathe new life into your exhausted fundraising effort. The foundations, donors, and friends who gave you production support will welcome the news and may be willing to kick in additional support for promotion. You can also return to funders who turned you down before, this time armed with a PBS commitment letter and the confidence of a national air date.

To prepare for public television, first produce a concise but compelling information packet. Include a synopsis of your program, credit list with cast (for documentaries, too) and bios for key personnel, photos, awards, and reviews. Play to your show's strengths as a *television* program. Consider including a statement about its intended audiences and your ideas for promotional angles. If relevant, include any special information about yourself or your show's subject that will help a programming scout sense that something unusual and important awaits her in the videotape she's about to watch. Have a stack of videocassettes ready to go (the number depends on how focused or widespread is your strategy) for inclusion in your initial or follow-up packet.

The basic communication tools you relied on for fundraising and production are still essential: a telephone (there will be days you will not wander far from it), a reliable answering machine or message center, computer, fax, and modem.

This is a good time to get your library in order. Order a copy of the *Public Broadcasting Directory* ($15 from the Corporation for Public Broadcasting)—an invaluable guide to the PBS labyrinth, its related organizations and programming services, and state-by-state listings of member television and radio stations and their key departments. Renew the subscriptions and independent producer memberships you let lapse during production mania, starting with those publications and organizations that provide up-to-date information on series solicitations and other public television opportunities.

Renew your personal contacts. One seasoned producer observes that in the same way most fundraising is based on contacts, personal relationships with public television personnel is a building block for a career as an independent producer. She continues that choosing to attend a public television meeting over a film market might be a setback in the short run because of the missed chance to sell your film, but a better long-term investment in developing a personal and collegial relationship with public television decision makers.

Finally, dust off your television set and watch public television. Programmers are frustrated by independents who do not themselves watch public television but are nonetheless convinced that their show is *perfect* for PBS. Do your homework before pitching your program. Especially with series, acquaint yourself with at least a couple of seasons' worth of programming

Now let's survey the terrain.

A TELESCOPING LANDSCAPE: ROUTES TO NATIONAL AND LOCAL CARRIAGE

The fondest dream of many independent producers is a national PBS "feed" broadcast to all stations across the country on the same date and at the same time. It is easy to see why so many independents have committed themselves to this path, even though the competition for a coveted spot on the national schedule is fierce. A national feed is much more efficient than pitching your program station-by-station. You are likely to get paid (although rarely what you feel your program is worth). A national air date is prestigious and will help you line up publicity and additional underwriting. Your parents will finally be able to explain to their friends what it is you do. Best of all, you will realize your desire of reaching hundreds-of-thousands—maybe millions—of viewers in their homes.

On the other hand, many experienced producers, wary of pinning their hopes on a national PBS broadcast, instead build their PBS campaign from the ground up—beginning early in their career with their local public television station. A local or regional strategy may make sense if, for example, your show is *not meant* for a national audience, which is true of the most innovative work. The nature of your program and its target audience may argue for a market-by-market approach. Whether it is your strategy of choice or default (i.e., rejection), a local approach will help you develop personal relationships with stations that will serve you well from one project to the next.

If your project received federal funds from the National Endowment for the Humanities, Corporation for Public Broadcasting, or a CPB-funded organization like the Independent Television Service (ITVS), then it must be offered to PBS for free, typically with the exclusive right to air four times in a three-year period. But even these programs have no guarantee of getting on PBS, which can snub a program that is underwritten and offered by a federally funded agency as easily as they dismiss a program submitted by an independent producer.

NATIONAL BROADCAST: THINK SERIES

The National Program Service (NPS) is the PBS entity that creates the core schedule that goes to member stations. NPS programs serve a national viewership, while member stations focus on programs to serve local community interests. Glance at your local public television station's lineup. You are likely to see a combination of NPS programs (signature series like *Masterpiece Theater* and *Nature* and special series like *Baseball* and *The Great Depression*, as well as pledge-drive, children's, and other specials) and non-NPS programs that stations have produced or acquired from a myriad of other sources. The NPS schedule is dominated by series for obvious reasons: they attract loyal followings, save money and resources by being marketable as a package, and are more likely than single program one-offs to be shown by member stations.

How can you get your work on public television's national, prime-time schedule? Your best shot—although still a long shot—is through an existing *anthology series* that acquires works by independent producers. Two of these are *P.O.V.* (an acquisition series of non-fiction work with an annual call for submission and payment of $425 per minute) and *Alive TV* (an acquisition *and* commissioned work series of half-hour programs encompassing a range of new genres and short experimental work, now paying a minimum of $500 per minute). These series provide quality packaging and aggressive national publicity campaigns, and pay fees that rank among the highest offered throughout public television. Non-fiction producers might also want to check into other national series such as *The American Experience* and *Frontline*. Keep an eye on trade publications for other national series solicitations.

If your work falls outside the scope of an existing series or you have tried but been rejected, you can go directly to *PBS Programming*, whose three content areas are: News & Information (i.e., factual programs, including News & Public Affairs and Science & History); Drama; Performance & Cultural (here is where you will also find the "How-to's"); and Children's Programming. Start by sending a letter and information packet with videocassette to the PBS Office of Program Man-agement in Alexandria, Virginia. Expect a turn-around time of three to six weeks. Follow-up telephone calls during that period, if any, should be placed sparingly and should never take the place of materials that stand on their own. Decisions are made jointly by the programming departments. Be prepared for rejection.

But, if PBS wants your show, your relationship has only just begun. Do your best to negotiate an acceptable acquisition fee. PBS determines this fee on a case-by-case basis. Try to get the best air date you can to coordinate a national publicity campaign. Consider lobbying for an on-air video or audio tag at the end of your program, such as a 1-800 number for purchasing a videocassette or a national hotline for more information on the subject. Keep in mind that strict PBS guidelines govern such promotions. Expect to re-cut your program to meet packaging decisions and conform to the technical guidelines outlined in *The Red Book*, available from PBS Program Management. If you know someone who has been funded by ITVS, ask to look at the ITVS *Program Producer's Handbook*. The media arts center in your region may have a copy in its library. It is not for sale or intended for use by non-ITVS producers, but the handbook is a useful interpretation of PBS guidelines that also govern ITVS programs. Once PBS has given you a Program Acceptance Form (PAF), it may take months for your program to go on the air.

PBS Fundraising Programming commissions and acquires works from many sources, including independent producers, but with a bottom-line mandate of raising money for stations. Formatted around station pledge breaks, these specials must demonstrate profit on investment—as well as meeting the NPS core schedule's criteria of quality and national interest. A current topic helps. If the little-known book you based your program on just became a runaway best seller, if your show's host has just been catapulted to national celebrity status, or if you can already see the natural pauses for an intercut pledge-break script, send your packet (with a sales spin) and a tape to PBS Fundraising Programming.

After PBS, the largest supplier of programs to public TV stations is the Boston-based American Program Service (APS) whose precursor is the Eastern Educational Television Network/Interregional Program Service. APS sells "acquisitions" programs to public TV stations through twice-yearly teleconferences and an annual market. Station-presented programs are offered free through a Program Exchange.

Here is how an acquisition works. Call APS and tell them about your program. If they are interested, they will ask for written information and/or a videotape. If they agree that this program is of national interest and appeal, negotiations can begin. Their price depends on how much money they think stations will pay for your show. If the fee does not suit you, you may be able to make it up with outside underwriting or negotiating an on-air promotion to boost videocassette sales. Once you have a deal, APS will put your program on the block and see how many stations respond. If enough stations want to buy, your program will go to contract. If the interest is not there, your deal is off.

You can also find a regional springboard to a national audience in the regional programming services: Central Educational Network (CEN) in Des Plaines, Illinois; Pacific Mountain Network (PMN) in Denver; and Southern Educational Communications Association (SECA) in Columbia, South Carolina. The regionals are funded by membership dues from stations in their regions, but provide programs nationally via a satellite "soft feed" for stations to broadcast if, how, and when they want. You can buy inexpensive satellite time (charges vary, starting with nonprofit vs. for-profit rates) and the regionals will provide publicity support through their own communication network with public television stations. Through a combination of fundraising for the satellite uplink, lining up an underwriter for publicity, and promoting videocassette sales on air, your investment just might pay for itself.

Let's look at an alternative programming consortium tack used for independent producer Micha X. Peled's *Inside God's Bunker*, a chilling portrait of Hebron's militant Israeli settlers. Because of the film's red-hot topicality in the wake of the Hebron massacre, Peled was reluctant to wait for the next P.O.V. cycle to try for a national air date. Unable to get a broadcast even on his local public television station, Peled decided not to waste time going directly to PBS. Instead, the film's London-based distributor sold the forty-minute English version to Program Resources Group (PRG), which placed it in an "International Dispatches" programming strand and distributed it to a consortium of secondary stations in markets also served by a primary station. Lead station WLIW in Long Island wrapped the program with a studio discussion for optional use by participating stations. Through this alternative route, Peled's documentary, which was funded by European TV and had already been broadcast in fourteen other countries, found its way to American television audiences.

As you plot your national broadcast strategy, remember the five *minority consortia*, funded by CPB to acquire and package works by and about culturally specific minorities, and distribute them through the public airwaves. The consortia include: the National Black Programming Consortium in Columbus, Ohio; Native American Public Broadcasting Consortium in Lincoln, Nebraska; National Latino Communications Center in Los Angeles; National Asian American Telecommunications Association in San Francisco; and Pacific Islanders in Communications in Honolulu. Each consortium has its own structure, but they all work closely with independent producers and, at this writing, all of them have funding programs. If your work receives a production grant, that consortium holds the broadcast rights. Consortia curate and package thematic series of independent works and other TV specials. Then—just like you, but with the advantage of established collegial credentials—they pitch their programs to PBS, APS, the regionals and individual stations. The minority consortia increasingly act as co-presenters within existing series such as P.O.V. in a shared effort to cultivate community-based press coverage, and woo crossover audiences.

WORKING WITH A "PRESENTING" STATION

"Independent" does not have to mean "alone." You may want to look for a *presenting station* to serve as your entry to a national broadcast. Doors that are closed to independent producers (such as the APS Program Exchange) swing open for stations. Programmers see a show in a different light if it comes with station backing, a signal that the first hurdle—will stations want this program?—has already been cleared. The financial arrangement depends on the audience, prestige, and programming niche your show is likely to claim for your presenting station. The station may offer you a fee, pick up the costs you would have incurred if PBS had accepted the program directly from you, and lead the charge on your publicity campaign. Conversely, in these financially strapped times, the producer may not only go unpaid, but effectively have to pay the station for its presenting role by covering all of the station's costs.

Independent producer Dorothy Fadiman has a longstanding relationship with San Jose station KTEH. The station presented her hour-long documentary *Why Do These Kids Love School?* to PBS, where it was picked up quickly and packaged as part of a back-to-school cluster of programs examining education. Her film had a national prime-time feed, and continues to have a television life in re-broadcasts. As the presenting station, KTEH negotiated a 1-800 promotional tag at the end of the program. Fadiman says that the re-broadcasts, coupled with the on-air promotion, have led to brisk and continued sales to educational markets. The revenues are shared by PBS, the station, the producer, and the distributor, which ranks her documentary among its most active titles. Especially important to Fadiman was the energetic publicity work that KTEH directed toward its fellow stations and the local and national press. In contrast, both KTEH and Fadiman struck out with PBS when it came to her Academy Award-nominated, half-hour documentary, *When Abortion Was Illegal: Untold Stories*. With PBS unresponsive (her CPB Gold Medal for Independent Production notwithstanding), the film first found its way to the national airwaves through a "Women's Health on Public Television" series programmed by KCTS in Seattle, and distributed by the Public Television Outreach Alliance via the Pacific Mountain Network. Subsequently, it was picked up for a "Women's Voices" series co-presented by APS and P.O.V.

While a public television station is the most obvious presenting entity, this role is also played by the minority consortia, media arts centers, festivals, and other independent groups that package individual programs into series and—as an intermediary on your behalf—shop it around.

LOCAL BROADCAST: THINK AND ACT LOCALLY

Many veteran producers caution that it is a mistake to delay the important relationship-building contacts with stations until you have stacked up enough national rejections. Your decision on whether to head directly for the stations depends on such factors as the time of year you finish your program or whether you can reach your intended audiences more effectively region-by-region.

To arrange local air dates, your first contact will be with station program directors (their titles vary). Do you have a personal contact there? Having a station insider hand your material to the program director is more effective than a cold submission. One producer with moxie enlisted a prominent television critic, who had lauded the film while on a festival jury, to put in a good word to the local program director. A letter of support from a television columnist or other opinion maker may add weight to your case.

Program directors defy generalizations. Talk to other independents and it will not take long to get a handful of names of programmers with a reputation for openness to new ideas, a curiosity about new independent works, a flair for putting on shows that give a local counterpoint to the PBS feed, or an instinct for creating series from programs drawn from various sources. Dip into your archive of *The Independent* to check out Michael Fox's March 1995 article, "In the Program Director's Chair," which profiles highly regarded public television programmers in Los Angeles, Kentucky, Seattle, and St. Paul/Minneapolis.

Let us trace the experience of independent producer Ellen Bruno with her two half-hour films *Samsara: Death and Rebirth in Cambodia* and *Satya: A Prayer for the Enemy*. With *Samsara*, her shotgun mailing of scores of letters and a videotapes to major stations was costly and time-consuming. Most stations were uninterested and only a handful had any money to pay. When a station accepted her film, it was almost always for an ongoing independent showcase or a special series being curated by the program director. Painstaking as it was, this approach got her festival award-winning film on television in regions throughout the country. Bruno returned to those program directors several years later when she completed *Satya*, and virtually all of them snapped it up. *Satya* went on to a national broadcast premiere on P.O.V. following its local broadcasts on stations such as KQED in San Francisco (*Docs of the Bay*), KUHT in Houston, and KLRU in Austin (both of Bruno's films were included in series presented by the Southwest Alternate Media Project), and WNYC in New York, in a program of selections from the Human Rights Watch Film Festival. Good things can come from a good relationship with a station. A future co-production agreement? A station offering to present your next project to PBS? An unexpected spin-off in Bruno's case was an approach by a station who wanted to commission her to make a ten-minute piece.

THEY WANT YOUR PROGRAM, BUT WHEN WILL IT BE SHOWN?

Once your program is *accepted*, throw your resources behind creating and carrying out a publicity campaign that will get your show *seen*. In the words of one consultant, independent producers should not leave their promotion up to anyone else but take on "as much of the publicity as they can stomach."

First, Get The Best Air Date You Can Get. Bargain for the best air date you can to make a coordinated publicity effort possible. For a national broadcast, your ideal will be "same night and time" carriage on the core schedule, which member stations have a tacit agreement to carry. Be prepared to compromise. But if you have a persuasive programming angle you may have luck in getting carried the same day throughout the country, if not the same time. It is no accident that Skip Sweeney's 1980s personal video classic *My Father Sold Studebakers* was carried on Father's Day, nor his follow-up piece, *My Mother Married Wilbur Stump*, on Mother's Day.

Now, Line Up the Stations. Once you know your air date, draw up a target list of your most important markets, generally based on their size or on demographics that make them a natural for your program. Allowing as much lead time as possible, call or write the program directors of the stations on your list. Your message should be brief and to the point: tell them the date of your program, give a brief description emphasizing any special appeal your program will have in that market and offer to work with the station on publicity. Ask if they plan to air the show or first need a preview tape, which you can send that day. Your task, which may take fifteen minutes or a month, is to convince the program director that your show will be well reviewed and received in that market. Enclosing a favorable write-up or two may prove your point. Follow up with a phone call or letter and, without badgering, move toward a commitment to air your program, and, if possible, to broadcast on the same date as other stations so you can include them in your national publicity strategy.

PUBLICITY: THE FINAL FRONTIER

Here is another advantage to being part of a national series: the series, not you, will pay for a nationwide publicity campaign. Series usually hire outside public relations firms, and ask you to be available for interviews and provide a preliminary press release, photos, and other basic promotional materials. For one-shot specials, however, the lead is usually taken by the producer, the presenting station, or even the program's underwriter. In all cases, expect to work in varying degrees of closeness and intensity with publicists and station program information (PI) directors.

PBS does not promote everything on its schedule, but is charged with getting basic promotional materials into the hands of the stations so they can do the press work in their own markets. The producer is responsible for generating and paying for these materials, as outlined in "Producer Promotion Requirements," available from National Press Relations. Whether you or PBS does promotion, here is what the stations need:

- a basic news release (that they can reproduce on their own letterheads for local press efforts);
- brief program description for use in station program guides

and newspaper listings;
- a photo;
- promotional spots of various lengths; and
- a highlights clip and videocassettes for the PBS press offices.

PBS provides stations with a press preview feed a couple of weeks in advance so stations can start working the local TV critics. The National Press Relations offices in New York and Los Angeles hit the major press in those two cities, as well as national wire services and syndicates, national monthlies and weeklies (including *TV Guide*) and major newspapers. With six to ten weeks' lead time, these offices can also pitch feature ideas, set up interviews with producers, and arrange press screenings as appropriate.

Depending on how your program gets on public TV, you might find yourself working with the National Press Relations offices of PBS, *Alive TV*'s public relations firm, the APS programming and marketing information director, your presenting station, or PI directors at stations in different parts of the country. Value their experience and guidance, but for maximum coverage, do not stand on the sidelines.

Give yourself a crash course on publicity. Read the "Promotion" chapter of this book. Go to your public library and look up important monthlies, weeklies, and dailies. Compile a list of entertainment magazines, general magazines with TV columns, specialty publications that relate to your program's subject, and national radio programs. Call them and find out how they work, getting information on their deadlines, editors, and critics. Tell them about your program and ask if you can send them a press kit and videotape. Create a deadline-driven calendar and get to work, using the telephone and press kits with cover letters to make your pitch. Give suggestions on how a review, an interview with you or someone in your program, a feature story, or a critic's choice highlight will interest their readers or listeners.

Work directly with the stations. Purchase labels from PBS and send out additional mailings to PI directors at stations in your key markets. Seek their advice on how to best publicize your program in the local market. Ask for names and phone numbers for local critics and press you can approach directly. Make story suggestions for the station's program guide.

Finally, don't forget to call home! Make a regional sorting of your own mail list of funders, supporters, friends, and family, and other contacts (get personal mail lists from people in your program, too). Send them postcards listing the public television air dates in their region. Few things will be as rewarding to those who helped you along the way as the knowledge that the work they believed in all along stands on the threshold of breaking through to television audiences.

[Editor's Postscript: This chapter was written against a backdrop of tremendous structural change in the mid-1990s. Political pressures, legislative antipathy toward funding public broadcasting, and the PBS quest for a programming stance that will distinguish it from the commercial network line-up have triggered a restructuring process at PBS, the extent of which is not known as we go to press. Details will change, but the basic tenets outlined in this chapter—that there are many routes to getting your work on public television, each with its own rewards and costs—will undoubtedly remain intact.]

CHAPTER 6

THEATRICAL DISTRIBUTION OF FEATURE FILMS

David Rosen
with special thanks to Steve Reynolds

Filmmaking, perhaps more than any other art, is a social act. Not only does a film emerge from the collective participation of tens (sometimes hundreds) of people, but it needs to be seen by an audience to realize itself as a work of art—let alone commerce. Theatrical distribution is the process by which a film moves from its completed form as a print to its exhibition at a movie theater.

Theatrical distribution involves two distinct aspects—distribution and exhibition. In this chapter, we will concentrate on the distributor's release campaign as well as the exhibition process. While reference to the dominant Hollywood system will be made, special attention will be paid to the theatrical release of independent films—lower-budget specialty or art films, be they inherently commercial or non-commercial productions.

Theatrical distribution is but one, and usually the most important, form of distribution for certain kinds of films. Specifically, the theatrical market is dominated by dramatic or narrative films that are produced and exhibited in 16mm and 35mm and are feature-length, running ninety minutes or so. Due to social as well as economic factors, other film forms (like documentary, experimental, and short-subject) receive only occasional theatrical release. Other forms of distribution—such as cable and broadcast television, non-theatrical exhibition, and home video—may be more appropriate for showing these types of film/video productions. Additionally, due to the significant expenses associated with theatrical distribution and exhibition, self-distribution is very difficult to successfully implement. Because of this, theatrical self-distribution—"four-walling"—will be briefly considered at the end of the chapter.

When this chapter was first published in 1989, the independent film scene was fundamentally different from that found today. Then, independent features—and especially narrative films—were conceived of as specialty films. They were emphatically not mainstream movies, and even the most commercially successful effused a deep humanistic, social consciousness; they echoed the spirit of the turbulent and progressive 1960s. Many of the filmmakers, distributors, and exhibitors shared the broad culture and values of that halcyon era.

Today's independent film scene is far more commercial. Like so many aspects of the culture industry, the demands of the marketplace profoundly influence creativity. The unexpected success of *sex, lies & videotape*—it grossed an estimated $26 million!—fundamentally changed the independent film business. A sizable audience was identified and, with it, independent films matured into a significant movie-industry genre, like action-adventure or children's films. Because of the significantly lower costs of production and marketing associated with independents, the financial performance of a relatively successful indie can be superior to that of most studio releases.[1]

This development led the studios to either acquire the most aggressive independent distributors (e.g., the Disney takeover of Miramax, the Turner buyout of New Line and Castle Rock) or start their own indie or lower-budget divisions (e.g., Gramercy by Universal/Polygram, Searchlight by Fox, Sony Classics by Columbia). The more mainstream "micro-major" distributors attempt to "cream skim" the yearly crop of independent films (through pre-sale financing deals and other mechanisms). In response, a new generation of boutique indie distributors—like October and Zeitgeist—have emerged to complement more established companies like Samuel Goldwyn and New Yorker. These, and many others, are keeping alive the perhaps less commercially viable but more quirky, maverick, off-beat, aesthetically original, and socially conscious films that have been the hallmark of independent filmmaking over the last two decades.

HISTORICAL OVERVIEW

The history of independent film distribution and exhibition is one of struggle by relatively small entrepreneurs, usually woefully under-capitalized, trying to gain operating space within a highly oligopolistic industry. Their fate is analogous to that of the independent filmmaker.

The current form of theatrical distribution took shape during the 1920s and has remained relatively intact ever since. During the early period, the "Big Five" Hollywood studios (Paramount, Warner Brothers, M-G-M, Twentieth Century Fox, and RKO) operated twin business units in production/distribution and exhibition. The majors organized their exhibition circuits along regional, non-competitive lines.

Together with the "Little Three" (Columbia, Universal, and United Artists), the studios gained effective control over the film market. They dominated through practices that involved full-line "block booking" (e.g., the studio forced the non-major exhibitors to acquire a season's supply of new releases without seeing them or having the ability to reject undesirable ones), "first-run zoning" (e.g., fixed tiers for film releases) and admission price discriminations. These practices were principally applied to independent exhibitors who were dependent on the studios for product, but not to the Little Three studios. This situation remained in place until 1948 when the Supreme Court, in the *Paramount* decree, ordered the studios to divest their exhibition units.

Nevertheless, from the Depression through the early 1950s, "B" filmmaking was the locus of activity for independent producers and distributors. During the Depression, movie-house ticket sales fell precipitously and the double-bill was created by independent exhibitors to lure back audiences by offering two shows for the one admission price. While the majors' A title was the main attraction, the low-budget B film emerged to supply double-bill programs.

The principal "Poverty Row" micro-studios included Monogram and Republic, the two most important, and Grand National during the 1930s; Producers Releasing Corp. during the 1940s; and American-International Pictures during the 1950s. Added to the first-tier list were the literally dozens of tiny operations with such names as Tiffany-Stahl, Sono Art-World Wide (later bought out by Fox), Majestic, Mascot, Chesterfield, Puritan, Invincible, Victory, Allied, and Liberty. These micro-studios produced a wide variety of crime thrillers, adventures, teen fare, westerns, and patriotic war movies. The audience for B films were working- and lower-class people who, with the coming of television, deserted the movie-house for the comfort of free television in their own living rooms.

Today, the film business has come nearly full circle from where it was in the 1920s. Spurred by the Reagan administration's easing of regulatory restraints and other factors during the 1980s, the dominant media conglomerates—and especially the Hollywood studios—have not only (re)gained control over the major exhibition chains, but through a series of strategic acquisitions, have gained control over the distribution of more acceptable, mainstream independent films. And, not unlike the experience of three-quarters of a century ago, a new generation of "mini-micro" studios have emerged to counter marketplace hegemony by distributing the works of non-mainstream independent filmmakers.

THEATRICAL RELEASES, 1980s-1990s

Over the last decade, motion picture theatrical releasing has followed a relatively cyclical path, surging forward and then back only to rise up again as overall market conditions shifted. Output grew by 36 percent between 1982 (with 361 releases) to 1988 (when it hit record high of 491 releases), only to contract over the next four years (dropping to 385 in 1990) and to bounce back through the 90s to reach 462 in 1994. Table 1 details this decade; Figure 1 presents it more graphically.

TABLE 1

Motion Picture Performance:

Movies Released: Studio vs. Independent Share, 1982-1994

Year	Movies Released*	Studio Releases**	Independent Releases	% Independent
1982	361	150	211	58.4%
1983	396	166	230	58.1%
1984	408	152	256	62.7%
1985	389	138	251	64.5%
1986	419	133	286	68.3%
1987	489	122	397	81.2%
1988	491	153	338	68.8%
1989	458	157	301	65.7%
1990	385	158	227	59.0%
1991	423	150	273	64.5%
1992	426	142	284	66.7%
1993	450	156	294	65.3%
1994	462	184	277	60.0%

*	Includes new and reissued movies
**	Includes MPAA members companies
Source:	Motion Picture Association of America

FIGURE 1
MOVIE RELEASES, 1982-1994

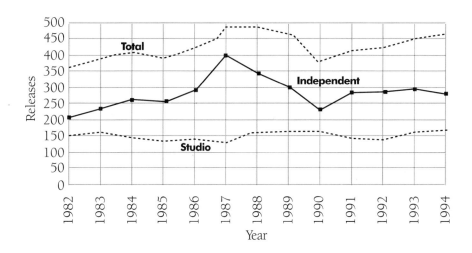

Independent films account for approximately two-thirds of total movies released. During the early 80s, independents made up less than three-fifths (fifty-eight percent), but as overall output surged during the mid-80s, the share of independent releases skyrocketed to more than three-fourths (eighty-one percent) of the total, only to again fall to its current level. A small handful of the principal distributors of the period (e.g., Goldwyn, First Run, New Yorker, and Skouras) are still in business, but many (e.g., Cinecom, Island, Avenue, Orion Classics, and Miramax) have gone out of business or been absorbed by a major.

The ebb and flow of overall film output as well as that portion comprising independent fare is tied to a number of factors, including the emergence of new ancillary outlets for motion pictures (e.g., home video and cable in the 80s), the multiplexing of movie theaters, and shifts in demographics (especially the maturation of baby-bombers). As the major restructuring of the in-home entertainment market gets underway with cable, satellite, and telephone companies providing more programming options, a surge of independent production and theatrical releases is likely to occur once again.

THEATRICAL DISTRIBUTION

In a formal sense, theatrical distribution commences after a filmmaker has completed post-production and secured an agreement with a distributor. Distribution usually consists of the development and implementation of a marketing campaign followed by the actual release to a movie house. Perhaps most important, the theatrical release provides the necessary push by which a successful release into the other ancillary markets, especially home video, cable, and foreign, is effected.

The U.S. motion picture distribution system has been and continues to be dominated by a handful of Hollywood studios. As indicated in Table 2, its structure remains nearly identical to that of the 1920s, with today's "Big Six" and "Little Four" controlling approximately ninety percent of the $5.25 billion 1994 theatrical box office gross. The power of these companies over the market—and especially over independent film releasing—cannot be overestimated. Historically, each year only a handful of independent films break out, becoming the darling of the critics and achieving strong box office sales. Today, the major studios control not only the major blockbuster movies upon which the business is built, but control the handful of successful independent films as well.

Studios distribute movies produced in-house (usually on a contractual basis with an established producer who has an "out-put" deal with the studio) or acquired from an outside source. Such outside sources include movies from the mini-majors as well as established "independent" producers. On rare occasions, as with Warner's release of Stand and Deliver or Columbia's release of I Like it Like That, a studio will pick up a low-budget independent film that does not have high-powered connections.

An independent filmmaker will more than likely secure a distribution deal from one of the smaller micro-majors or Little Four or a classics division of one of the Big Six. These companies specialize in handling lower-budget, more idiosyncratic art, crossover, documentary, and foreign-language films. Table 3 breaks into three tiers many of the leading distributors of independent films. In addition to the companies identified, a host of established and startup independent distributors are releasing specialty films, including Drift, First Run, MK2, New Yorker, Shadow Distribution, Skouras, Stranger Than Fiction Films, and Upstate Films. (These companies need to be distinguished from the more mainstream independent distributors, such as Savoy, RKO, and Hemdale, who do not normally release specialty or art house fare.)

TABLE 2

The Studio Distribution System:
The "Big 6" and the "Little 4"

Distributor	Parent Company	Related Holding*
BIG 6		
Disney/BuenaVista Touchstone Hollywood Miramax	Disney	Cable network, home video
Columbia TriStar SonyClassics	Sony	Movie theaters, TV production, home video
Paramount	Viacom	TV production, movie theaters, TV stations, TV production, cable networks
20th Century Fox Searchlight	News Corp.	TV network, TV stations, home video
Warner Bros. Triumph	Time Warner	Cable systems, TV production, home video distribution
Universal/MCA Gramercy	Seagram/Matsushita	TV network, TV production
LITTLE 4		
Gramercy MGM-UA	PolyGram/Philips and Universal	Propaganda Films
Samuel Goldwyn	Samuel Goldwyn	TV production, Movie theaters
Turner** New Line/Fine Line Castle Rock	Turner	Cable networks (CNN, TMC, TBS)

* Holdings are presented to illustrate vertical integration and are not intended to suggest a thorough analysis of a company's varied holdings (including consumer electronic products, telecommunications networks, newspaper, magazine, book and new media publishing companies, theme parks, and other entities), domestic and global.
** Time-Warner recently announced their plans to acquire Turner.

Source: *Praxis,* 1995

TABLE 3

Specialty-Film Distributors

Tier	Distributor	Recent Releases
Tier #1	Columbia/Sony Classics	*Vanya on 42nd Street, A Man of No Importance*
	Disney/Miramax	*Like Water for Chocolate, Pulp Fiction, Clerks, Ready to Wear, Tom & Viv*
	Turner/New Line/Fine Line	*Dumb & Dumber, The Mask, Hoop Dreams, Short Cuts*
	Goldwyn	*The Wedding Banquet, 32/Glen Gould, The Madness of King George*
	Gramercy/Polygram-Universal	*Priscilla, Shallow Grave, Panther*
	October	*Last Seduction, The War Room, Ruby in Paradise*
Tier #2	Castle Rock	*Top of the World, Two Small Bodies, Alligator Eyes*
	First Look Pictures	*The Secret of Roan Inish, Party Girl, La Scorta, Bhaji on the Beach*
	I.R.S. Releasing	*One False Move, My New Gun, The Beans of Egypt, Maine*
	Northern Arts	*Tokyo Decadence, Skipping Razors*
	Seventh Art Releasing	*Making Up!, Consuming Sun*
	Strand Releasing	*Macho Dancer, Natural History of Parking Lots, Crush*
	Tara	*Freedom on My Mind, Dr. Bethune, Berkeley in the Sixties*
	Trimark Pictures	*Dead Alive, Federal Hill, Curse of the Starving Class*
	Zeitgeist	*Poison, Wittgenstein, Coming Out Under Fire*
Tier #3	Angelika	*The Trial, Blessing*
	Arrow Entertainment	*My Life's in Turnaround, Sofie*
	Circle Releasing	*Blood Simple, The Killer, Dark Obsession*
	Kino	*Daughters of the Dust, Visions of Light*
	Rainbow Releasing/Jaglom	*Eating, Mistress*
	Roxie	*Red Rock West, Ishi*
	Shadow Distribution	*Latcho Drom*

Source: *Variety, FILMMAKER*, and *Praxis*, 1995

MARKETING & RELEASE

For independent filmmakers who strike a deal with a distributor, the release campaign involves the development of the overall release and marketing campaigns. The distributor must determine the release strategy, select the city/cities and theater(s) for the opening and rollout, and book the designated theaters. In addition, the distributor will prepare the promotional and publicity materials and create the artwork and trailer. Most important, distributors secure collections of box-office rentals for ticket sales.

The overall campaign strategy is all-important for the film's theatrical performance. Such a strategy begins with a candid assessment of the film's strengths and weaknesses—its market appeal! Usually, such a strategy has been informally agreed upon by the filmmaker and distributor at the time the deal was struck; all parties involved should know what kind of movie they've got. A distributor's failure to correctly assess a film's appeal can be disastrous. A small company operating on a tight budget has little money available to substantially revise the campaign.

At the heart of the strategy is a preliminary assessment of audience most likely to see the film. Such an assessment involves two issues. First, the likely audience's composition or character has to be specified. Is the audience only an art house, women's, gay, ethnic, racial, religious, or regional group, or does the movie have crossover potential to reach a larger constituency? Second, an estimate as to the initial and long-term audience performance—number of tickets likely to be sold—has to be made. This is a tricky, imprecise science usually based upon the distributor's knowledge of how other, comparable films have done on a regional or national basis.

Once a strategy has been agreed upon, appropriate marketing and promotional support materials need to be developed. Such materials include a presskit, with black-and-white cast photos and production stills, background materials on the principals, and, where available, favorable reviews or feature articles that might have appeared if the movie was in a festival or competition. In addition, a "one-sheet" or poster has to be designed and printed, a print ad has to be created, and a theater lobby display, sometimes including a special marquee and flag, has to be prepared. Also critical is the production of the trailer, the short clip with appealing cuts from the movie with voice-over narration for showing in movie theaters in advance of the opening.

Distributors will often test the effectiveness of either the movie itself and/or the various components of the campaign through appropriate market-research techniques. Pre-screenings are used to measure audience reactions to the film's final cut or the score. In addition, focus groups are used to determine which poster design is more appealing or better represents the film. Similarly, exit polls are often conducted during the first weekend screenings to determine audience response. These techniques help the distributor better calibrate the campaign.

Critical to the effectiveness of these marketing elements is novelty and presentation quality. Especially with lower-budget films, it is essential to promote those strong, unique elements in a presskit or art work. The competition for reviews and audience attention is intense and, for an independent film to stand out, it needs a unique hook. Such a hook could be the film's innovative storyline, that it is the filmmaker's first feature, that it was made on a shoestring budget with great ingenuity, that it demonstrates technical wizardry, or spotlights a major Hollywood talent. The distributor will look for anything to help the film stand out from the flood of movies competing for attention.

The hook helps stimulate word-of-mouth. Before the film opens, the distributor will organize screenings for critics and, usually, for members of appropriate target-audience segments. Critics' reviews that appear at the time of the film's release often make or break a movie—they are the guideposts of popular consumption. Given the high costs of print, radio, and television advertising, distributors depend on favorable reviews to attract the initial audiences. If the initial audiences like the movie and, in turn, tell their friends that they *must* see it, a hit movie begins to take shape. With ongoing newspaper ads, which usually incorporate excerpts from favorable reviews, audience interest is further stimulated.

Successful films, however, usually attract interest among distributors, other filmmakers, theater owners, film critics, and even informed filmgoers before the formal distribution process commences. This early awareness—the film's initial (and hopefully favorable) buzz—is invaluable to an independent film's commercial performance. Increasingly, this buzz is taking place even before the first day of principal photography, the official commencement of production. How the film is packaged, if a star is attached, if the script is hot, and other factors directly affect presale financing. And such financing, by distributors for home video, television, and foreign markets, is essential to get the movie made. Generating early (and effective!) attention is the principal function of such pre-launch venues as the Sundance Film Festival (perhaps the single most important festival for independents) and the Independent Feature Film Market (IFFM), presented annually in New York City by the Independent Feature Project.

THEATRICAL EXHIBITION

Analogous to the marketing strategy is a distributor's release strategy. It is based on a candid assessment of the film's performance potential. Key elements of the strategy include: deciding in which market(s) to open the film; determining how many theaters to open in; determining how long to wait before a rollout and how wide the release should be. For an average release, opening costs for the top nine markets alone can run from $150,000 to more than $500,000. Underscoring every decision is a need for creative flexibility so as to be able to quickly respond to unanticipated developments encountered during the release, particularly during the most critical early phases of the launch.

The most important factor in implementing a successful theatrical release is securing the right movie house. While this sounds easy enough, competition among distributors for a choice venue is often intense. Even though there has been a nearly thirty percent increase in the number of screens during the 1980s (from 17,675 in 1980 to approximately 25,000 in 1994), there is usually only one—or, in larger markets, a handful—of choice art houses that regularly show specialty films.

The exhibition markets in the United States are organized along four tiers basically conforming to the size of major cities (see Table 4). Specialty films usually open in New York City and rollout to other cities. On occasion and depending on the particularities of a film, a distributor might choose to open in, for example, Seattle because of its strong moviegoing tradition, or another market appropriate to the film's story. However, and with some exceptions, nearly eighty percent of the total revenues earned by a specialty film come from the top nine markets—tiers 1 and 2.

Within some of the larger markets there are a few alternative or non-commercial movie houses that provide quasi-commercial exhibition to specialty films. Such theaters as the Film Forum in New York or Pacific Film Archives in Berkeley are successful examples. In addition, with the spread of multiplex theaters some screens are being programmed with art films.

TABLE 4

U.S. Specialty-Film Theatrical Release Tiers

Tier	Markets
Tier 1	New York—usually for initial launch and attracting national press attention. Los Angeles—for West Coast launch and attracting film industry attention.
Tier 2	Includes Boston, Washington, D.C., Philadelphia, Chicago, San Francisco, and Seattle—these are the smaller major markets.
Tier 3	Includes Atlanta, Austin, Baltimore, Cleveland, Dallas, Detroit, Houston, Minneapolis, Salt Lake City, and Tucson—these are larger smaller markets with sophisticated moviegoers due to presence of major universities or state capitals.
Tier 4	Includes the multitude of smaller cities like Des Moines, Norfolk, Richmond, and Rochester.

Source: D. Rosen, *Off-Hollywood: The Making & Marketing of Independent Films*, IFP/Sundance (1987), Grove Press (1990).

A good working relationship between the distributor and the exhibitor is critical, especially in the second- and third-tier markets. Guaranteeing a theater's availability on a pre-set date is essential for the execution of a successful campaign. The momentum generated at the initial launch has to be maintained through careful planning and coordination. Most independent distributors rely on a network of sub-distributors throughout the country to handle relations in smaller markets. These sub-distributors coordinate co-op ad arrangements, print distribution and, all important, box office collections.

It is important to understand that the economics of theatrical distribution and current market conditions—especially industry consolidation—works against the interests of small distributors and independent filmmakers. Exhibition agreements are structured as "step" deals—after taxes and the movie house's overhead costs (the "house nut") are deducted from the box office gross ticket sales, then the exhibitor and distributor split the net proceeds according to agreed-upon percentage terms or steps. The conventional 90/10 deal has the exhibitor initially getting the lion's share of the net revenues and, with each week that the film plays at the movie house, the proceeds dispersion formula shifts to the distributor's favor. Netting it all out, the distributor traditionally averages approximately forty-five percent return of box office gross revenues—the "rental."

In today's marketplace, the relatively high supply of annual new films being released gives the exhibitors a powerful weapon to quickly drop a film that does not demonstrate "legs" or appeal during the first-weekend launch. Often a distributor's commitment to the film and favorable critical reviews can help the film buy time until favorable word-of-mouth brings in the audience. Unfortunately, all too many films fail to hold a movie house past the first or second weekend.

SELF-DISTRIBUTION

Some independent filmmakers will resort to self-distribution if they fail to secure a commercial distribution deal. Self-distribution is traditionally referred to as four-walling and is a very expensive, time-consuming, and risky way to release a movie. However, it can work. (For a detailed discussion of this topic refer to Joe Berlinger's chapter in this book).

Self-distribution usually takes one of two forms—vanity screenings or genuine self-distribution. With regard to the first, on rare occasions a resourceful independent filmmaker will four-wall or rent a local theater for a specified period in order to qualify for an Academy Award nomination, to help generate critical attention and, hopefully, demonstrate to a distributor that the film has commercial potential. *The Ballad of Gregorio Cortez*, a classic independent film, effectively utilized this technique to secure a very advantageous deal with a major distributor.

Genuine self-distribution can be an effective way for an independent filmmaker to get a film out. Historically, however, this method has been more effectively exploited by genre filmmakers (e.g., horror, wilderness, action, teen) than specialty or art filmmakers. Recently, Haile Gerima has been effectively self-distributing *Sankofa*, targeting African-American neighborhoods and community groups for support.

To work effectively, this approach usually involves a market-by-market or region-by-region release plan, and requires significant financial investment. In addition to rental costs for multiple theaters (including projectionist, ticket-taker and candy-counter person), the producer has to create a highly professional advertising campaign and have the resources to buy sufficient print (and sometimes radio or television time) to promote the movie. It often happens that these four-walling expenses are greater than the movie's "negative" costs.

CONCLUSION

Theatrical distribution is the first window through which a movie enters the feature-film distribution pipeline. Successful exhibition is invaluable to a film's performance in all ancillary markets, including home video, pay cable, foreign, non-theatrical, and, in time, video-on-demand. It is a difficult and expensive form of distribution, but its results—especially when successful—are the dreams upon which the movie business are built.

For independent filmmakers, the current theatrical distribution market is—again!—poised for significant change. The movie business is historically cyclical, and is now beginning to be rekindled by major changes in distribution technologies. During the mid- to late-1980s, the film business was buoyed by the explosive growth of home video and, to a lesser extent, cable television. An enormous number of movies, both new and catalog, were required to meet expanding demand. This helped independents secure financing through pre-sales and other deals with distributors and home video companies, among other means.

As the home video market achieved near-saturation in the early 90s, demand for new product fell. Following *sex, lies & videotape*, a new generation of independent films achieved remarkable box-office sales. Some of the most recent high-performance, mainstream indies follow: *Pulp Fiction* topped $60 million; *Four Weddings and a Funeral* topped $52 million; *The Piano* topped $40 million; *Menace II Society* grossed nearly $30 million; *Jason's Lyric* topped $20 million; and *You So Crazy* topped $10 million. (*Variety* estimates that in 1994 twenty-two independent releases achieved box-office grosses of more than $1 million.) Concomitantly, the relative strength of the leading independent distributors grew (in part due to the value of their libraries), leading to their acquisitions by the majors.

In this environment, the successful production and release of more expensive independent films ($5 million+ "negative" costs) will become more difficult. Distributors will look for lower-budgeted movies with "stars attached" and be less willing to take risks on first-time directors, or more offbeat movies that do not seem to meet a prescribed formula of successful performance. In effect, many contemporary independent films (what has been dubbed "mainstream independents") challenge the very spirit of independent filmmaking.

This is an operating contradiction within the independent distribution scene: original films are what critics champion and audiences come out for, but, being unpredictable, distributors are more cautious about backing them. Nevertheless, with the likely explosion in video distribution to the home during the rest of the 1990s—with increased cable channel capacity, direct broadcast satellite (DBS), telephone company video delivery, and movies on CDs—a further upswing in independent movie production and theatrical release is probable.

These factors will likely fuel the emergence of a three-tier structure for independent filmmaking. The top tier will be those financed by a pre-sale deal with a major specialty distributor (whether the studios maintain their specialty arms is an open question); the second tier will be composed of those that secure a distribution deal after completion and/or a distribution agreement from a smaller company with limited capital; and, finally, the third tier will be those features that fail to secure a commercial distributor—or lack the necessary wherewithal for self-distribution.

For those in the second and third tiers, this video-driven environment will require filmmakers to return to the innovative, risk-taking, and lower-budget mode of filmmaking that characterized the mid-1980s and today's guerrilla indies. While more challenging, and probably less financially rewarding, these constraints will probably help keep alive a new wave of creativity and ingenuity that has historically been the hallmark of independent film.

Notes:

[1] In 1994, New Line had a financial performance superior to that of the major studios. Based on a cost-to-gross performance ratio, it topped the industry at 126%; the majors performed much more weakly—Paramount (87%), Disney (59%), Universal (41%), Warner (23%), TriStar (-3%), and Columbia (-33%) [*Variety*, January 9-15, 1995].

CHAPTER 7

THEATRICAL SELF-DISTRIBUTION, OR, GIVING UP YOUR LIFE FOR A YEAR CAN YIELD RESULTS

Joe Berlinger

n some circles, our film *Brother's Keeper* is more famous for its self-distribution effort than for the film itself. After all, it earned almost $1.5 million at the box office—an impressive box office gross for any independent film, let alone one without the benefit of a marketing and sales campaign waged by an established distributor with clout, contacts, and know-how. The battle for that box office gross was hard-won, and it took more than a year of our lives. Would my partner, Bruce Sinofsky, and I do it again, knowing what we know now? Definitely. After all, upon the conclusion of our theatrical release, *Brother's Keeper* went on to a successful home video release (Fox Lorber), was broadcast on PBS's *American Playhouse* (our primary source of post-production financing), and was televised in seventeen countries worldwide.

Before we began showing *Brother's Keeper* on the festival circuit, the film might not have seemed a likely candidate for theatrical distribution. First of all, it is a nonfiction film—yes, a documentary. For years documentaries have been viewed as even more noxious to distributors than foreign films. For instance, *Variety* reported that documentary features account for only one-tenth of one percent (.1%) of the total 1994 national box office receipts. Secondly, the film is about a small rural community in upstate New York and four illiterate dairy farmers, one of whom was accused of murdering his elderly bed-mate brother. At first look, this is not an auspicious scenario for boffo box office.

In January 1992, we premiered the film at the Sundance Film Festival where it won the coveted Audience Award. Then when we received extensive feature coverage and glowing reviews in such publications as *Variety*, *The Hollywood Reporter*, *Premiere*, and *The New York Times*, we fully expected to walk away with a sweet distribution deal and a nice chunk of change as an advance. Some distribution offers were made but respectable advances were not part of the proposed deals. In general, distributors offered us piddling advances or none at all. And most of those distributors wanted to release the film in 16mm which would automatically ghettoize the film to a limited number of art houses.

Most important, no one seemed to have a concrete, specialized marketing plan to handle our odd little film. Some distributors acquire a large number of independent films relatively cheaply and indiscriminately. They then toss them out into the marketplace, and it is sink or swim: the movies that immediately generate good box office are followed up on and nurtured with strong advertising campaigns and aggressive bookings. The rest are abandoned to their fate—and box office oblivion. We feared that without tender loving care, our film might be pulled by a distributor before it had time to find its audience.

It became obvious that if *Brother's Keeper* were to succeed in the marketplace, self-distribution was the only way to go. Bruce and I knew that only we would give the film the passionate, personal marketing and sales campaign that the film needed in order to find its audience. As with the production of the film itself, our self-distribution of *Brother's Keeper* was an unlikely success story of overcoming the odds without help. We produced the film on weekends and evenings while holding down full-time jobs, and we did it without any financial assistance or co-production monies (until *American Playhouse* stepped in with completion funds after seeing a rough assembly of dailies). With self-distribution we believed that our enthusiasm and determination more than compensated for our lack of distribution experience and know-how.

What follows are some lessons and thoughts provoked by our particular experience with *Brother's Keeper*. In writing this chapter, I used the following guideline: "Gee, I wish I had known this when we started." For us, the process of self-distribution involved reinventing the wheel because information is closely guarded. By and large, we set out on this journey without a road map. Perhaps the lessons outlined below can help you make a more informed decision than we did.

DISTRIBUTORS CAN BE (AND OFTEN ARE) DEAD WRONG.

The single most important factor in the success of self-distribution is your deep, strong, and unshakable belief in your film. The fact that distributors and, later, some theaters pass over your film, does not mean that it is not marketable. The history books bulge with stories of films that distributors thought were duds but that went on to critical and box office success. Conversely, innumerable "sure-fire hits" have bombed at the box office, creating ulcers and unemployment for many a distribution executive. The lesson: It is almost impossible to predict success, so if you *really* believe in your film, do not accept a lousy distribution deal.

Self-distribution should not be considered a last resort. You should think of it as a viable option, along with (one hopes) other distribution offers. If you want a bigger advance, or if you feel that the distributor does not really understand or appreciate your film, or that the marketing plan is not consistent with your vision of the film, then self-distribution might be the way to go.

THERE ARE (MUCH) EASIER WAYS TO MAKE A LIVING.

Before you turn down those no-advance distribution offers, however, be fore-warned: there are easier ways to make a living than self-distribution. In fact, putting the funding together to get your film made might seem like a piece of cake in comparison. Self-distribution is not for everybody. The established distribution system is ruthless to low-budget, offbeat films. You are the first to be pulled off the screen by the theaters and you are the last to be paid. Prints, advertising, and professional promo materials are expensive. And the work is all-consuming.

Before you dive into self-distribution, ask yourself if you are willing to expend the time and energy needed. Bruce and I spent literally a solid year distributing *Brother's Keeper* to the exclusion of all other work. When the critical success of *Brother's Keeper* began to attract offers to direct new projects, we needed tremendous willpower to turn them down. We had to take ourselves out of production just as the time was ripe for us to sign new deals. In order to succeed, we devoted ourselves one hundred percent to distribution. We hoped that those offers to direct new projects would still be around in a year. It is a risk you should be prepared to take.

Why do it, then? If a distribution deal does not materialize, there is no choice—self-distribute or give up the idea of a theatrical release. For others (as with us), self-distribution is better than accepting a bad deal. It assures you creative control over every aspect of your film's marketing and promotion. This control was especially important and gratifying for us. From poster design to trailers to press releases, our imprint—for better or worse—was on everything. Self-distribution is also a great way to learn the distribution game. You will be much more savvy the next time you sit down to hammer out a distribution deal.

THINK ABOUT MARKETING RIGHT FROM THE START, OR, IMAGE IS EVERYTHING

The most successful self-distribution effort begins long before the film is finished. Thinking about marketing even before you expose your first frame of film will pay off with valuable dividends—either landing you a better distribution deal, or giving you the tools to launch a successful self-distribution effort.

Here are some ways to think about marketing right from the start.

• *Title.* Some film titles just grab you. Others are a bore, or are so personal that they have no meaning to the viewer. Try to come up with a snappy title that takes on a life of its own. *Brother's Keeper* as a title came to me early in the production. I had been dragged to synagogue by my father-in-law one beautiful September morning during the High Holy Days. Since my Hebrew is less than perfect, I was flipping through the Bible to keep the boredom at bay. I just happened to come across the passage about Cain and Abel and immediately realized that *Brother's Keeper* was a perfect title. It felt right, and Bruce and I never seriously considered another option.

• *Tag line.* Almost as important as the title is the movie's tag line. In a few short words, you have another chance to tease your potential ticket-buyer into seeing the movie. Most people loved our choice of "A Heartwarming Tale of Murder." Although the tag line did draw audiences, it also elicited some strong reactions from viewers who thought it was misleading—that it implied Delbert Ward had, indeed, murdered his brother Bill. Our belief is that the tag line suits the film well; both are full of ambiguity. After all, murder is generally not considered a heartwarming activity. So, the tag line could imply that Delbert is guilty or innocent—or both. It conveys both the tenor of the film (heartwarming) and the 'plot' (murder). And frankly, a little bit of controversy is good for publicity.

• *Stills.* While you are shooting your film, take plenty of stills. Bring a photographer along (and make sure you appear in some of the pictures.) The stills should be as evocative (if not more!) than the film.

• *Behind-the-scenes footage.* As long as you are taking stills, do yourself a favor and grab some B-roll of you and your crew working (a consumer Hi-8 machine will do). If your film has a special angle, and you have success in getting television press for your film during its release, you will be glad you have this footage. With the proliferation of EPKs (Electronic Press Kits), segment producers have come to expect behind-the-scenes footage. It could mean the difference between landing a story and losing one. With our B-roll in hand, we ended up on CNN's *Show Biz Weekly* and on *Entertainment Tonight*, among others.

• *Press Kits.* Start creating the elements for your press kit from Day One. Think carefully how to position your film in the press materials. We were surprised to see just how much of our written material was picked up and reported—in some cases verbatim—by the press. If your press release, synopsis, bios and the director's statement are well-written, editors and reporters will be more likely to feature your film in their publication. Try to get any press you can about the making for your film—even from hometown papers—and include clips in your press packets.

•   *Logo and stationery.* Your logo is one of the most important elements in your marketing campaign. You do not, however, have to spend a lot of money on graphic designer fees to come up with an effective logo. One day while flipping through my typeface book, I discovered a type called Caslon Antique that evoked antique type used 200 years ago. That discovery led us to use our title *Brother's Keeper* as the star of the logo. It was a simple, easy, and inexpensive solution that served us well.

A couple of years ago I attended the IFFM (Independent Feature Film Market) as a buyer. The marketing literature that landed in my box was appallingly amateurish: sloppy handwritten flyers, out-of-focus photos, and press releases with typos and grammatical errors. It was a real turn-off. I could not help but wonder how good the films could be if the marketing was so bad.

While not every filmmaker can be a marketing expert, you must make sure that everything you create conveys a professional image—from press releases to flyers, from logo treatments to postcards. You want the world to take you seriously. As a self-distributor, you have no track record and your film is an unknown quantity, so many theaters will ask for some promo materials before they decide to book your film. Therefore, the more professionally you present yourself, the more confident a theater will feel, and the more likely they will be to book you.

YOU NEED AN ORGANIZATIONAL STRUCTURE

As simple as it sounds, many people who ask my advice have not thought about creating an organizational structure to service their release. It does not have to be fancy—after all, we started marketing *Brother's Keeper* in my small Brooklyn apartment, and we cleaned and shipped prints from Bruce's house in New Jersey. Even-tually, we moved into an office as our release expanded and we knew we could pay rent.

Like any small business, you should determine areas of responsibility for each member of the company. Bruce, Loren Eiferman (my wife), and I worked full-time with a part-time assistant (who later became full-time once the release was in full swing). The hours could be absolutely grueling. At the height of the madness, there were many nights when we rolled into bed near dawn.

How are you going to keep track of which theaters you have contacted? Who will negotiate the terms of the bookings? Who will take care of contracts and bookkeeping? How will you do your photocopying? What about a phone system—will you have a simple voice mail system or someone who will answer the phone during business hours?

How will you handle print and poster shipping? Will you hire a service, or will you do it yourself? We chose to do it ourselves because we wanted to be in control of what marketing materials were shipped and to know at all times where our prints were. We felt we would maximize our print collection by handling the shipping ourselves. Shipping can be a nightmare—be prepared to track down lost prints and posters.

It is also crucial that you develop a plan to get paid and to track money. You must create professional invoices and send them regularly. You need to figure out how to deal with not getting paid, which unfortunately happens more than you will like. In fact, the aggressive pursuit of money due you is perhaps the most unpleasant task of distribution. Two years after the theatrical release of *Brother's Keeper* ended, we are still trying to collect our share of the grosses from a number of theaters. As you struggle to collect monies owed you, the bills will mount. Then you, in turn, have to juggle paying *your* creditors.

DO YOUR HOMEWORK/EXPECT TO REINVENT THE WHEEL

The first decision you will have to make is whether to book the film yourself, or hire an independent booking agent. The advantage of an agent is that he/she presumably has connections and a track record and you can be free to work on marketing and publicity. (If you do decide to go with a booking agent, make sure you check carefully that the agent can indeed deliver what he/she promises.) The major downside to a booking agent is that you are giving up a sizable piece of the pie, since the booking agent will want a percentage of your revenue. Because there were two of us—and we are control freaks—we decided to book the film ourselves. We were able to share responsibilities. I tended to focus on marketing and publicity, and Bruce tended to focus on booking and transport—although we swapped hats on many occasions.

A small handful of distribution executives were very generous with their advice when we started doing our homework. However, by and large, distributors tend to hang on tight to their information. Therefore, you have to do your home-work, and you will often feel like you are reinventing the wheel.

Do not despair! The information *is* out there. When we could not find a list of theaters that play art films, we made weekly trips to a specialty magazine store that carries out-of-town papers, purchased newspapers from other cities, and looked at the movie page to determine which theaters were playing our kind of film. Then, we'd call the theater to find out who owned it and/or booked it (information is often in the ads), and then called the bookers.

At the risk of stating the obvious—all theaters/markets are not alike. In some cases you will be required to pay for all the marketing and advertising. Some theaters require less investment and carry less risk. They take care of the bulk of the advertising, but the payout will not be as good.

Some theaters are calendar houses—they set their schedule months in advance and print detailed and unchangeable schedules. Even if your film is doing extremely well, a calendar house cannot extend your run (unless they have more than one screen).

Most theaters operate with open engagements and respond to the demands of the marketplace. Theoretically, they will hold on to your film as long as it keeps selling tickets. One of the frustrations, however, of self-distribution is that even if your film is doing well in an open engagement, the established distribution companies will often demand that the theater pull your film prematurely to make way for their films. The theater, not wanting to offend a regular supplier, usually acquiesces, thus denying you the chance to fully exploit that particular market.

Theaters can be very territorial. If they do not premiere a film in their city, they will not take it as a "move-over," and if they also have screens in other cities, they might not book the film at all because of the snub in their home market. For instance, when we decided to open *Brother's Keeper* in New York City at the Film Forum, we alienated a booker for another New York theater who also books more than thirty theaters nationwide. We had a good run in New York, but we lost quite a few good venues because of our decision.

You cannot make sweeping generalizations about theaters. Independent art houses are not necessarily kind-hearted and nurturing places for filmmakers; nor are theater chains always cold, unsympathetic, and bureaucratic. We encountered some theater chains that were terrific. The Nickelodeon in Boston—part of the Loews Theater chain at the time—was one of our best venues. They were great to work with; they gave our film attention and care; and they paid us promptly.

On the other hand, some privately owned small art houses were horrible and, to this day, we are still trying to collect from some of them. By and large, however, most art houses get high marks from us—they are usually in the business because they love good movies.

PLAN AHEAD

Self-distribution requires a lot of lead time. Calendar houses book at least four to six months in advance, so give yourself plenty of time to pitch the movie, close the deal and get the dates you want. Outline a strategy for release. We started out by releasing the film in New York and San Francisco. New York is *the* crucial venue. If you do not develop an audience in New York (and get some good reviews), you will probably have a hard time building momentum in other cities. In fact, if you bomb in New York that could be the death knell for your self-distribution campaign. On the other hand, doing well in New York gives you immediate clout in the market-place. Many theaters in the smaller markets read the ads in the *Village Voice* religiously to gauge how the independent films are faring.

If you don't want to take the calculated risk of opening in New York, you can try to begin your release in smaller cities and build toward the major markets. And if you do well, it might help you secure better venues in the bigger cities. Ultimately, though, in order to have a significant self-distribution release, you must open—and succeed—in at least one of the major markets: New York, Chicago, Los Angeles, and, to a lesser degree, Washington, D.C.

Festivals can be an important adjunct to your self-distribution effort. They can generate reviews before you begin your release. Those reviews, in turn, can be used to sell the picture. If your festival screening immediately precedes your release in that particular city, the festival press coverage can boost your own marketing. Be careful, however, not to get lost on the festival circuit. First of all, with the proliferation of festivals worldwide, the circuit can be a drain of time, money, and energy. Also, be aware that in some markets, the press coverage that accompanies festival screenings might eliminate all possibilities for additional coverage when you release the film theatrically at a later date. By that time, your film will be old news. So, in some markets it is better to pass on festival press coverage and to hold out for your theatrical release if the release date does not coincide with the festival dates.

TURN A NEGATIVE INTO A POSITIVE

As a self-distributor you will be operating with several strikes against you before you even get started, especially if your film is a documentary. Use your ingenuity to transform those obstacles into advantages.

For instance, it is likely that you will be working with a minuscule budget, which means that paid advertising beyond the minimum level that some theaters require—especially in big cities—is prohibitive. Unless you are going to spend tons of money, most advertising is like whistling in the wind.

Many theaters require that you do some advertising with small display ads and/or by inclusion in group ads or co-op listings. But after those minimal expenditures, spend your money wisely by doing grassroots marketing, which is labor intensive, but cheap. Identify groups that will find your film interesting. For instance, we marketed *Brother's Keeper* to professional associations and community groups: from law schools to advocacy groups for older people, from psychology associations to rural organizations and civil liberty groups. Recruit some interns to pass out flyers at other theaters and to post flyers in university hangouts. Create a buzz by having friends stand in line for other movies and loudly talk up your film. The downside of grassroots marketing is that it is very labor-intensive. Therefore, the number of cities you can handle at any one time will be limited, which can significantly slow down the momentum of your release.

Create lots of "homecoming" screenings—go back to your childhood town, your cinematographer's college, your leading man's summer camp—and relentlessly pursue that local angle. I grew up in Chappaqua, New York, went to Colgate University in upstate New York, and lived in Brooklyn. My parents were living in Florida. Bruce's childhood home was in Newton, Massachusetts; he attended college in Amherst; and during filming he lived in Montclair, New Jersey. That gave us seven excuses to create homecoming events surrounding our openings in those markets.

If I have not driven this point home yet, I will say it again: *press, press, and more press*. Feature articles, blurbs, photos and captions, reviews, TV appearances, radio interviews—they are all *better* than paid advertising, and they are free. Hire a publicist for the more routine tasks like setting up press screenings and distributing press kits. You should, however, make sure that you take a very active part in creating your own spin on the film. Figure out a unique, catchy angle on how your project came about. For us, it was the now over-used story of weekend no-budget filmmakers financing a film on credit cards. Every film has a story—you must find it and exploit it.

KNOW WHEN TO SPEND MONEY

Even though your budget is small, there are certain items that you should not skimp on: film prints, posters, and trailers.

• *Prints.* 35mm prints are more expensive than 16mm, but infinitely more useful. If you shot on 16mm, seriously consider blowing it up to 35mm (a major expenditure—about $40,000 in our case). If you try to distribute with 16mm, you are relegating yourself to a limited number of art houses—approximately seventy in number nationwide—which limits your potential gross. On a purely practical note, 16mm prints get damaged more easily than 35mm prints do. But, of course, a 16mm print is one-third the cost of a 35mm print.

Only strike as many prints as you will need, but do not skimp. It takes solid planning to figure out your print schedule, and you do not want to lose a date for lack of a print. Prints do get lost or delayed in shipping, so you should have one or two extras for back-up. We started out by striking five, and then upped it in increments of five to ten, fifteen and finally thirty prints. At $1,600 a pop, that is another $50,000 investment.

• *Poster*. We lost some important dates early on because we did not have good movie posters. Theaters want and expect standard-size posters, and frequently they will not book the film without them. When we first started the release, we printed half-sized posters to save money, but we quickly discovered that our cost-saving measure had actually lost us money. For instance, a prestigious theater in Providence, Rhode Island was ready to book *Brother's Keeper* until they found out that we did not have the right size posters. We did open in New York without posters. As a result, I ran around putting together make-shift displays that did not quite look professional and needed to be redone by hand at the start of each engagement—a big waste of time.

• *Trailers*. Most theaters ask for trailers. If effective, they can be one of the best means of promoting your film. A trailer is like a free two-minute commercial shown to your target audience. By the time we realized we needed a trailer, our negative was tied up with the 35mm blow-up, so we had to act fast and creatively. It occurred to me that a testimonial from Spalding Gray might work. He had presented the Audience Award to us at Sundance, and in his speech he related an anecdote that later became the makings of our trailer. In his signature style, he explained that *Brother's Keeper* had enthralled him so much that he couldn't even leave the theater to go to the toilet despite desperately needing to pee.

So when we had to produce a trailer quickly, we contacted Spalding and asked him if he would relate the anecdote again on film. Shot in our "documentary" style in his writer's studio in the Hamptons, the trailer itself became a cult mini-film and generated its own buzz.

DEVELOP A THICK SKIN

This is as much of a life lesson as a distribution lesson: everyone says no. Therefore, do not take it personally. And—perseverance pays.

As an example, we urged Karen Cooper, the head of Film Forum, to present *Brother's Keeper*. We screened the film for her in New York, and she gave us a firm no. Although that could have been the end of the story, when the film screened at the Berlin Film Festival, we persuaded Karen to watch it again, this time with an audience. The energy of the crowd (who loved the film) convinced Karen to take it on, and as a result, *Brother's Keeper* began its theatrical life at the Film Forum—in our opinion one of the very best venues in the country.

The Spectrum Theater in Albany seemed like a good bet for *Brother's Keeper*. Munnsville, New York (the village of 499 that is the locale of the film), is only 100 miles away, which gave the film a strong local appeal. The theater presents a well-balanced mix of Hollywood movies and specialized independent films. One of the owners proved to be a very nice guy, but he did not believe that *Brother's Keeper* would find an audience. We worked hard over an extended period of time to convince him that he should give the film a shot. We talked with him on the phone frequently, sent him reviews, sent box office results from other markets, and eventually he relented and agreed to book it. As it happened, Albany turned out to be one of our best cities. We played there for seven weeks and on a per capita basis it was one of our strongest markets.

In one instance we played David to Disney's Goliath. The battle ground was the Coolidge Corner Cinema in Brookline, Massachusetts. When the theater split the screen between *Brother's Keeper* and *Aladdin*, Disney flexed its distribution muscles and demanded that *Brother's Keeper* be pulled. (A split screen is when the theater schedules two different films at alternating times for the same screen on the same day.) For once the little guy won when Coolidge Corner stood up to Disney and refused to abandon *Brother's Keeper*.

You will run into similar battles all along the way with theater owners, managers, and bookers. Since there are more films than ever and screen space is always at a premium, other distributors ruthlessly negotiate for bookings. Theaters will sometimes treat you and your film poorly because they do not want to offend distributors who provide them with a steady flow of desirable films.

Unfortunately, many theaters will take months to pay or will never pay at all. Again, do not take it personally. Keep your cool, continue to send invoices, and make frequent phone calls.

NOTHING BEATS THE PERSONAL TOUCH

When *Brother's Keeper* opened in New York at the Film Forum, for the first three weeks Bruce and I showed up at the two main evening shows. We talked to the audience at the end of the screenings, answered questions, and exhorted them to spread the word about the film. We firmly believe that our personal appearances significantly increased interest in the film.

On the third weekend of the run, we had to make the decision of whether to stay in New York or go up for a screening at Toronto's Festival of Festivals. Lured by the romance of a major festival, we decided to go to Toronto on Friday. By Saturday morning, we realized that the festival was not as important an event for us as we had expected. So I agreed to stay while Bruce hopped on a plane back to New York in time to make the 6:00 p.m. and 8:00 p.m. screenings at the Film Forum.

Some of the best moments were when we brought the stars of the film—

the Ward Brothers themselves—to screenings. Because we did not want to exploit them and we feared they would not enjoy the limelight, we decided not to bring them to the New York City opening. But as the film rolled into upstate New York where the Wards had become local celebrities, the brothers themselves expressed interest in appearing at screenings within a two-hour radius of their home. Even though they did not speak much, the Wards' presence drew big audiences and made the screenings into 'events.' After a five-month hiatus, *Brother's Keeper* reopened in New York City, back by popular demand. By this time the Wards were enjoying their public appearances so much that we brought them to New York, giving the press a new excuse to write about the film when it otherwise would have been treated as old news.

With each personal appearance, we enhanced our marketing efforts by selling hats, T-shirts, buttons and posters. As long as they are of good quality, these items serve as excellent marketing tools, and they generate ancillary income.

Most important to remember is that the bigger markets (New York, Los Angeles, Boston, Chicago) are not necessarily more lucrative than the smaller markets. College towns are great places for specialized films, and the college press is eager to write big feature articles if you are willing to show up in town and do a Q & A session. Treat Boise like New York City. Tender loving care in the smaller markets can result in substantial box office numbers. We earned more at the box office in Albany then we did in Los Angeles. And twenty percent of our total box-office came from the hinterlands of upstate New York where art films rarely appear, let alone do well. In the two nearest theaters to Munnsville—Oneida to the north and Hamilton to the south—*Brother's Keeper* has the all-time house record, out-grossing *E.T.*, *Star Wars*, and *Jurassic Park*.

In its 13 months of theatrical release, *Brother's Keeper* played more than 250 cities across the country and grossed nearly $1.5 million at the box office. As exhausting and challenging as it was, our self-distribution campaign allowed us: (1) To learn the distribution business inside-out; (2) To get to know our audiences directly—a unique and fulfilling experience; and (3) To earn a respectable profit through our own hard work. We often wonder what kind of business *Brother's Keeper* would have done in the care of one of the major independent distributors (e.g., Miramax, Fine Line, Goldwyn) with their infinitely larger P & A (prints and advertising) budgets. But, while more established distributors might have gotten higher grosses, they probably would not have marketed the film with as much enthusiasm, determination, or ingenuity as we did.

CHAPTER 8

NON-THEATRICAL DISTRIBUTION: THE EDUCATION, INSTITUTIONAL, AND CORPORATE MARKETS

Ericka Markman

any markets fall under the definition of non-theatrical. In this chapter we look at the three largest of those markets—education, institutional, and corporate. The income potential from the non-theatrical market is small relative to home video and cable, but it can be remarkably steady. Whereas products for the consumer market have a relatively short lifespan, popular titles in the non-theatrical market become perennial sellers, generating income year after year. Ninety-nine percent of schools, libraries, hospitals, and corporations have VCRs and regularly use videos in the classroom and for staff training.

Few producers can expect to recoup their full production investment from non-theatrical sales. Even a top-selling video in the non-theatrical market is unlikely to sell more than 1,500 units per year (compared to hundreds of thousands in the consumer market). However, education, institutional, and corporate sales represent a strong potential secondary market for your product. A title that catches on in the non-theatrical market can enjoy a shelf-life of five to seven years—or longer.

The education, institutional, and corporate markets are described collectively as non-theatrical, yet each one is quite different and has unique needs and buying criteria. Non-theatrical customers are institutional buyers who integrate video into their training and educational programs. For example, a tenth grade biology teacher will buy videos to supplement her classroom lecture and a hospital training administrator will use videos to train her staff in the latest OSHA regulations. Because non-theatrical buyers purchase videos for workplace use rather than recreation, they have specific buying criteria. That tenth grade biology teacher needs a video that fits into her basic biology curriculum and the training administrator needs the latest—not five-year-old—OSHA regulations. A key element to success in the non-theatrical market is meeting these criteria of timeliness and specificity.

No video producer should overlook the potential of non-theatrical distribution. But, to be truly successful in this arena, you must be aware of its needs and guidelines. The purpose of this chapter is to help you identify which of your projects have the highest potential in the non-theatrical market and to position them for the greatest possible success.

HOW TO CREATE A PRODUCT WITH NONTHEATRICAL POTENTIAL

First of all, you are the creator. Create the work that realizes your vision. However, if you want to maintain the option of marketing into the non-theatrical arena, begin researching that market even before you start production.

To determine if your product does have potential for non-theatrical use, educate yourself about what products have traditionally performed well in these markets. Non-fiction videos account for more than ninety percent of education, institutional, and corporate sales. Keep in mind that content is extremely important.

If you see a good fit between your product and the non-theatrical market, inform yourself at the outset about content and format requirements. You can save yourself considerable time and money by anticipating ahead of time whether and how you will have to modify your product

Some of the most important guidelines to observe are:

- Establish content appropriateness and accuracy.
- Limit running time to thirty minutes or less.
- Maintain cultural and ethnic diversity, including gender equity.
- Present a balanced political perspective.
- Keep profanity, nudity, excessive violence, or other potentially sensitive material to a minimum.

Buyers take the above guidelines very seriously. Many wonderful videos have been rejected by buyers because they violate one of the above guidelines. For instance, I once tried to sell a series of award-winning French language videos to the state of California for a state-wide school adoption. The series was rejected on the grounds that the teen-age onscreen characters drank wine, even though wine is clearly an important part of French culture.

In addition, find out what content requirements there might be for the subject you are covering. If you have produced a video on the rainforest, which you would like to sell into the high school market, find out what curriculum guidelines exist for rainforest education at that grade level. Research and evaluate what other products cover the subject and which do so successfully for your target market.

THE EDUCATION MARKET

The education market can be divided into two segments:
    (1) Kindergarten through twelfth grade (K-12); and
    (2) Colleges, universities, and graduate schools (higher education).
    Day care centers and home schoolers also use videos but probably account for less than 10% of video sales in the education market.

Kindergarten through Twelfth grade (K-12)

The K-12 market represents a potential audience of more than 100,000 schools and almost 55 million students. Each year, these schools spend an estimated $75-$100 million on video product. Video is widely used in the classroom. In fact, more than ninety-seven percent of the country's schools own at least one VCR, and teachers plan to increase video usage in the future.

The school market has experienced tremendous change over the past decade. As recently as ten to fifteen years ago, most schools bought programming in film format. Because film was so cumbersome and expensive, a centralized media buyer purchased one copy of a program for a whole district and cycled it through the schools. With the appearance of video, which is both a cheaper medium and easier to display, buying became a more decentralized process. Now, most buying decisions are made at the school building level by teachers, librarians, media buyers, or principals. Product is shipped by the distributor directly to each school. Most schools now have their own video collections rather than relying on loans from the district office, which means more units can be sold of each title.

The bad news for producers is that the transition to video format resulted in a significant drop in prices. Educational video prices are informally pegged to sell-through prices of consumer videos. Consequently, the average price of a thirty-minute educational video has declined from $300-$400 five years ago to about $75 in 1994. Another factor affecting the drop in prices is reduced funding for schools. Most schools have felt the impact of budget-cutting. Media expenditures have been cut along with other services. As a result, schools have become increasingly price-sensitive and value-conscious. In real dollars, the education market has shrunk over the past four years; it is expected to continue declining slowly over the next five years.

All of the above means that it is more difficult for producers to recoup their full production investment from school sales. Instead, many producers are modifying videos that they originally produced for a consumer market. As a result, the number of original titles produced for this market is declining and the competition among distributors for high-quality educational videos has grown.

At the school level, purchasing decisions are usually made by a teacher, librarian, or media buyer. Teachers use videos to supplement lectures and lesson plans and have very specific criteria about program format and content.

When producing or modifying a video for this market, consider the following:

(1) *Follow the curriculum.* Most importantly, the video must directly support the teacher's classroom activities—ideally by correlating with a curriculum. Many states publish curriculum framework guidelines. Schools have more money to purchase materials that comply with these frameworks. Curriculum trends are usually set by California, Texas, and Florida; many smaller states correlate their guidelines with the larger states' guidelines. You can get copies of the guidelines by calling the state departments of education.

(2) *Follow the funding.* Each year the federal government allocates funding to youth education and assistance programs. These funds support a variety of programs, some of which involve media acquisitions. In recent years there has been a strong emphasis on subjects such as substance abuse prevention, AIDS education, violence intervention, self-esteem, school-to-workplace transition and multi-culturalism. For more information on what subjects will be funded in the future you can contact the U.S. Department of Education or review the Education Funding Research Council's *Guide to Federal Funding for Education.*

(3) *Length is also very important.* Since the standard class period is forty-five to fifty minutes, the ideal video will run fifteen to twenty minutes, but no more than thirty minutes.

(4) *Suitability.* Schools are very conservative. It is very important that videos used in the classroom reflect cultural and ethnic diversity, and gender equity. Media materials must not have excessive profanity, nudity, sexually suggestive situations, or violence, or present material that could be considered racist or sexist, or promote negative ethnic stereotypes.

(5) *Teacher's Guides.* Every video for the school market must be accompanied by a teacher's guide. Discussion or activity guides help teachers integrate videos into their teaching plans, and nearly 80% of teachers use them at least occasionally. A teacher's guide can be a brief overview of the video, which also features a list of suggested activities and discussion topics for the classroom.

Marketing to schools is largely the domain of fifteen to twenty educational distributors who reach buyers through a combination of direct mail, telemarketing, print advertising, sales representatives, and exhibits at conferences. The major trade journals for this market include: *School Library Journal, Media and Methods, Curriculum Administrator, T.H.E. Journal,* and *Science Books & Films.* There are several major conferences each year, most of which are organized around a curriculum area (e.g., National Science Teachers Association conference and National Council for Social Studies conference). Many of the conferences now feature other media including computer software and CD-ROM. The National Educational Media Network, held annually in Oakland, is an excellent festival for meeting distributors.

HIGHER EDUCATION: COLLEGES AND UNIVERSITIES

The higher education market of more than seven thousand institutions—most of which are two-year and four-year colleges and universities—spends approximately $50 million annually on video products for classroom use.

With a universe of fewer than ten thousand institutions, the higher education market does not offer the same potential as the school market. Like schools, colleges and universities have been hurt by funding cuts, and buyers are extremely value conscious. Video prices are comparable to those in the school market, at an average price of $75, down from $300-$400 five years ago.

Unlike the school market, which once bought media through a centralized process, the college market has always been relatively decentralized. Professors and department chairs have more discretion than grade school teachers about how they will teach a subject and are the primary decision-makers for purchasing textbooks and other media. Professors, and sometimes media buyers, make the buying decisions. In general, videos are used in higher education for supplementary purposes—to supplement the lecture or lab rather than to teach a core concept.

Videos that are successful in the high school market often have crossover potential into the college market, and vice versa. In addition, series developed for PBS are often popular in higher education. For instance, the Annenberg/CPB-sponsored series *Art of the Western World* has had a long life in art history classrooms as well as on PBS.

One growth area is distance learning and telecourses. Telecourses, developed for the part-time student who lives off-campus, offer an entire course in a bundle of videocassettes, textbooks, and workbooks. As the demographic profile of an average college student shifts from a four-year full-timer to a part-timer, the need for flexible distance learning is growing. Use of video has grown accordingly.

The higher education market is reached in much the same way as the school market—through distributors who use a combination of direct mail, telemarketing, and print advertising. The college market is not large enough to support sales representatives, nor do distributors commonly exhibit at conferences.

With the exception of *Library Journal*, there are no trade journals for higher education media buyers as there are in the K-12 market. Professors subscribe to the major publications in their field of study.

THE INSTITUTIONAL MARKET

Libraries

There are approximately sixteen thousand public libraries in this country. About three-quarters of these libraries have video collections. Libraries spend an estimated $15-$20 million on video acquisitions annually. Since libraries purchase videos primarily on behalf of their patrons, their buying decisions reflect consumer interests.

Libraries have been badly hurt by state and local budget-cutting. Some have been closed down, many have been cut back. Without a mandate to build video collections, many have stopped buying videos. Most traditional non-theatrical distributors no longer find direct marketing to libraries cost-effective, and instead rely on wholesalers like Baker & Taylor and Ingram.

The head librarian or media librarian makes the purchase decision for her library, on behalf of her patrons. Most library collections represent a mix of feature films and how-to titles, with a smattering of higher quality documentary and educational programs.

The key to library sales is favorable reviews in a handful of trade journals, namely: *Library Journal*, *Video Librarian*, and the *Video Rating Guide for Libraries*. In addition, there are two national annual conferences that draw thousands of public and school librarians each year—American Library Association and ALA Mid-Winter—plus statewide library conferences.

Community and Religious Groups

Community and religious groups, like churches and the local PTA chapters, also buy videos for Sunday schools, after-school activities, guidance and counseling programs, and discussion groups. These groups buy general interest programs, with a special emphasis on guidance subjects such as substance abuse and personal ethics. This market may represent sales of as much as $25 million annually, although it is difficult to evaluate since so many groups buy through consumer channels.

Some distributors market to religious and community groups through direct mail and telemarketing. However, most of the purchasing takes place through retail outlets and wholesalers. If you or your distributor can arrange for your product to be carried by a major wholesaler like Baker & Taylor, the community, religious, and other special interest groups will have access to your product.

Prisons

Prisons buy videos, too. Many inmates work toward high school and college equivalency degrees through correspondence courses. Videos are also used in counseling and therapy sessions.

THE CORPORATE TRAINING MARKET

According to a recent *Training* magazine survey, corporations spent $50.6 billion on staff training and development in 1994, and $1.8 billion on off-the-shelf materials (books, videos, computer courseware and other pre-packaged training products). Video was the most popular form of information delivery, used by ninety-two percent of companies polled.

There is no question that video is considered an important training resource. Companies use videos both to motivate staff and to improve skills. Unlike the school market, tough financial times have not hurt video sales to corporations. In an era of downsizing and restructuring, corporations have an even greater need for training and retraining their employees. In the corporate arena, a well-trained and informed work force is a valuable commodity. Video and other forms of media training are very cost-effective. As a result, companies are less price resistant than schools, and price points for corporate videos are much higher—starting at $300 and going up from there.

In a larger company, the people responsible for staff development (e.g., human resources or training departments) make purchasing decisions. In smaller companies, it is often the president of the company or a high-level manager. The most common subjects for video training are general communications skills and other productivity training such as Total Quality Management (TQM), team-building, and time management. In addition, companies use videos to provide specific staff training. The Annenberg/CPB series *The World of Chemistry*, which teaches basic concepts of chemistry, sells perennially to the corporate market.

Companies buy directly from distributors and also from wholesalers such as Baker & Taylor. Some of the leading distributors in this field are CRM Films, Blanchard Training and Development, and Video Arts. Each year the foremost human resources and development association—American Society of Training and Development—sponsors an annual conference at which many distributors exhibit. The two best general sources of information on the corporate arena are American Society of Training and Development and *Training* magazine.

THE HEALTH CARE MARKET

Hospitals, health care centers and emergency service providers such as EMS and police forces are considered part of the larger corporate training market, but they require very specialized kinds of programming. The ever-changing health care landscape calls for a continuing stream of new and up-to-date information for patients, plus staff training in OSHA regulations, health care procedures, and issues. Health care information is one of the growth areas in the non-theatrical market.

According to the American Hospital Association, there are 6,500 hospitals and 550 HMOs in this country—and that number is growing. The average hospital spends nearly $13,000 annually on off-the-shelf materials for staff training alone—totalling annual expenditures in excess of $80 million. Psychiatric and mental health facilities also purchase videos.

Patient relations staff purchase videos to explain medical procedures and options to patients. Staff development personnel and nursing departments purchase videos that provide information on new medical procedures and OSHA regulations, as well as health care issues. Because this information—particularly staff training—is need-to-have, video prices remain high.

Health care video distributors can be divided into two general categories. Distributors like the American Journal of Nursing (an adjunct to the magazine) and Medcom-Trainex market products that are highly technical. Distributors like AIMS Media, Pyramid Film & Video, and Fanlight Productions market a broader array of products, which range from technical to general interest treatments of health care issues. AIMS, Pyramid, and Fanlight also distribute to the education and institutional markets. Distributors reach their customers primarily through direct marketing—direct mail and telemarketing—and advertise in trade journals as well. Buyers track the results of major health care festivals, and will often buy titles that have been praised by reviewers or judges.

SELF-DISTRIBUTION VS. FINDING THE RIGHT DISTRIBUTOR

Every producer has two options: to self-distribute his or her product or to work with a distributor. The advantages of self-distribution are obvious—no one is going to care about your video quite as much as you do. If you have the skills, resources, and desire to handle your distribution, you will probably be successful—and you will save yourself the considerable distribution fee. Distributors often retain as much as seventy-five percent of net sales to cover their costs and profit, and pay producers the remaining 25%.

In order to self-distribute product, you will need to set aside funds for a marketing budget. The costs of advertising in trade journals and exhibiting at conferences begin roughly at the $1,000 mark and rise from there. Direct mail, too, adds up quickly. Depending on the size and specifications of your mailing, estimate that your costs will start at $0.75 per piece and move up from there. Depending on how ambitious your marketing plan is, you should budget marketing expenses in the low five figures.

There are good reasons that most producers ultimately turn their video over to a distributor. First of all, most producers would rather spend their time producing than marketing. Secondly, distributors are presumably more expert at marketing since they do that exclusively. Finally, with only one or two products, you will not realize any of the economies of scale that distributors do. For example, it is clearly more cost-effective to mail a catalog that features fifty videos than one featuring only two or three. Most distributors spend 15-25% of their revenues on marketing—potentially in excess of one-million dollars annually. It is hard to compete with this level of spending.

If you do decide to work with a distributor, take the time and necessary steps to find the right one. Your distributor will play a key role in determining the success or failure of your product. Follow these steps to start your search:

- Read the *AV Marketplace* or a similar directory of distributors and develop a list of likely candidates.
- In addition, compile a list of exhibitors from key festivals and conferences.
- Call the distributors and request a copy of their catalogs. Look for prod ucts with content and format similar to your own.
- When you have narrowed the field, mail a copy or description of your video along with a cover letter to the director of acquisitions. Often the president of the company serves as acquisitions director, or can pass your letter on to the appropriate person. Be sure to apprise them of any awards or reviews the video has received.

(More information on finding and evaluating a distributor is provided in Debra Zimmerman's chapter on "How to Choose a Distributor.")

MARKETING YOUR PRODUCT

Even if you do decide to work with a distributor, you should start the marketing process yourself—immediately. This is really important. When you consider how much money you have spent producing your video, it is foolish not to commit a small percentage of that amount to making sure it achieves its maximum distribution and sales potential.

Two important first steps are:

- *Send out review copies and press releases* of your new product to reviewers at the major trade journals. Do not be afraid to sell yourself or your product. Make your video more interesting to reviewers by linking it to recent news worthy events.
- *Screen at festivals*. Many distributors attend festivals expressly for the purpose of acquiring product.

Festival screenings, editorial reviews and word of mouth can help build an early audience for your product, which will give you greater leverage when negotiating with a distributor or help you in your own distribution campaign.

CONCLUSION

To summarize, the non-theatrical market is a medium-sized and basically mature market—steady and fairly predictable. Few producers have retired on their earnings from non-theatrical sales. On the other hand, many have discovered a strong second life for their videos after cable or television broadcasts.

The non-theatrical market is not appropriate for every product; it is truly contentdriven. But if you do see a good fit between your video and one or more of the markets described above, I encourage you to pursue the opportunity. It requires little to no financial investment—just some good research and planning—and offers the potential of a long-term payoff. With the right video you could enjoy steady revenues for several years. More importantly, you will be reaching a diverse and interested audience who need the information you can provide.

CHAPTER 9

TAKING IT TO THE STREETS

Suzanne Stenson Harmon

udience development goes by a variety of names—outreach, community media education, social marketing, niche marketing—all depending on the level of one's involvement with the community in question. The underlying principles are all similar and beg one basic question: Who is your production *for*, and further, why?

This chapter intends to provide you with background and concrete action steps for developing a strategic communications plan with the core audience whose lives or work your production addresses. Research, partnerships, focus groups, development of materials, and dissemination of information (including via the Internet) are all ways you can forge links between your program and its core audience, with an intention to go beyond a general promotional message.

"Community" is defined very broadly here. A community can be a local geographic area, a regional concern, a topical interest, or a demographic label, (e.g., Japanese-American GenX'ers in Appalachia who have children). A group of individuals, organized or not, constitute a community if they share concerns, attitudes, behaviors, or interests. The more tangible or concrete their shared concerns, the greater the potential for impact.

While many of the tools provided here can be adapted for mainstream media, these tools are most effective when productions speak to a specific issue or audience and do so with a purpose. This is often the case with ethnocentric media or projects that are self-defined as social change agents.

BACKGROUND

In a larger view, audience development is the ideal forum for advancing overlapping goals of media literacy, education, empowerment, and representation. A production can achieve greater levels of authenticity and accurate representation through the direct involvement of a community. Furthering these connections through screening, discussion, and dialogue, the community itself can begin to embrace the power of media, gain validation of their own experiences, and begin to see the ways in which they themselves might become more critical media consumers (at the least) or become involved in media-making themselves (at best).

In the same way that publicity and promotion cast a wide net, outreach casts a deep one and can be one of the cornerstones of overlapping distribution strategies that give a production a longer and more fruitful life. A recent ITVS production for public television broadcast, Billy Golfus's *When Billy Broke His Head...And Other Tales Of Wonder*, for instance, was created with an intent to serve the disability community. Postings about the broadcast were distributed to community service organizations, and I learned anecdotally that a young man with paraplegia viewed the program with his parents after having learned of it through his community newsletter. Their comment to him was, "Now we finally understand what you've been going through." In turn, the parents recommended the program to their parenting support group, who brought it to the attention of the National Association of Protection and Advocacy Services (NAPAS). NAPAS showed *Billy* at their national conference, and subsequent inquiries were directed to the educational distributor. Sales have been brisk.

Long after the review section of your newspaper has hit the recycling bin, there may still be a legion of people who were so profoundly affected by your production that it can gain a meaningful afterlife, and continue to act as an catalyst for change in small or complex ways.

As you might guess, outreach can also serve as a principle for uniting distribution to different markets. Whether your plans include theatrical release, nontheatrical or educational uses, broadcast, home video, or cable, audience development finds the people who care about the issues or ideas you present and can simplify a unified strategy for all markets. As with most things, if you know who your audience is and how to reach them, your chances for success improve.

All of this ambition contains two major qualifiers: (1) You should devote the same energy and resource development to your audience that you devoted to your production; and, (2) Lay your groundwork well. While most of this chapter is concerned with unabashed energy and ambition, there is one warning that applies to all that follows: Do not attempt a concerted outreach or audience development campaign unless you intend to devote the time and resources to follow through. Outreach has the potential to make deep, strong, and very personal connections with people who devote their lives to the subject you are addressing. If promises (real or implied) are not honored, for whatever reason, they are guaranteed to haunt you far longer than a poor review.

RESEARCH

Research is an important element to finding appropriate community partners. From the moment you begin your production research or development, keep accurate and comprehensive records of whom you talk to, organizations or associations they reference, contact information, and anecdotal information about the issues or concerns those contacts share with you. These all become valuable pieces of information down the line and can help you make efficient use of your time, and theirs. There are several ways to identify individuals or institutions who might be appropriate partners:

(1) As you talk to people in the field, ask them where they get their information. When you follow the trail of communication, you may realize that most people get credible information about their field of interest from one or two places. These venues become priority targets for involvement. You should consider their appropriateness early, rather than late.

(2) The Internet: There are several search engines you can utilize to call up vast amounts of information on a particular topic. Some of the more powerful search tools can be found on the World Wide Web, which is navigated by a number of software tools. The two most popular are Netscape and Mosaic, which each have links to searchable databases or indices. (See resource list for Website addresses.) The Mosaic and Netscape sites operate using keyword searches, while Yahoo and IGC have browsable indices. Via keyword searches, you can identify and locate organizations whose work coincides with your production. You can also discover spaces for online discussion to monitor public attitudes and opinions on the topic, and links between affiliated issues.

If you are not yet familiar with the Internet, I strongly recommend that you become acquainted. It should not be viewed as a be-all and end-all. However, the Internet has become a place where millions of people worldwide go for information, and, within the electronic universe, where topical communities form. The cyber-community could easily be its own chapter here, with the myriad of information-gathering resources, not to mention imminent distribution and promotional possibilities. Your local bookstore probably has several more complete directories, many of which include utilization advice. (Some are listed in the bibliography at the end of the book.)

Internet environments can change rapidly, but the compilation of resources may become venues for postings or discussion when you are ready to implement your release strategy. Bookmark these resources for later, and note the administrator of the site who, as gatekeeper, can assist you in getting the word out.

(3) *The Encyclopedia of Associations* is available at many public libraries in

the reference section and can direct you to issue-based institutions (there are several subject-oriented indices). The multiple volumes are thousands of pages long, and this is a labor-intensive process, but is more thorough than the Internet, as many institutions are not yet online.

What are you looking for in your research? I call organizations the intermediary audience; some organizations or associations focus specifically on issues of representation within the field of interest, and I find that these folks are usually ahead of the game on what film, video, and television have to offer a community (beyond entertainment). On a program like *Stolen Moments: Red, Hot + Cool* by The Red Hot Organization, the audience development plan included AIDS service organizations and youth-serving organizations (particularly within the African American community) since the intent of the program was to raise awareness about HIV/AIDS with African American youth. The largest and most well-endowed intermediary was the Centers for Disease Control, which contributed their five thousand-entry database of AIDS service organizations. Speaking to them early was essential, because when the release of the program was imminent, I went back to my contact and apprised her. She forwarded me to their National AIDS Clearinghouse's Online Department, who posted information on the program daily, online, to state departments of health and human services and the general electronic AIDS community. This proved useful in reaching rural people especially (Kansas took an inordinate interest), and ultimately impacted the broadcast carriage of the show.

When doing research I encourage you to be thorough. Look for small, grassroots organizations as well as large associations. Particularly within communities with marginalized economic status, smaller organizations may not be connected to the national databases and indices, and are generally very appreciative of the opportunity to become involved.

The more invested a community is in your production, the more likely its involvement in your distribution and outreach plans. Some ways a community might become invested in your production are as onscreen talent, in advisory capacity, through the contribution of financial resources, by making in-kind contributions, or simply through an overlap of interests including shared or similar experiences. In the best of all worlds, you as a producer plan to (or already do) have an intimate knowledge of the community for whom you are producing, and intend to gain further and deeper knowledge during your production process.

PARTNERING

Partnering is destined to become the buzzword of the next millennium. Funders, activists, and entrepreneurs are all actively engaged in seeking partners, facilitating partnerships, and creating partnership opportunities. A word to the wise: *Partnerships are only useful if all parties reap a benefit.* The role of outreach in this process is a creative expansion of possibilities, harnessing the power of communications and the visual media. Successful partnerships can bring communities together, educate and inform, further the distribution of your production, and/or add one more tool to the variety of methods that activists or communities utilize for social change.

Your direct intermediary audience consists of a broad range of potential partners, and should be a stepping stone to a broader group of individuals, who will view, attend, or purchase your program. In the case of *The Uprising of '34*, produced over a six year period by George Stoney, Judith Helfand, and Susanne Rostock, the intermediary audience was broad: southern grassroots organizations, archival associations, historic societies, and trade unions. By reaching out to these organizations early, and including them in the production process (to locate stories, to spread word of the research and development process, to raise money, and to engage in focus groups) the audience development process for the broadcast (and subsequent educational release) was greatly eased. The producers went back to the hundreds of organizations that had been engaged throughout the production and apprised them of the releases. The result was a committed group of information gatekeepers who spread the word throughout their respective worlds via print, word-of-mouth, online, and at conferences and other gatherings.

Partners can engage in a variety of activities to support your production and their programs. Some options are:

- Lending their name to promotional materials and events;
- Hosting screenings or focus groups (either public or limited to portions of their membership or staff);
- Including information in their communication with their constituency (this might include online postings, features in larger publications, mentions in newsletters, provision of a berth at conferences or meetings, etc.);
- Financial assistance to carry out an educational program with their members;
- Office space or other in-kind resources (such as a staffer to help you in your work).

Community-based organizations possess differing degrees of media awareness. It's important to delineate and emphasize the ways in which all parties can benefit from the proposed partnership. It's also important to realize that some social issue media projects have utilized some organizations' resources exclusively as a tool for promotion, and that there are people who feel "burned" by the experience. Cultivate your partners consciously, with an eye to the future and to the enhancement of long-term relationships.

THE TOOLS OF THE TRADE

The most useful tool in community-based outreach is time, which to most of us means money. Outreach requires one-on-one contact with leaders in the community, provision of material about the production, visits to their location or meeting sites (if you can afford it), and a volume of time on the phone, tracking people down, holding discussions, and following up. Your time might also be spent in setting up screenings, writing print materials, coordinating mailings, or hustling the show to newsletter editors.

If you have money but do not have time, consider yourself fortunate; and then consider hiring somebody who can do this work for you. As producer or director, ask yourself if you are the best person to represent your work to disparate outside interests. Usually the answer is yes, but sometimes a work becomes larger, broader, or different from what you conceived and it's possible that an outreach strategy might benefit from a contractor's distance from the project.

When you are looking for somebody to rep your production for community use, look for someone who: (1) Has a working knowledge of the nonprofit community and its communication methods (preferably within the field of interest addressed by your production); (2) Is highly interested in the production; (3) Is extremely energetic and thorough; and (4) Is someone you trust.

Once you have identified potential resources, secured personnel, and engaged your partners, you can get to the work of enacting a release strategy. This process can be a lengthy one of review, feedback, materials development, shipping, follow-up, and scheduling. Optimally, you should allow yourself at least six months for the process, or longer if you wish to coincide with conferences, events, or ambitious dissemination.

For makers who are determined to hit the festival season (which, as you may know, can also suck up major amounts of time and money for prints or dubs), you may want to consider starting one campaign and then the other, depending on your resources. If you choose to mount activities for industry exposure and public involvement, consider local opportunities for doubling-up your audiences at scheduled screenings or creating materials with dual uses.

Create different versions of your print material for each intended audience. Include consistent descriptive information with venues and dates listed. Also include opportunities for organizations (or individuals) to plug in (e.g., "Things You Can Do"). You might also consider two or three descriptions of differing lengths in order to make it easy for editors to cut and paste.

Issue-oriented conferences can be a wonderful way to bring large numbers of people to your production. *Positive: Life With HIV*, an ITVS series executive-produced by Juanita Anderson for AIDSFILMS, Inc., has taken me to three AIDS-specific conferences and more are planned. Generally, conference attendees are focused on the issue at hand, and this alone, instead of the day-to-day operation of their organizations. A conference is an excellent place to distribute material, screen tapes (where possible), and talk to a wide variety of people.

If you have good working relationships with the convening organizations or individuals, larger presentations can lend credibility and exposure to the project. Consider requesting a room to use specifically for viewing and/or discussion of the work; coordinating the cablecast on the in-room television systems that many major conference-equipped hotels enjoy; or offering the work (or a trailer) to incorporate into a plenary session or presentation.

The conference experience for *Positive* has included the SkillsBuilding Conference hosted by the National Minority AIDS Council and the National Association of People With AIDS, the AIDS Update Conference and the national meeting of the National AIDS Fund, formerly the National Community AIDS Partnership. Occupying a table to disseminate information at the first two conferences brought inquiries from a broad cross-section of AIDS service providers and advocates, ranging from the National Catholic AIDS Network to a local initiative in Oakland, California. In both cases, we provided a tear-off card for easy reply and received several hundred over the following four months. At the National AIDS Fund conference, the series was screened for local community leaders and the Fund has signed on as an official partner to the national broadcast and to local educational activity.

The Internet can also be used for broader outreach and it is constructive to work with a computer-literate individual or organization with a server who can create a World Wide Web page specifically for your production. This allows you to publicize, or list, this site with groups or indices that are found online, and readers can browse your information to find precisely the information they are looking for. The World Wide Web site for ITVS consistently averages four to five thousand readers a month, with varying numbers for production-specific pages. The Web site for Montana Public Television registers forty thousand 'hits' per month. Clearly it is not feasible to talk with that many people individually.

There are also Usenet newsgroups and thousands of discussion groups whose members subscribe precisely because they care about the issue. It is very likely that there is already a discussion group on your topic—no matter what it is—and these individuals will want to know about your production. If you begin to generate a high level of interest in your production, and it is highly issue-oriented, look for the discussion group and cultivate subscribers' interest carefully. If you can't find a discussion group, you might want to create one, as it can also be a great way to inform large numbers of people about your progress. Especially within commercial services (such as America Online and Compuserve), discussions on a particular topic can be short-lived. Create a careful and methodical buzz while observing each community's own 'netiquette.'

One last consideration that you might give to support outreach is the development of a viewer's guide, whose cost can often be offset by corporate or foundation support. A viewer's guide can be framed to answer the questions that you will likely be asked over and over again: How does this piece intersect with our work? What are the points of this production that are relevant to the issues we work with? Can you give me some tips for using this work in a group discussion setting? I'd love to get involved but what can we do?

I strongly recommend that you involve representatives from the target audience in this process. Their credibility, insight, and intimate knowledge of potential pitfalls (everyone has his or her skeletons) can help you avoid making egregious errors in your approach. Outreach is all about involvement and forging alliances.

The following is a sample budget template containing the basic items you will need to launch an outreach effort:

OUTREACH BUDGET ITEMS

TEMP STAFF	Temp staff generally run at least $8-$10 per hour, although you may be able to convince friends to pitch in here.
OUTSIDE SERVICES	Mailhouse, web developer, etc.
CONSULTING	Researcher negotiated according to job. Writer negotiated according to job. Designer negotiated according to job. Proofreader, generally between $12-$20/hour.
PRINTING	Variable.
TRAVEL	Conference Fees—variable. Lodging—variable. Airfare—variable.
OFFICE EXPENSES	Variable.
PHONE/FAX	Don't forget to include online charges.
POSTAGE/SHIPPING	Variable.
COPYING	Variable.
PROMOTIONAL REEL (OR TRAILER)	Variable.
DUBS	In bulk, generally around $3.50/hour.

FOLLOW-UP

As mentioned above, audience development has the potential to forge strong alliances. When you start to spread the word, you will soon realize that it is critical to make your follow-up as easy as possible. *Kontum Diary*, produced by Steven Smith, is a one-off offered to public television stations individually by ITVS. One of the direct mail recipients, a veteran in Cleveland, reposted the press release to the Veterans Forum on Compuserve and subsequently received more than three hundred inquiries to his personal mailbox. We worked with the Forum administrator to develop answers to the inquiries. Also a result of direct mail and online postings, inquiries to ITVS numbered in the hundreds. It was important to have ready-made information to send out, a paragraph at-the-ready for e-mail, and information with the receptionist regarding educational distribution.

The creation of event-specific materials can ease the flood in some cases, creating a way for you or your colleagues to respond quickly and easily to requests. Additionally, some of the discussion above regarding the creation of Internet discussion spaces can be useful for large numbers of people who are trying to accomplish similar activities.

CONCLUSION

Audience development is a bold step in forging communities across issues. The process of bringing together producing communities with communities of distribution, education, activism, advocacy, and organizing is an exciting and energizing process.

It is clear that collectively we harbor a deep need for community and relationship-building. Most of us also fear and loathe the ways in which most media address these concerns. A small but growing group of leaders within seemingly disparate spheres is beginning to recognize the power of working together to create a real movement. In the words of ITVS executive director Jim Yee, "Make it real."

CHAPTER 10

HOME SWEET HOME VIDEO

Milos Stehlik

 ifteen years ago they all laughed at the idea that a majority of Americans would be watching movies that appeared on a black plastic cassette in their own homes, and on their own television screens. Skeptics said: "It's not the same as looking at movies in a darkened movie theater"—and they were right. But today 78% of American homes—a total of 73 million homes in all—have VCRs, and Americans rented some 3.5 billion cassettes in video stores last year.[1]

Today those same laughing cynics are talking about digitizing films and delivering them on a little disk that will be played back in their "home theater" (or, in a more urban environment, on the little television set in their kitchen). They might even send these same films reeling down the information superhighway.

Faith Popcorn[2], the prognosticator of trends, said that a dominant new social trend was something she called "cocooning." People do not go out so much anymore. The battle of the 90s is the struggle for leisure time in an over-programmed life. The home becomes the castle, and our connection to the outside world is largely electronic.

Home video—or home entertainment—provides the major share of Hollywood film industry revenue. Home video's ascent to this position has been a roller coaster ride. Events and developments that had potentially beneficial repercussions for independent film- and videomakers have come and gone. There was a brief time when home video provided pre-production funding to independent features, but the plug was pulled in the late 80s.[3] There was a time when independent features that had run their course as theatrical and television releases, could be resold to the new home video medium. That time is largely gone. There was a time when independent home video companies grabbed money made in office products or real estate, threw it into glossy marketing, and hoped that millions would rush out to buy a new documentary about whales in the same way they snapped up Jane Fonda's aerobics routines. Today the money is gone, the companies are gone, and the whale documentary languishes in litigation in a California bankruptcy court. Gone are Vestron, Pacific Arts, Media Home Entertainment, Nelson, Virgin Vision, Embassy, Academy Home Entertainment, and a dozen other independent video companies.

What makes home video different? Why is its brief history so volatile? There is one constant, cardinal rule: home video is a consumer-driven medium. The customer has—and exercises, to his or her best ability—choice to rent or not to rent, to buy or not to buy. The entertainment—and sometimes information—of the 90s comes in a rectangular box. Home video responds quickly to consumers' social, political, and cultural attitudes and trends.

A MINIHISTORY OF HOME VIDEO

The Hollywood studios dominate home video as they dominate theatrical distribution and television. Home video is a part of their vertical marketing strategy along with theatrical release or foreign sales. Home video is a significant share of a film's earnings path. As the studios learned the value of home video, they poured substantial promotional dollars into assuring that the major companies would control the largest market share. Films were established through promotion at the box office so that from the first theatrical release movie "product" would flow smoothly through the theatrical–international sales–home video–cable TV pipeline.

Even the counter at which the consumer picks up his rental copy of a videocassette was cleaned up and streamlined. The point of purchase—the point at which the consumer makes the rental or purchase decision—is today consolidated and dominated by chains. The chains applied a mass market, McDonald's-type formula to home video. If the place where America bought hamburgers did not have to look like a greasy spoon, so the place where America got its home video (the video store being the Mom and Pop dream of the 80s) did not have to be a dank basement with a Dolph Lundgren poster on the ceiling. The way to every American's heart and pocket book was through a squeaky clean suburban strip-mall video store where even the most violent Steven Seagal knock-off can easily pass for family entertainment.

This streamlining has made navigating the home video waters much more difficult for any independent producer. There is a positive side. The overall risk of releasing an independent feature is more leveraged because that risk is spread across more than one market. A feature that flops at the domestic box office can still recoup some of its investment from a home video release. One of the more instructive pastimes is reading the trade ads of video manufacturers as they engage in blatant distortions of truth in representing an unreleasable theatrical B-feature as a major box office event that "played all the major markets" (Peoria, no doubt, included).

POSITIONING FEATURES FOR HOME VIDEO RELEASE

A feature is still best positioned in the home video marketplace by theatrical play-off. The theatrical release establishes the film's identity and confers its value, including the value it will have in the home video market. Critics and journalists review and write about films when they play theaters, then recycle these reviews for the home video release. Critics do not, as a general rule, review straightto-video releases. Those straight-to-video releases that do bypass theatrical runs are most often straight genre (action) films, or films that failed in theatrical tests and will now exploit the star value to salvage the film in home video release. Examples include: Emir Kusturica's French-American co-production *Arizona Dream*, which failed in theatrical tests and was then released by Warner Home Video hyping the cast of Johnny Depp, Faye Dunaway, and Jerry Lewis; or *It's Pat*, the failed *Saturday Night Live* spinoff feature.

The negative side of the maturation and consolidation of home video is that a distributor usually buys and controls all rights. A home video release is timed to benefit from the money spent marketing the feature in theatrical release. Columbia (now Sony) bought Robert Rodriguez's homespun feature *El Mariachi* for theatrical release via Columbia Pictures, and for home video release via Columbia/TriStar Home Video. When Miramax bought *Pulp Fiction* and *Clerks*, Miramax did the theatrical release, television, international sales, and home video. The revenue from multiple markets tends to benefit the distributor since any advance to the producer will very likely encompass all rights, home video included.

The few independent distributors remaining who do not control or have a permanent home video licensing deal with a major studio are having a difficult time. All distributors realize that they have to act like studios if they are to survive. They have to control the picture from pre-production through home video release. The strategy of once-quasi-independent distributors like Fine Line (owned by New Line, which is now owned by Turner Entertainment) is to produce more, acquire less. They also need to control the library of films they own. Distributors who once had their films in home video licenses across several video manufacturers are rapidly consolidating and getting their rights back as the rights expire. It is a smart long-term strategy. The videos can be successfully rereleased. And there are, undoubtedly, new home video technologies on the way so that the films can be repurposed. Both completed and previously released films/videos and raw footage are seeing new life as a result of new technologies like CD-ROM. Film is re-edited, reshaped and repackaged into new product. Similarly, works that had their initial life on videocassette will be repackaged for the new video disc.

HOW HOME VIDEO WORKS

The maturing of the home video marketplace means that there now is a more highly evolved economic and marketing formula. Theatrical features are first released to home video as so-called "rental" product at a high price—somewhere between $80-$100. The video store pays less than this retail price (normally 25%-30% less). Generally the video manufacturers do not sell directly to video stores, with the exception of larger chains. Instead, the manufacturers sell to so-called two-step distributors. There are a half-dozen of these with distribution centers scattered around the country, including: Baker and Taylor, Ingram, Major Video Concepts, Sight and Sound, and ETD.

Through weekly mailers to their customer base and by telemarketing, these distributors "pre-book" titles scheduled to come out and then place the consolidated orders with the manufacturers. The weekly mailers consist almost entirely of ads that are paid for by the manufacturers. The ads, as well as rebates from the manufacturers, are very expensive and represent a significant income source for the two-step distributors. The distributors are obviously under considerable pressure—and sometimes quotas—to rack up large numbers of units on the major releases from the studios. The manufacturers do not leave promotion of their titles entirely up to the two-step distributor. Manufacturers mail directly to the video store retailers items like brochures, product announcements, posters, "screeners" (advance copies of the video with violators "Not for sale or rental"), standees, counter-top displays, and other promotional paraphernalia. Huge promotional sums are spent on these efforts.

The release pattern for new rental home video product parallels a theatrical release. There is a "street date"—the day when a new home video release will be in the stores, with all of the marketing and public relations muscle focused on that street date to build (or re-build) consumer demand. Depth of copy—and knowing how many copies to buy—is a major concern for video retailers. The supermarket merchandising of home video undoubtedly leads to homogenization in the marketplace. Video retailers feel they must have enough copies of a major release in order to compete, which in turn leaves them with fewer purchasing dollars to spend on slower-renting and, in most cases, more intellectually interesting and challenging releases. After interest in the newly released video has died down it is sold off as a "used" tape to brokers who recycle them to other stores or video vending machines; or the used tape is sold directly to the consumer.

Because of the right of first sale doctrine, the producer receives a royalty on the initial sale of the video to the store. There is no profit participation in the rental revenue of the tape (except in several maverick tape-leasing schemes). This is true for the U.S. home video market, but it is not the case in all foreign home video markets.[4] The idea that a store can charge a rental fee for a videocassette from which the film producer receives no share bothers some independents but is actually a naive fear. If the video rented so well, the video retailer would naturally purchase more copies. Instances of video stores getting rich from renting an independently produced video unfortunately do not exist.

INDEPENDENTS AND HOME VIDEO

A major benefit that home video offers to independent producers is direct access to the consumer. Some producers court this access aggressively, occasionally with strikingly positive results. Others remain fearful. I am always baffled by the producer who made an independent (and unknown) first feature without theatrical play-off and says, "I want my tape sold to consumers. I don't want it sold to stores." This still happens, although infrequently. The number of consumers who can be persuaded to plunk down $59.95 for an unknown first feature is limited unless the consumer has a chance to see the tape first (rent it) and is thus persuaded to own it. In fact, selling that feature to video stores will be very difficult, simply because the stores will have to wait a long time, often years to get back their $40 or $50. Video stores are first and foremost necessary cogs in the Hollywood machine.

Independents who made very successful forays into packaging their work for home video include James Broughton and Barbara Hammer. Todd Haynes's reputation was buttressed with the home video release of *Poison*, as was Jennie Livingston's with *Paris Is Burning*. There are some underground filmmakers like Nick Zedd, whose audience knows him almost entirely through his home video releases both independently and through *Film Threat* magazine.

Occasionally a studio will release a major film at a sell-through price the first time out. The perception here is that the film is collectable enough that consumers will instantly want to buy it rather than rent it. Carefully planned and promoted, these are major success stories like *Dances with Wolves* or *Forrest Gump*.

THE SELL-THROUGH REVOLUTION

During the last five years home video has undergone a second, smaller revolution. This is an explosion of video sell-through: consumer purchase rather than rental of home video. There are two aspects to this.

The retail price of a theatrical feature first released at a high price point as rental product is dropped some six months or a year later. The title is now no longer rental product, but rather sell-through product. This price reduction is often a part of a seasonal or thematic promotion (Mother's Day, Easter, Christmas, baseball season, etc.). The magical sell-through price is $19.98, but this is rapidly spiralling downward to $14.98 and $9.98. Fueling this downward price trend are rack jobbers who push videos into (and through) mass merchants. Sell-through experience reveals that most Americans purchase their videos in general stores. The manufacturer gets quite a bit less than the $19.98 here, with the discounts given to the rack jobber averaging 60-70%. Obviously volume is everything. It is unlikely that a more challenging independent feature—one that cannot be rolled out in mass volume like the studio release of a 1940s B-Western and sold through Target, K-Mart, Best-Buy, or some other chain—can make any money at even the $19.98 price level. For the moment, independent home video labels are maintaining sell-through prices of $24.95-$29.95—but not higher.

NONFICTION VIDEO

The consolidation and homogenization of the home video market place has also had an impact on non-theatrical (non-fiction) video. A documentary like *Hoop Dreams*, which sold more than 120,000 video copies at $96.98 is—plain and simple—a miracle. This is particularly extraordinary because the home video world views non-fiction video (sometimes called special interest video) as video that delivers "information." Personal documentaries do not have a separate consumer profile and thus tend to get lost in a quagmire of music concert videos, tapes about doll collecting, health, or psychic instruction.

Merchandising of non-fiction home video centers on "brandedness." The imprimatur gives the video its special sales value. This means *National Geographic*, *Nickelodeon*, *Nova*, *Smithsonian Institution*, or narration by Meryl Streep or Robin Williams. How many stars are there left in Hollywood who have not done their own exercise video? Occasionally a tape will create its own brandedness, as *Abs of Steel* has. Another bit of home video history: amid great controversy, PBS tried using its logo as a brand in a now failed distribution effort with the defunct Pacific Arts Video, which included some independent documentaries and features.

Cable television networks have also become attuned to home video as a vertical sell-through market. A & E, The Discovery Channel, Showtime, WGBH-Boston are all licensing programs for home video release as well as cablecast. The home video programs are then sold through a combination of on-air promotion, through the cable network's in-house magazines, and through outside distributors. Television networks, too, are recycling their programs into home video markets, with spinoffs of everything from news programs like *Nightline* to daytime soap operas and episodes of *The Brady Bunch*.

A similar kind of vertical integration pattern is affecting the music industry. A new music release, including jazz, blues, and classical, now often includes a VHS and laser disc release alongside the release of a CD or tape cassette.

Many former record stores (now CD outlets) sell video and laser disc. This softening of retail boundaries will inevitably continue as bookstores move into selling information technology (CD-ROM). At first this would seem to be a positive sign: more outlets means more possibilities for placing independent media work. In fact, it simply means that the market (and the consumer) is more confused. Video is everywhere. You can rent it or buy it at the grocery or drug store, the service station, catalog, bookstore, gardening center, or traditional video store. Cheaply recorded public domain films or cartoons sell for $2.99—which confuses a consumer who may then balk at an independent half-hour documentary selling for even $29.95.

The truth is, independent film and video has never—including now—travelled well in a mass market environment. Independent work requires special and often expensive handling. It needs an educated (or educable) consumer who looks for stimulation, challenge and information—rather than 110 minutes of electronic diversion.

THE PARALLEL VIDEO UNIVERSE

Parallel to the explosive growth of the commercial home video industry, a small, specialized home video distribution structure has evolved and survived into the 90s. It is marginal to the studio-driven home video business in the same way that small press publishers are marginal to the mass market commercial publishing business. Cassette sales here are counted by the hundreds, not by the hundreds of thousands or millions. The pioneers here are distributors who came to the home video field from the theatrical art film distribution side like Kino, New Yorker, First Run, Meridian, Fox Lorber, and others; or those who carefully cultivated a specific market niche like fine arts (opera, ballet, jazz) or boating (Bennett Video). Manufacturers court the mainstream distributors like Major Video Concepts, ETD, or Ingram and the video retail chains like Blockbuster, Tower, or Hollywood Video. Manufacturers also rely on catalogs and alternative distributors like Facets, Critics' Choice, or Barnes and Noble and on independent video stores that have committed to foreign, independent, or documentary sections. From this diversity of outlets they are able to piece together modest, but viable distribution strategies for foreign and independent features, classics, compilations, and animation.

Several hundred mostly independent video stores have also evolved around the country. They are concerned not only with depth of copy, but breadth of copy. One view of this kind of video store is as a perpetual repertory cinema, as a repository and source of video culture. Quentin Tarantino's emergence from a video store clerk to pop culture icon and one independent who has "made it" has helped fuel the myth that if you are around Sam Fuller and Aki Kaurismaki (and Quentin Tarantino) tapes long enough, something is bound to rub off.

Art film distributors like Kino, First Run Features, and New Yorker Films have found economic salvation in releasing art films (mostly foreign films, but occasionally independent features) to home video markets. Other independents like Fox Lorber, Water Bearer Films, MPI, Mystic Fire, and World Artists Home Video have valiantly fought the good fight to broaden the market for foreign and independent features and documentaries. Non-fiction video has spawned its own alternative home video distribution industry including classical, jazz, blues, ballet, and other dance and opera (Kultur Video, Video Artists International, View Video, Rhapsody Films).

Parallel to this are dozens of home video labels that serve the specific interests of special interest groups like railroad buffs, hunters and fishermen, sailing and boating enthusiasts, cult and grade-Z movie collectors, horror and science fiction fans, and those interested in spiritual and New Age issues, doll collecting, bluegrass music, home remodeling and other how-to. Many of these labels have catalogs, advertise in special interest or collector publications, and sell by mail directly to the consumer as well as through catalogs, stores, or other outlets. This includes hundreds and thousands of video titles on travel, cooking, gardening, home repair, antique collecting and restoring, music instruction, art. There are also experiments in retail sell-through of home video. New York now features two retail stores, How-To-Video, that specialize in the sales of only instructional videos; Suncoast Video is a major chain that does not rent, but only sells, videos and laser discs.

Sometimes home video moves from the alternative distributors into the mainstream. Gay and lesbian video, for example, once the exclusive province of small independent home video distributors is now more frequently released by larger companies. Examples include *Adventures of Priscilla* and *Savage Nights* by Polygram and *Go Fish* by Hallmark Entertainment.

What is new and exciting about these developments is that learning and information is now audiovisual and not purely text-driven. Programs can bypass the monolithic and homogenized mainstream distribution systems by going directly to the consumer.

There are other—isolated—success stories. Maverick titles like Peter Greenaway's documentary *26 Bathrooms* or the Joseph Campbell *Power of Myth* series or the films of Charles and Ray Eames on video were surprising hits for non-fiction films although even here one could argue that all three had some "brand-edness."

A number of independents have set up video labels for their own work. Successful examples here are the Maysles Brothers with their *Salesman, Grey Gardens* and series of art documentaries; photographer/filmmaker Danny Lyons; and filmmaker Jon Jost. It needs to be stressed that these are very low-key operations that take a long-term view and count on home video as purely ancillary income. They rely on other catalogs, libraries, or truly first-rate video stores to provide the majority of sales. Others, like filmmaker Ron Mann, have set up an Internet home page that describes their work and offers it for sale.

These independents do not get suckered into the tempting notion that by cleverly packaging and pouring money into advertising, a serious independent media work can suddenly sell tens of thousands of copies. The cemetery of expensive efforts to mass market video that had a limited audience to begin with now occupies quite a few acres. The idea of self-publishing or self-distributing home video to cover a substantial portion of the production cost remains a dream. Some companies have tried a high-profile approach to marketing independent releases, mostly by spending substantial sums for advertising in distributor mailers. Fox Lorber Home Video (*Brother's Keeper, Through the Wire, Thank You and Goodnight*) has now cut down substantially on this flamboyant approach, focusing instead on niche-oriented marketing and direct personal sales contact with distributors and customers.

Experimental film or video, which is most marginalized by the mainstream culture, understandably has the most difficult time. With few exceptions, collections of short films are also a difficult reach despite truly noble efforts by some distributors to creatively package. Yet even here there are surprises. Home video releases of theatrically established collections like *The Animation Celebration, The Quay Brothers*[5] or *Computer Dreams* (computer animation compilation) have done well in the sell-through home video market.

Libraries—most of which now have video collections—have not been an enormous source of purchasing strength for independent home video, yet are a growing home video market. A number of foundations, including the MacArthur

Foundation, National Video Resources of the Rockefeller Foundation, and most recently the Revson Foundation's Jewish Heritage Video Collection, have made major investments to try and turn local public libraries into responsive and responsible collections of independent videos. All have distributed subsidized collections of independent work in thematic packages (Native American Video, Latin American Video, etc.) to public libraries at lower-than-non-theatrical cost. In addition, National Video Resources has focused efforts to teach librarians about building media collections that reflect both a historical and contemporary heritage.

THE HOME VIDEO FUTURE

Technophiles, futurists, computer-geeks, and the robber barons of the end of the millennium are busy predicting the imminent demise of the videocassette. The future is digital, they say, but the consumer jury is still out.

Those of us who remember the promises of infinite media options once touted by broadcast and cable television know that the distribution future of independent media is not dependent on technology or hardware or on systems of distribution controlled by conglomerates. Instead, the successful models of distributing independent work are almost always alternative structures—targeted marketing, building grassroots constituencies, postering, and telephone-trees—that overcome the marginalization of independent media by the mainstream consumer culture.

In this alternative media universe, home video—or whatever replaces the videocassette—is an important element. Home video is more than an ancillary media market—it is now a primary means of reaching the consumer. Because home video breaks down the boundaries between producer and consumer, the home video revolution is alive and well. The revolutionary idea of delivering a film or video directly to the consumer on his home ground is a major social shift. At the same time, home video has educated the consumer to choice. It is no longer the blanket "We go to movies on Saturday nights." Home video introduced the possibility of an informed sensibility. In spite of what is playing at the multiplex, educated consumers now know that at a video store (or, possibly, a library) they can check out an independent feature, an instructional video on home repair, a documentary on the Gulf War, or a compilation of European animation. By educating the consumer, we educate the gatekeeper. That is the challenge.

Notes:

[1]*Video Business*, April 14, 1995

[2]Faith Popcorn, *The Popcorn Report* (1991)

[3]Columbia TriStar Home Video provided production funds to a number of independent features in return for home video rights.

[4]The Supreme Court has ruled that the act of purchasing a tape transfers the ownership of that property (though not the copyright) to the purchaser, who is then free to re-sell or rent it. Videos are in this sense no different from books, moving vans, or rental chain saws.

[5]According to First Run Features, the two volumes of *The Quay Brothers* animation have sold a total of more than 10,000 cassettes—an impressive number for a collection of surreal animation.

CHAPTER 11

CABLE DISTRIBUTION

Michael Fox

able television is almost as ubiquitous in the home entertainment environment as broadcast television, video rentals, and pizza. But 'twas not always so.

Cable television systems were first established in the late 1940s to deliver television signals to rural areas with poor over-the-air reception. For a fee, homes were connected to a master antenna, which transmitted signals over coaxial cable. Thanks to a shielded copper wire, even residents of remote areas could join in the communal postwar embrace of prime-time programming and home-appliance commercials.

For the next fifteen years, the function of community antenna television (CATV) was simply to extend the signal to outlying areas. Cable was wired into just three percent of U.S. homes at the end of 1965, and claimed 1.6 million subscribers.

Then cable operators began to take a more proactive attitude, toying with creating original programming rather than merely carrying network fare. With its multiple-channel capacity as well as the ability to pick up distant signals via microwave technology, cable suddenly had the potential to compete with broadcast television. CATV channel capacity increased from three to twelve, and MSOs (multiple systems operators) who owned and operated several cable systems sprung up. Broadcasters recognized the challenge, however, and convinced the FCC to regulate the cable industry, effectively locking it out of big cities and discouraging its expansion. Nonetheless, eleven percent of the nation's homes were connected by the end of 1972 and 7.3 million people subscribed to cable.

That year also marked a change in philosophy at the FCC, which eased its constraints on the cable industry. Of equal importance was the development of

Home Box Office (HBO), the first successful pay-television channel. The entrepreneurs behind HBO reasoned that enough people with perfectly fine reception would subscribe to cable in order to watch exclusive programming. Professional boxing proved a big draw for HBO. Recent movies, uncut and shown without commercials, also were a huge inducement (this was before the home-video era). Americans reveled in the heretofore-unknown thrill of bare breasts and swear words emanating from their television sets.

Several communications satellites were launched in the next few years, providing cable with an affordable means of reaching viewers nationwide. In 1975 HBO became the first service to deliver its programming via satellite. WTBS, Ted Turner's Atlanta-based station, was right behind, staking its claim as the first "superstation."

A tidal wave of new, specialized cable programming services followed. Many of the upstarts offered niche programming such as children's shows, wall-to-wall sports, twenty four-hour news, and religious programs. This strategy of "narrowcasting" was the antithesis of broadcast television, which offered lowest-common-denominator fare intended to attract the largest possible audiences.

Technical advances—which enabled cable systems to expand their capacity—and marketing innovations helped fuel rapid growth. Tiered pricing, with one fee for a basic cable package and a surcharge for premium channels, proved an effective method of adding viewers. By 1980, sixteen million people subscribed to cable and twenty one percent of U.S. homes were wired.

But not all the new networks struck gold. After all, as late as 1978 the entire industry generated a paltry $5 million in advertising revenues. The enthusiasm of network founders and their bankers was not always matched by viewer turnout. Lower-than-projected ratings and income resulted in debt, failure, mergers, and/or revised programming philosophies.

The shakeout in the early 80s was followed by sweeping deregulation in 1984. By this point, CNN's coverage of the Iran hostage crisis and ESPN's ubiquitous presence in bars had integrated cable into everyday life. Most of the big cities became wired in the 80s and subscribers signed up in droves. The turning point arrived before the end of the decade, when cable penetration finally topped the critical fifty percent mark and national advertisers wholeheartedly embraced the medium.

By 1991, Turner Broadcasting System's four twenty four-hour networks (TBS, TNT, CNN, and C-SPAN) garnered a larger share of the viewing audience than each of the Big Three networks. While the rolls of subscribers continued to swell, operators were deluged with complaints of rate gouging and poor service. Congress and state legislatures finally took note of the abuses of deregulation, and passed measures to limit rates.

CABLE PROGRAMMING SERVICES

Although cable continues to build its share of the audience, the major developments of recent years are related to programming. Cable has achieved credibility on a par with the Big Three television networks, thanks to consistently excellent showings in the Emmy Awards. HBO has been honored for its classy original fact-based films, such as *Barbarians at the Gate* and *Citizen Cohn*, while Showtime received kudos for some of its movies. As a result, top-notch directors and major stars will now work in cable movies without loss of prestige—which in turn brings more glory to those networks.

On the other hand, network reruns have become the programming of choice for Lifetime (*thirtysomething, Designing Women*) and USA (*Murder, She Wrote, Wings*). Talk shows and stand-up comedy (which are cheap to produce) and infomercials (which typically purchase slots after midnight) comprise a surprising amount of cable programming. This is certainly a long way from the exciting commercial-free adult programming that cable television promised in the 1970s, and which motels listed on their marquees to lure guests. Indeed, cable is often as limited and predictable as network television.

Most cable stations aim for a niche that is specific enough (e.g., The Sci-Fi Channel, The Comedy Channel, MTV) to distinguish them in a crowded field yet broad enough to draw a large audience. Their aim is to post the kind of ratings and demographics that will convince both cable operators to keep them and advertisers to sponsor them.

This is especially true for basic cable services, which are advertiser-supported and included in a package (which also contains the local broadcast channels) provided for a monthly fee by the cable operator to the subscriber.

Pay TV is commercial-free and is offered to the subscriber for an additional fee. Here is a brief description of the major services and those of greatest interest to independents.

HBO—The most popular premium channel in the country devotes the lion's share of its schedule to Hollywood movies, bolstered by original movies, boxing, and Wimbledon tennis. It has also commissioned documentaries such as *Dear America: Letters Home from Vietnam*.

Cinemax—HBO's sister channel shows mostly movies, skewed to a slightly younger audience.

Showtime—HBO's primary competitor offers movies, a sci-fi series, *Outer Limits* and comedy series such as *Twisted Puppet Theater* and *Full Frontal Comedy*.

The Sundance Channel—Thanks to Robert Redford's annual festival, this Showtime-owned channel has the cachet of a brand name for independent work.

However, there is no connection between films that air on this channel and those selected for the festival.

The Movie Channel—Also owned by Showtime, this network offers more movies, including classics and R-rated films.

Bravo—"The film and arts network" airs foreign and independent movies and a broad range of cultural programming (opera, ballet, theater). Bravo also offers excellent British programs like *The South Bank Show*. Offered as a basic service in some areas.

Independent Film Channel—Bravo's offshoot, launched in September 1994, presents films made outside the Hollywood studio system, including documentaries, shorts, and animation. This and the Sundance Channel are obvious targets for independent filmmakers.

The Disney Channel—Family entertainment, from Bob Hope comedies to *Mr. Smith Goes to Washington* to children's shows.

Even in the post-shakeout era, dozens of basic services still exist. Here are the largest ones.

USA—Closely resembles independent broadcast stations, with its roster of reruns.

Lifetime—Aimed at women. In early 1995 announced a renewed commitment, to the tune of $100 million, to produce original made-for-cable movies.

Arts & Entertainment—Mix of documentaries, dramas, movies and performing arts.

MTV—The music video channel commissions bumpers and IDs from animators.

Nickelodeon—Programming for children and their older siblings. In the evening, *Nick at Nite* offers reruns of vintage shows.

The Discovery Channel—Documentaries spotlighting the themes of nature, science, history, people and places, world exploration, and human adventure. One of the most hospitable networks to independents.

A complete listing of cable program services and buyers is available from the National Academy of Cable Programming, which operates under the auspices of the National Cable Television Association. Their annually updated publication, *Producer's Source Book: A Guide to Cable TV Program Buyers*, costs $60. Call (202) 775-3611 for details.

PUBLIC AND LEASED ACCESS

Although cable networks joust with each other for viewers, there is no competition between cable operators for subscribers. The way that cable spread through the

United States was that local governments awarded exclusive franchises, typically for fifteen years. (New York and Los Angeles are so big that the areas were divvied up between a couple of operators.) Each company assumed the cost of laying cable and connecting homes, then had exclusive rights to sell the service.

Every cable operator chooses which program services it will carry, with that decision limited by channel capacity and predicated on subscriber preference (i.e., ratings). However, operators have nothing to do with the actual programming, and neither acquire nor produce shows.

As one of the conditions of receiving a franchise, most municipalities require cable operators to offer public access programming. The aim is for the community and its members to have affordable and easy entry to the "airwaves."

That access is provided on a first-come, first-served basis. Many cable operators provide a studio and equipment, with a city-appointed board actually managing the program. Producers can produce shows in the studio, or they may bring in tapes produced elsewhere. Production values for public access shows are typically bare-bones. No commercials are allowed on public access.

For independents, public access is one of the most accessible and under-utilized media. Viewership is tiny (albeit loyal), self-promotion is the only avenue for publicity, and, of course, payment is nonexistent. Public access is an alternative if all other broadcast and cable outlets have turned down a piece, or for additional airings after a work has completed the theatrical–cable–public television distribution cycle and the rights have reverted to the maker. Public access is also a likely venue for student films.

Most cable operators also offer leased access. Producers pay for time and are allowed to sell commercials during their show. The most successful programs typically encompass racy material and flamboyant local personalities with cult followings.

It is possible to syndicate a program to public access stations, however this involves approaching each station on an individual basis. Although some assert that the odds of getting on the air are better this way than by applying to the well-known cable programming services, it is a time-consuming approach that is most appropriate for fringe programs with low production values.

Access has taken on a more visible and controversial profile recently as the number of programs produced by racist groups has increased. (A 1991 study found fifty seven different hate shows nationwide on public access.) Community television certainly was not conceived as a forum for attacks on minorities; producers, meanwhile, claim First Amendment rights. The clash has moved to the courts.

SELLING TO CABLE

One might expect cable services, with their endless need for programming, to view independent filmmakers as a valuable resource and supplier. However, keep in mind that cable services are aiming for the broadest audiences. With so much money at stake, their programming choices have become nearly as mainstream and conservative as those of the broadcast networks. Having said that, there are opportunities for independents.

With respect to features, most programming services prefer to deal with distributors (for finished films), and agents (for proposals). Distributors are perceived as having more experience with the market, and a more realistic grasp of license fees. They are also more adept at the logistical details of contracts, insurance, and other matters. Agents, meanwhile, serve as a clearinghouse of sorts, ostensibly weeding out the talented from the not-so-talented.

Network schedulers work at least two months in advance. Therefore, the lead time is shorter for finished films obtained via acquisition than through production. Payment is determined on the basis of either a flat fee or per subscriber. A flat fee is a negotiated, fixed price while per-subscriber fees are determined by the network's average number of subscribers on the film's playdates. Although the latter is more cumbersome to monitor, it is a means of sharing the risk and finding a fair price in a world of variable subscriber totals.

Documentaries are the programs most commonly acquired directly from filmmakers without intermediaries. As with any query (such as an application for a foundation grant), it is basic that you know the field. Consider only those networks that air original work and aim your pitch at those whose programming is consistent with your proposal.

In addition, each programming service has different priorities. One may require exclusives, and another may allow a theatrical window. TBS, for example, does not negotiate back-end deals (such as home-video rights) on original programs it develops with indies. TBS views the work as an asset they want to own as part of their library. However, since TBS provides the entire budget, the filmmaker does not need to raise funds from other sources (from sale of the home-video rights, for example).

Similarly, the Discovery Channel covers the full production budget in exchange for all rights. The motivation in this case is marketing synergy, since Discovery will develop the CD-ROM, video, and/or book to tie in with the show.

Typically, cable networks prefer to receive ideas in writing as the initial step. If they are interested, they will request a detailed, honest budget with a treatment. Development of the script is the next stage, followed by funding of the production. In almost all cases, the network retains final cut.

Keep in mind that the lead time of networks such as TBS is usually more than two years; that is, they are currently developing films that will not air for at least two years.

It is also important to understand the concept of windows, which refers to periods of availability in different markets. The order of distribution for features, for example, is theatrical, followed by pay cable, home video, and broadcast television or basic cable. The sequence varies for documentaries, although HBO typically allows a theatrical window prior to its cable premiere.

Once a link has been skipped in the chain, it is usually lost forever. Once a program has aired on PBS, for example, most premium channels will not buy it. Therefore it is crucial to plot and choreograph the distribution strategy. (For more on this topic, refer to Marc Mauceri's chapter on "Sequencing.")

Previous experience producing a documentary for a network will enhance a producer's chances of getting another project approved (assuming it was a positive experience for the channel). But it is no guarantee. HBO financed and produced Rob Epstein and Jeffrey Friedman's *Common Threads: Stories From the Quilt* in 1990. That film won the Oscar for best documentary, yet HBO was initially hesitant to get involved with the filmmakers' most recent documentary, *The Celluloid Closet*. After Epstein and Friedman obtained much of the funding elsewhere, HBO eventually agreed to ante up the rest of the budget (fifty percent) in exchange for the pay-television rights.

Independent filmmakers should be aware of a pair of new funding sources. HBO provides completion funds (and a licensing fee) for four or five documentaries a year to be aired on Cinemax's *Vanguard Cinema* series. Michel Negroponte's *Jupiter's Wife* was one of the first films to benefit from HBO's largesse at a cash budget of $100,000 (excluding salaries).

The Independent Film Channel has a fund dubbed IFCheap (IFC Helps Emerging Artists Produce), which is designed for development and finishing funds for independent features. The sentiment is admirable but, at the moment, moot; the fund is financed from profits, which the new channel probably won't generate before 1997 at the earliest. However, the IFC does produce shorts.

A PEEK INTO THE FUTURE

The rapid acceptance of fiber optics and compression technology has expanded the capacity of the cable operator to the point that a five hundred-channel universe is a real possibility. Meanwhile, the entry of the telecommunications companies into the home entertainment industry—with their potential ability to deliver programs to consumers over telephone lines—represents a direct threat to cable. Both developments offer the prospect of movies-on-demand, spelling a serious challenge to home video stores.

Interactive television is the latest gimmick to generate attention. Despite the hype, however, interactive programming has yet to prove that it is an innovation that can transcend home shopping, game shows, and children's programming.

The vast appetite for programs would seem to represent an opportunity for independents. Of course, that is what many people said when cable first began making inroads. The current environment offers a replay of sorts. All three systems mentioned above require enormous investment, from laying fiber optic cable to installing interactive set-top boxes in millions of homes. Consequently, programming sources will continue to target the broadest possible audiences, which is not always consistent with the themes, topics, and points of view favored by independent filmmakers. Not everyone is thrilled about unimaginative programs, of course, as evidenced by headlines such as "150 Channels and Nothin' On" and "50,000 Channels and Nothing to Watch" that appeared in the early 90s in publications as varied as *Business Week* and *The Progressive*.

Yes, many independent filmmakers have benefited from the prominence of cable, and will participate in its continued evolution. But given its enormity, the cable system has barely tapped the vision, energy, and creative power of independents. A dramatic change in philosophy is certainly possible, but seems unlikely.

CHAPTER 12

VIDEO ART: STAY TUNED

Kate Horsfield

ost people involved with video wince at the inappropriateness of the phrase video art. This is a term that has become somewhat out of favor since the 1980s when video expanded to include new videomakers, new agendas, and new audiences that are not specifically affiliated with the art world. While video tapes were considered 'art' when they originated in the art world in the mid-60s, other kinds of independent video began at the same time.

Video art could refer to several genres or types of work: experimental video, performance video, documentary video, activist video, narrative video, community-based video. Each genre represents a different quality and set of values and lately it has meant a different audience as well. Experimental and performance video are usually more art-based in terms of their focus on innovative visual substance and non-narrative content; while activist and community-based video is usually less concerned with visuals and more concerned with delivering information or including new videomakers in the process—as in educating at risk youth, or organizing communities to take direct action.

For the past thirty years, video has moved back and forth between prioritizing form over content/content over form—innovative experimentation on one side and social issues or political critique on the other. This seesawing effect is not random and uncoordinated, but is a direct response to the emergence of postmodern cultural theories. As theories change, they bear influence on who makes video, what it should look like, and who it is for. From the beginning, video art has meant more than one type of approach to using the technology for expressing a variety of ideas. So a little history into the development of the medium might be helpful here.

A BRIEF HISTORY

The 1960s revolt against the mainstream and the corporate structure encouraged artists to invent ways to take the art object (mostly sculpture and painting) out of the gallery (i.e., the commodified space) and into a more conceptually pure space where art could be experienced but not bought or sold. This was a repudiation of modernism and, in particular, the ways in which modernism fetishized the art object. So art practice began to change and new materials and new ways of working as an artist became possible. This opened the door for radically new art forms such as performance, installation works, and video.

During this same period, in 1965, Sony Corporation released the first portable video equipment—the porta-paks—for use in the industrial market. The porta-pak, while somewhat primitive in comparison to its progeny, the camcorder, represented a major opportunity for using television technology for personal expression—since obtaining any kind of access to television production equipment was virtually impossible before 1965. Television was controlled exclusively by the government (standards) and the corporate television networks (money and power).

Artists immediately saw creative opportunities in video and were among the first to purchase the new video equipment. They imagined uses for video that reflected a new sense of aesthetics and a new form of art making. Video was a frontier territory with no history and almost no critical dialogue attached to it, and many artists relished the freedom that this offered. There were three major conceptual groupings in video when it first became available: performance video, formalist video, and community-based video.

Some artists—like John Baldessari, Vito Acconci and Bruce Nauman—began to work with the new medium as an extension of ideas they had developed in other media such as photography or sculpture. Video became a part of a repertoire of processes and forms that extended the artist's vision. Each of these artists used video to record early performance pieces—usually in front of a single black-and-white video camera. These artists were already known in the art world and they provided video with a very important sense of credibility as a new medium. Even though most people did not know what video was, they were interested because of the artists who were using it.

Others came to the new medium because it represented the opening of the new era of electronics. These artists became involved in designing equipment as visualizing tools. Their work was more concentrated on the process of making images rather than the end product of producing tapes. Woody and Steina Vasulka, Stephen Beck, and Dan Sandin are examples of inventor-artists who began working in the 1960s with homemade synthesizers and other image-making tools. Their work was very performance oriented in the respect that it was primarily used as a live process of discovering images while working at a synthesizer. The process of generating original images was more important than making tapes composed of those images. These were the visionaries who were inventing handmade equipment that preceded the digital revolution of the 1990s.

Other communal and collective groups took a more activist stance in relation to the porta-pak and its ability to record reality. TVTV, Video Freaks, Peoples Video Theater, and Raindance focused on small and large events—antiwar demonstrations, a gay parade, behind-the-scenes organizing, and the Republican National Convention in 1972—forming a new kind of grassroots video documentary style that was low tech and high in the essences and immediacy of video. They focused on a socially inclusive media of ideas, people, and communities who were outside the limited representations of corporate television. Video was the center of communicating the countercultural ideals of the 1960s.

THE SEVENTIES

By the early 1970s, several video communities had developed across the country— New York, San Francisco, Buffalo, Syracuse, and Chicago all had thriving video communities. News of new work spread from one community to another. Everyone was very interested in screening everyone else's video. So the first distribution consisted of "bicycling" tapes—usually through the mail or under the arm of a friend and fellow videomaker—from one group to another. This small-scale distribution was extremely important because screening tapes helped videomakers see themselves and each other as a part of a very active community with links across the country. This was a very modest but very important kind of distribution. The goal of distribution was not necessarily to make money from screening work, but rather to see work, have yours seen by peers, and become aware of developments in other parts of the newly emerging video field.

In 1970 the New York State Council for the Arts began funding video as they did other art disciplines such as painting, sculpture, photography, and film. Soon the National Endowment for the Arts and other state councils were also funding video. They funded production, via fellowships, and also exhibition and sometimes distribution via the media arts centers category. This new funding was a very significant development in the history of video. It was a commitment to the new medium, and an investment in videomakers and the media arts field. Videomakers, video screening programs, video distributors, and media arts centers have all been subsidized by government and foundation grants since the 1970s. This funding has kept the video screening programs and collections going and the field growing larger.

In the two decades between 1974 and 1994 as the whole media arts field grew, the number of videomakers increased and many colleges and art schools developed video and media programs. There were jobs in colleges for videomakers, and schools were turning out lots of interesting young videomakers. Many screening venues appeared in museums and alternative spaces. There were even a few strands for independent work on public television, like *Image Union* on WTTW in Chicago and *Alive TV* in Minneapolis. And the media arts field produced its own very important showcase for independent and community-based video, Deep Dish Television, on cable access channels around the country.

Two organizations were formed in the 1970s to exclusively distribute video art—Electronic Arts Intermix was founded in 1972 and the Video Data Bank was founded in 1976. The Kitchen also distributes video but they were primarily formed as a presenting organization for new music, performance, and video.

RECENT HISTORY

While government and foundation funding has kept the media arts field growing, earned income from distribution of tapes has also grown. While it is rarely true that a videomaker will make back through distribution what he or she has put into production/post-production of a tape, earned income from tape distribution has been increasing year by year. All video distributors have reported similar increases in earned income. An example is the Video Data Bank. In 1984 earned income from the rental and sale of all tapes was $84,000 and in 1994 earned income had climbed to $310,000. Simultaneously, in 1994 government, foundation, and other funding support for the VDB was $156,000. So you could say that it took $1 of public and private funding to generate $2 of earned income. But the growth in earned income represents a very positive interest and a demand for video. It is a hopeful sign that video has caught on and is getting more popular with its audiences. From 1976 to 1989 the typical audience and screening venues were in alternative spaces, media centers, film and video festivals, and museums. While these are still the main user groups for video, educational institutions—particularly screening as part of the curricula in universities—have also become major users of video. The intellectual community in academia is the biggest supporter of video— art departments, journalism, film and media programs and more recently feminist studies, Black studies, and Queer studies.

It comes as no surprise to anyone that video has never been a marketable commodity in mass market systems such as public television, cable television, or video stores. The content is usually too "hot" and opinionated and it is too visually daring for the restrictive formats of television. Video began as a resistance, an alternative to the commercialism of television, and to mainstream thinking itself. Video is the medium of the marginalized—those who are left out of mainstream television—the artists, the poor, the handicapped, the intellectuals, at-risk youth, and genderbenders. Video shares the attributes of other art practices in that it is part of an intense personal and intellectual investigation that tends to disregard convention.

THE VIDEO COMMUNITY

From the 1960s on, the media arts field has operated as a small community of film- and videomakers, programmers, distributors, funders and festivals. This sense of community was a major component of the media arts field—from its inception in the 1960s to the late 80s. Making money was not nearly as important as gaining appreciation for your work from your peers, getting a few important museum and festival screenings and the occasional government grant. Audience members were usually your friends. This smallness offered a sense of community—everyone knew of everyone else—and this provided a buffer against the marginalized position of video in reference to the larger and more well-known art and media disciplines such as painting or film.

While the protective community grouping provided opportunities for videomakers to be familiar with each other, it also kept them isolated from interacting with other parts of the art world. There are the media artists and the visual artists—carefully partitioned just like the funding categories of the National Endowment for the Arts. A few alternative spaces brought film- and videomakers together in programs, but hardly ever did painters and sculptors work with videomakers. Why is this important? Artists who achieve prominence in video are often not known in other areas of the art world, much less among the general public, unless they work in other media such as photography, drawing, film, or installation. Some artists who began making tapes and then moved on to making larger works have achieved major recognition in the art world—Bill Viola, Gary Hill, Dara Birnbaum, Doug Hall, and Martha Rosler. But most videomakers are not known by other members of the art world and individual members of the media arts field, and have almost no name recognition outside a small circuit of people. This makes it very difficult to draw audiences from the visual arts for artists in the media arts field. And it makes it difficult to promote the similarities between the media and visual arts.

THE FESTIVAL CIRCUIT

The festival circuit plays an important role in bringing people together for discussion and the presentation of new work. Probably the most important festival in the

United States in the 1980s was the American Film Institute/National Video Festival. This festival brought many videomakers to Los Angeles to the American Film Institute campus to premiere their work. It was a very prestigious festival and it was intellectually elegant. It had curated sidebars that featured new ideas and developments in video, Latin America and Eastern Europe. And it had a catalog with critical essays by important members of the video and film community. This festival peaked in importance in 1989—the year it premiered Marlon Riggs's *Tongues Untied*. The next year the festival began to decline, and though it still exists, it has lost its ability to bring video people together as an interesting working community.

Unfortunately no other festivals have achieved the status of the National Video Festival, but there are still important festivals for video such as the IMAGE Festival in Atlanta, the New York Video Festival, Charlotte Film and Video Festival, and Images Festival in Toronto.

Europe has always had an enthusiastic response to performance and video from the United States. Recently the foreign markets have been big purchasers of video. Europe has many video festivals, including two of the most important for video anywhere: the Worldwide Festival in Den Haag; and the VideoFest in Berlin, which is held at the same time as the very prestigious Berlin Film Festival. These festivals feature work from several European countries, Canada, Australia, Latin America, and the United States.

Tongues Untied represented some major accomplishments and changes in video that had occurred by the late 1980s. New individuals and groups began to use video in important new ways—to communicate urgent social messages such as AIDS awareness and safer sex information, ethnic or racial pride. Tapes were produced that encouraged activism or compassion and understanding rather than visual appreciation. Narratives shifted to the relationships between the personal and the political such as Rea Tajiri's *History and Memory* (1991). Voices spoke from a multicultural perspective. Production and access shifted away from the individual to groups that included urban projects for underprivileged youth, such as Branda Miller's *talk about droppin' out* (1989), made as a collaboration with youth from Madison High School in Boston. Many, many important tapes were produced as a cultural parallel to the AIDS activist movement in addition to Marlon Rigg's *Tongues Untied*. A few of these are: *DiAna's Hair Ego: AIDS Info Upfront*, Ellen Spiro; *they are lost to vision altogether*, Tom Kalin; and Stuart Marshall's *Bright Eyes*.

This new work was produced with the intention of linking video with new audiences outside the arts community—audiences in community centers, churches, labor and health groups, gay rights and activist meetings, public libraries, and K-12 schools. Each tape had a special audience to match with its process or content. "Audience outreach" became the operative words for distributors as they attempted to link the work with new audiences. New distribution strategies were developed to reach out to communities of Black and Latino youth, labor groups, people with AIDS, welfare mothers, environmentalists, prisoners.

Each video tape is made with a set of characteristics that affect a specific audience—audiences who come for discussions surrounding closed-circuit screenings in academia, prisons, activist groups, community centers; or other audiences that are reached through mass communication systems such as television or cable access. Some people think that only "good work" gets on television and the other work is shown in closed circuit screenings. Not true. The difference in distribution is not just a matter of whether the video is good, but of whom it was designed to appeal to. Some video is made to appeal to television audiences—and the videomaker chose the format, structure, technical requirements, and narrative line that makes it possible to present on television. Other videomakers want more intimate screenings with discussions of the ideas raised in the work.

Until very recently most videomakers did not expect to get their work programmed on television. Videomakers have always understood television to be very limited, entertainment oriented, and unable to present innovative, controversial, or difficult work. When experimental work has been programmed it was always relegated to a few independent program strands on public television, such as *Independent Focus* on WNET in New York; *New Television* out of WGBH in Boston; *Alive TV* from Minneapolis; *The Territories* in Houston and Austin, Texas; *Image Union* from Chicago; or the *Living Room Festival* from San Francisco. In 1994 we counted just thirteen public television strands for independent work.

In 1991, after a lengthy battle by independents, the Independent Television Service (ITVS) was created by a mandate from Congress via the Corporation for Public Broadcasting. ITVS was formed to get money to independents to produce innovative and challenging television for underserved audiences via the public broadcast system. With a multimillion dollar annual budget for programming, ITVS wields enough bucks to support independent film and videomakers in making a new kind of television that links independents to underserved communities. ITVS offers a much bigger pot of money for film and videomakers to make larger scale works. This is an opportunity that did not exist until 1991 in the media arts field.

Most videomakers do not produce their work with television audiences in mind. This is partially a result of the historical fact that there never was much opportunity for independent videomakers to screen on television. If they did get that rare opportunity, it cost a fortune to acquire the music and visual rights to the elements in the video. As Ellen Schneider, co-executive producer of P.O.V. said to me last year: "It took the independent field fifteen years of fighting to get twelve hours of work on national public television."

From the beginning, video was fixed at an intersection between the art world, the world of progressive politics and the mainstream. Drawing from each of these sources, video offers an original view of the world that can inspire, activate, lull, infuriate, and bore audiences. It flourishes in small screening venues because it needs the intimacy, interactivity, and commentary that audiences provide. When work is on television, you might make lots of money and get exposure to huge audiences but you do not get the benefit of an audience's direct response to your work. This will change as digital technology offers interactive response between the video-maker and the audience.

If you walk into a video store today and ask if they have any video art, or even independent video, you are likely to get a blank stare. In spite of an increasingly enthusiastic response to video in art venues and in academia, video stores have mostly not been interested in independent work. Because of the limited runs, high royalty payments to videomakers, and complex subject matter, video has been a hard sell to store owners who are considering only the bottom line. The mythical "home market," which hypes the idea of great numbers of sales to individuals who are collecting home libraries, has not panned out yet. If video is sold in stores or catalogs, it is usually bought by faculty members who do build up personal video collections for use in curricula.

As video nears its thirtieth anniversary, we can celebrate the accomplishments of many videomakers and many media arts organizations that go back to the late sixties and early seventies. And we can celebrate the sensibility and politics behind video as well. As we move further into a world organized around the corporate mentality, the complex ideas and original forms of video and other alternative communications that are not primarily driven by money and the bottom line become ever more important to the free debate and expression of democracy. We need fresh ideas, we need the debate and the challenge to convention that art and alternative media offer.

THE FUTURE

So what does the future offer for video art? Both high and low technology are offering important technological advances for video. Camera technology has delivered important improvements in the camcorder. This helps videomakers produce work of a better visual and signal quality and it makes it easier to get work broadcast. There have been great advances in editing technology. In the future it will be possible to edit for a very reasonable cost in non-linear digital software programs such as Quicktime, Macromedia's Director, or the Avid. Production will get cheaper, more accessible, and better through the new technologies. We hope that the high-end delivery technologies will also offer opportunities for video, particularly for distribution via the Internet and on digital server and satellite systems. The caution with this is that since commercial entities are developing the fiber optic and digital systems, they may be too expensive for use by independents. We hope that legislation will be put in place that guarantees a "public lane" on the national information superhighway that will allow for affordable non-profit use. All of this is currently under discussion by Congress and has yet to be finalized.

Since video was left out of three other technological revolutions that improved delivery of media—public broadcasting, cable distribution, and video stores—we hope that the decentralization and uncontrolled web of Internet communication will be a more promising arena for video to thrive. It is entirely possible that the new technologies could provide a huge audience for video and tremendous new electronic approaches to reaching new audiences and new buyers for video. But there is still a small worry that, as video becomes a partner to text and sound in the concept of multimedia, video might lose its current tenuous foothold on a separate identity. Stay tuned...

CHAPTER 13

FROM TAIPEI TO TANGIER: GETTING YOUR FILM PLACED AROUND THE WORLD

Nancy Walzog

O ne of the most difficult questions I am often asked is "How much money can I expect to make from international sales of my film?" Unfortunately, this is an almost impossible question to answer because there are many unpredictable factors that come into play when trying to project a program's foreign sales. As president of Tapestry International, an international distributor of quality documentaries, drama, performing arts, cultural, and children's programming, I must view programming with a critical eye toward what will be successful. But success, by definition, is subjective.

Success from a distributor's point of view is usually a combination of the project's potential for profitability and profile in the marketplace. Success for the independent producer may be based on other criteria. Do you need to pre-sell rights to recoup part of your production budget? Do you want festival exposure? Are you looking to showcase your directing skills when you pitch your feature-length screenplay? Before you begin your project, it is critical that you fully evaluate your goals and objectives so you can make the right decisions along the way. The time to start planning for international distribution is while your project is early in its development.

ANALYZING THE MARKETPLACE

Much like writing a business plan, the first step in planning your project is to analyze the marketplace. The international television environment is a rapidly changing landscape where there are literally hundreds of thousands of hours of programming with which to compete. Finding out how business is done and how the industry works will help you answer the following key questions: Is there a market for a project like mine? Are there any content or stylistic elements I can consider now in order to avoid potential pitfalls? Should I go with a distributor or try to make international sales myself? And most importantly, how much or how little can I rely on foreign sales to pay back my debt?

The main international markets for independent programming consist of television sales to the English-speaking territories (such as Australia, Canada, and The United Kingdom), Scandinavia, and the countries of Western Europe. Sales to major European broadcasters in foreign language territories such as France, Germany, Spain, and Italy can be lucrative. However, the odds of selling to these stations are very small due to the large quantity of their own production. Sales in other regions such as Latin America and Asia are also difficult due to the inherent cultural differences.

In general, the international marketplace is exploding right now as new regional cable and satellite stations are coming on the scene in areas such as Europe, The Middle East, Asia, and Latin America. Many familiar cable brands such as Nickelodeon, Turner, Disney, and Discovery have launched impressive cable networks in these regions as well. On one hand, there are many more opportunities for programming in general; on the other hand, programmers for these new outlets face increased pressure to be more commercial or ratings-driven. They must also manage a demanding twenty-four-hour schedule, thus making it almost impossible to consider a single title coming in directly from the producer.

Many stations are only interested in series. Series programming provides the continuity to build an audience from week to week. Buyers repeatedly tell us it is harder to buy and schedule a single hour than a fifty two-part series. Independent producers should consider the possibilities for limited series when developing their projects. As sellers, there is a limit to what we can do. It is difficult, if not next to impossible to create a slot for a program if none exists. If a client such as Discovery says during a meeting, "We don't buy any fiction," we do not push a drama on them—even if it is about whales!

The best approach is to find buyers who have been involved with projects such as yours. Find out who they are by asking your fellow filmmaker friends what stations have bought their films. Talk to distributors. Try to attend foreign film festivals and markets so that you can network. Read trade papers such as *Variety, The Hollywood Reporter*, and foreign trades such as *TV World* and *Television Business International (TBI)*. These sources will give you the latest profiles of new stations, recent deals, trends in the market, as well as semi-annual price guides detailing price per hour by genre in the various territories.

PREPARING YOUR PROJECT

You have done your homework. Now be honest with yourself and ask, "Can my project really be sold?" Television and video buyers are typically most interested in subjects with general audience appeal such as: history (war and political intrigue are always good bets), nature, science, human interest/adventure, light entertainment (such as magic, circus, music), children's/youth programming, and action-based drama. Special interest programming such as how-to/instructional series, cultural documentaries, short drama, experimental narrative, and performing arts are more difficult to place, but each of these genres can find a niche in certain markets. But be aware, the slots for independent films with limited audience appeal are very specific and you cannot count on selling your film broadly in all the territories.

That said, films by American independent producers are very much coveted and appreciated by international audiences because they are often some of the most imaginative, unique, and wellcrafted productions in the marketplace. Films such as *Silverlake Life*, *Dream Deceivers*, *Hoop Dreams*, and *I Like it Like That* have enjoyed impressive international exposure. Most distributors that specialize in distributing the work of independent producers are usually up-to-date on the stations and slots that are buying the work of independent producers.

Make sure you ask yourself what audience you are targeting—the first question a buyer will think of when trying to find a time slot for your film. Is your film made for teenagers? If so, you might want to be wary of foul language that might be too rough for broadcast standards. Will you have a narrator? This is the most universal style in documentary because it is easy and relatively cost-efficient to dub. Filmmakers must also consider differences in cultural and political perception of the film's subject. Gratuitous violence is frowned upon in many parts of the world. Often themes about a social issue in America have no relevance to an international audience. Try to imagine a Dutch woman or a Japanese man watching your film. Would they understand and care about its point of view?

As you go into production, make sure you continue to think about your film's foreign distribution. In this age of the clicker it is really important to think for television. Come up with an arresting opening sequence so no one will zap you after the first fifteen seconds. Television is a visual medium. Buyers often evaluate programs based on the opening minutes, much as their viewer would do at home. Nothing is worse than two minutes of credits over black with monotonous music under. I have seen wonderful films passed over because they got started too slowly.

The next issue to consider is running time. Broadcasters schedule on an hourly basis, with the bulk of their schedule in one-hour blocks, several half-hour slots, and very few slots longer than one-hour for programs other than major feature films. Broadcasters look dumbfounded at a documentary with a sixty six-minute length and ask, "How can I schedule something like this?" There is always the possibility to edit, but most producers are reluctant to let others edit their film, and buyers rarely have time to put in the extra work when they could buy something just as good at fifty six minutes.

When you actually begin production on your project, it is important that you consider all potential foreign uses of your program. In addition to television and home video release, there are growing multimedia opportunities such as video-on-demand offered through the phone companies, CD-ROM, and interactive. These ancillary uses must be considered ahead of time when you are negotiating the use of music, stock footage, underlying rights to story, screenplay, talent, etc. If at all financially feasible for your budget, negotiate now while these technologies are just beginning to ramp up. While on set, make sure a photographer (or friend, if your budget is tight) takes both black-and-white prints and color slides as if they were actual scenes from the film. Stage them if you have to; photos are that important. A photo is your only graphic image to "sell" your film prior to someone watching it. After a sale is made, good quality black-and-white glossies and color slides become a contractual requirement for the sale.

POSTING FOR FOREIGN

When you begin post-production, make sure you think international. While in the on-line room or lab, be prepared to create a textless (sometimes called a generic) master tape (D2, BetaSP, or 1") without opening titles, credits, subtitles, or lower third IDs of on-camera subjects or locations. Audio configurations on an international master vary depending on the number of audio channels available on your master and the program's genre and content. At a minimum, fiction should have a complete English mono mix (to be used as a guide for translation) and a separate mixed music and effects track, therefore allowing the flexibility to sub-title or dub. Documentary should have a complete English mono mix on one track with separate music effects, and dialogue with no narration on the second track. This will allow broadcasters to re-narrate and sub-title or overdub on-camera speakers. Most importantly, plan the creation of the international master with your editor and your lab in order to arrive at the most cost-effective and best approach for your particular film.

Also at this time, the producer should prepare a post-production transcription of the final master (not the shooting script). The "transcript/script/dialogue list" should contain the narration, if any, and all dialogue. This should ideally be matched to time code or, at a minimum, to exact running time in the program.

In addition, subjects/characters should be clearly identified and any visual references to locations included. You must also prepare a cue sheet listing all of the music contained in the program, the exact running time of cut, the use (theme, background, etc.), the publisher, and the composer and the performing rights society that administers the rights payments.

WHAT FOREIGN DISTRIBUTION ENTAILS

Before making the decision whether to sign with a distributor/foreign sales agent or handle your own foreign sales, you should first find out what foreign distribution entails and what kind of commitment you will be making if you choose to go it on your own. By now you probably already realize, through pursuing grants, pre-sales, distributors, etc., that the world of television works at a very slow pace. Add language barriers, time differences, cultural protocol, and long distance fax negotiations to the mix and you can imagine that it seems as though it takes an eternity to get a sale completed!

The foreign distribution process revolves around an annual schedule of markets and festivals where films are launched, business is initiated, and deals are negotiated. For the television and video business, the major markets are NATPE in January, Monte Carlo in February, MIP-TV (Cannes) in April, Sunny Side of the Doc (Marseille) in June, MIPCOM (Cannes) in October, The London Screenings in November, and MIP Asia (Hong Kong) in December. Of these, MIP-TV and MIP-COM are the most important of the markets. For feature films, key festivals and markets include Sundance in January, the AFM (Los Angeles) in February, Berlin in February, Cannes in May, The Independent Feature Film Market in September, and MIFED in November. Due to a weakened foreign theatrical market and the boom in ancillary markets such as television, multimedia, and home video, there is now much buyer crossover at all of these markets. There are also emerging markets specifically geared to interactive disciplines, such as MILIA in Cannes in January.

Producers should plan on concluding their negotiations with a distributor at least three months before the markets so that the distributor has enough lead time to prepare the film for its market launch. If at all possible, producers should try to attend a few markets and festivals so they can survey the marketplace and make future contacts.

Apart from occasionally bidding on the latest blockbuster hit television series or the hot new feature getting all the buzz, buyers are usually very routine in their approach to the markets. They know what time slots or theatrical releases they have, they know which distributors have that kind of product, and they use the markets as a way to browse through catalogs, to learn about market trends, to prescreen potential programming, and to catch up with other colleagues in the industry. Most of the serious decision making is done after everyone returns from the market. Distributors will then send out screening cassettes, follow up by fax and phone, and, hopefully, begin negotiations and close deals. But be warned, the sales process sometimes takes a year or more before the deal is signed and you actually receive money. Television buyers who like your program but do not have a time slot right now, will often come back to it a year or two later if they remember it. As distributors see their clients at least two or three times a year at the markets, we often learn of changes in the buyers' needs and remind them of programs they should reconsider.

Once you receive an offer, you will be amazed at how low some of the license fees are. License fees are based on a number of factors, most often the number of viewers or subscribers in a particular territory or viewing area. In some instances (usually in the higher-paying territories), there is more opportunity for negotiation. In the smaller territories and with public service television stations, rates are often fixed and set by the government.

Depending on the needs of the station, a license period usually ranges from one to four years with a fixed number of transmissions or "runs" during the license period. License periods are generally exclusive, meaning you cannot sell it to another station in the territory during the same time period. Length of license period, exclusivity, and number of runs can be negotiated to some extent and are often tradeoffs for money. Buyers, in almost all circumstances, create their own versions of the film subtitled or dubbed in the appropriate language and will bear the costs associated with the versioning. Whether a buyer elects to subtitle or dub depends on custom. Territories such as Latin America, Germany, France, Spain, and Italy almost always dub. Scandinavian and Dutch buyers will always subtitle. Other clients in Asia and other parts of Europe are more flexible depending on the program and their budget.

Now that the deal is negotiated, the distributor issues a contract and invoice and delivers the broadcast materials: dub master(s), a press kit that includes a clear concise synopsis describing the main plot and theme, captioned B/W still photos and color slides, English transcript, cast and credit list. Sometimes, distributors can negotiate a down-payment on the contract prior to delivery of materials. However, it is still customary for a broadcaster to pay the bulk of the license fee after receipt and technical acceptance of materials. This is why it is imperative to make sure your materials are in good order *before* a sale is made. Lastly, the process of collection begins, sending gentle reminders and not so subtle past due notices to clients. While most clients are very reliable, there is often intense bureaucracy causing payment delays due to lost invoices, expired tax withholding forms, and many other tiny details that must be followed to the letter.

Not only are distributors experienced in navigating through these complex issues, they have regular and ongoing contacts in the marketplace that it would take the independent producer many years and many thousands of dollars in travel to obtain. Distribution is a full-time job. Producers often start making a few sales themselves, only to find out how labor intensive and expensive the distribution business really is. At Tapestry, we have executives in all key areas of distribution—sales, legal, and materials servicing—who have many years of experience in handling the complexities of international licensing.

GOING WITH A DISTRIBUTOR

I hope that this brief outline of the distribution process has illuminated the major benefit of signing with a distributor—namely, you will have time to move on to producing your next project! When looking for a distributor, make sure you consider the appropriateness and the "fit" of your film with the distributor's catalog. Ask the distributor how he or she plans to market your film. Ask them at which markets they exhibit and how often they travel. You also need to know the typical terms of a foreign sales agency agreement/distribution contract. As a rule, distributors do not usually give advances against representation rights for single films and documentaries due to the considerable investment they make in time and effort to introduce a project into the marketplace. Instead, distributors offer a deal whereby they take a certain percentage (anywhere from twenty five to fifty percent) of gross sales derived from the sale of the film. The distributor usually advances the cost of sales expenses such as preview cassettes, mailings, printed flyers, advertising, promotion, shipping, and lab or post-production work necessary to fulfill a sale; however, these expenses are then deducted from the producer's proceeds from the sale(s) of the film. You should be very specific about the scope of deductible expenses when negotiating with your distributor. Occasionally there are performance guarantees along the way, but even these are rare for a single program.

Other key terms of representation are length of representation; approvals, if any; editing rights; and accounting/reporting. Given the long timeline for concluding international sales, any contract less than two years is not really beneficial for either party. The average contract is three to seven years. Most distributors require that the representation period be exclusive. Most distributors, including Tapestry, will not enter into non-exclusive distribution agreements because they cannot risk losing time, money, and reputation in the marketplace by offering a program that might later become encumbered with rights problems. Exclusive representation is also best for the producer because he or she can be more secure in knowing they will get the distributor's full concentration and that there will be no confusion in the marketplace. It is a small world at the markets and when more than one distributor is offering the same project, the buyers might well raise a red flag and think that it is not even worth pursuing the project because it might have rights problems later.

Approvals over key deal points is something to be negotiated with your distributor, but realize one important fact. Sometimes approvals tie the distributor's hands when negotiating for the sale of your film. A distributor will also have a more realistic and informed position on a potential offer based on his or her experience negotiating other similar deals.

A producer recently asked me, "How come you sold my film to Israel for only $500? Is it even worth it?" Remember now, Tapestry is only making 30%—150 bucks on the deal! For that, we sent out a screener, followed up to get a decision (twice!), drew up a contract, sent out materials, replaced the master damaged in transit, collected the $500 (less Israeli government withholding taxes), prepared a royalty report, cut a check, and paid thirty two cents to mail it to the producer. A good business decision? Maybe, maybe not... However consider the whole scenario. We offered the film to the other stations who could have paid more; they passed. Is it not in the producer's best interest to have her film shown in Israel? As a distributor we build our relationship with this new cable station hoping that they will continue to grow, thus being able to pay more to other producers in the future. Both the producer and Tapestry made a little money and the client was happy to get the show. A good distributor looks at the entire picture and tries to create a win-win conclusion in the best interests of everyone. Once I explained this to the producer, she understood why we would go through with the deal.

Hopefully, there is a basic trust between you and your distributor. Even more important than having deal approval is checking your potential distributor's references before you sign, and doing your research on the pricing of films similar to yours. Do not be afraid to ask questions anywhere along the way.

Edit rights and approvals over foreign versions are always sticky issues for independent producers because their films are their babies and rightfully so. Producers want to have their programs seen in the best possible way. Buyers, on the other hand, feel they know their market, can better decide what might have to be cut for time or censorship, and can create the best translation for their audience. Producer approval over these elements is never granted. Tapestry tries to protect the producer's interests by putting a clause in our license agreement with the buyer stating that their edited version and translation "will not substantially alter the tone, content or form of the original film."

Accounting reports and accompanying payments are generally sent to producers on a semi-annual or quarterly basis. This report itemizes the gross sales made during the period, distribution fees, withholding taxes, and deductible sales expenses. In addition, some distributors periodically send out activity summaries listing clients who are looking at cassettes or who have rejected the film.

CONCLUSION

Will you make enough money from foreign sales of your film to risk getting yourself in debt? Don't count on it. When raising your production budget, foreign sales should be considered "gravy," not the means by which to pay back large loans or lab bills. If you cannot pay for your production through grants and/or a sale to a U.S. broadcaster, you should seriously consider whether you still want to go ahead with the project. Another option is to pursue a pre-sale or co-production with a foreign broadcaster, but realize that co-production money is very hard to get. First, your project must be a perfect match with the buyer's needs. The buyer must justify why he or she is willing to pay a premium for a project that is a huge risk. The buyer is going to want to know that a responsible, experienced production team is at the helm and that a U.S. broadcaster is in place. The project's content must also have some sort of connection with the broadcaster and be able to tap into the interests of that particular country's audience. Following are just some of the major broadcasters that have a long track record of co-producing with independent producers: BBC and Channel 4 in the UK, La Sept/Arte in France, ZDF, WDR, and NDR in Germany, ABC Australia, and NHK Japan.

Knowing the possible obstacles in producing for the international market up front will allow you to go into production without compromising your ultimate vision. Part of the beauty of independent filmmaking in America is that producers have the passion and drive to go to the ends of the earth to make their project a reality. Going into the international marketplace with your eyes open will be the best thing you can do to make your film's international distribution a success story.

CHAPTER 14

FESTIVALS AND MARKETS

Peter Moore

ilmmakers make an amazing variety of films for an amazing variety of reasons. Whatever the genre or motivation, sooner or later everything boils down to a room full of strangers sitting in the dark and watching images projected on a screen. It does not matter if it is a computer-animated short, dramatic feature, political documentary, experimental video, class project, or instructional tape—films are made to be seen. And for an independent film, the first screening is almost always going to be at a film festival or market.

The choice of which festival or market premieres your film will determine whether this occasion turns out to be the first step in an incredible tale of critical acclaim, commercial success, and the approbation of your peers that culminates in a televised awards ceremony (cue the elaborate revenge fantasies about telling off all the people who didn't believe in you); or whether it is merely going to mark the only time your film will be seen outside of your living room. It's crucial to try to decide what you want for the film, even if wanting and getting are two very different things.

Though many factors are at work here, the most important thing is still the film itself. A really great film can, and usually will, survive the most badly bungled handling. Conversely, even the most carefully considered and managed festival strategy cannot give a really bad film more than a dead-cat bounce (this tastelessly vivid expression is borrowed from the world of high finance, where it is used to describe a momentary rebound of a doomed enterprise). Then there's the undeniable role that luck plays. How else can we explain why so many mediocre films are selected to be shown at prominent festivals and go on to become the objects of frenzied bidding wars between distributors, while other better and more worthy films are inexplicably ignored.

What I hope to do in this chapter is to provide some basic information about festivals and markets and try to answer some of the key questions you have to consider in putting together a strategy to get the most out of festivals and markets. For more comprehensive information about individual festivals, the essential reference work is the AIVF/FIVF *Guide to International Film and Video Festivals*.

WHAT ARE FESTIVALS AND MARKETS?

For filmmakers, festivals and markets are an opportunity to share work with an audience. For the general public a festival is an opportunity to see new and uncommon films and videos. For distributors, programmers, and other industry professionals, festivals, and most especially markets, are a chance to scope out the latest work. For filmmakers, the choice of which festivals and markets to attend will be affected by which audience you are more interested in reaching—whether you are looking for exposure or distribution. Along this continuum there are some festivals that can give you both.

Many festivals are competitive, or (as in the case of the Chicago and San Francisco film festivals) have competitive sections in which prizes and/or cash are awarded. These awards can be useful in promoting your film (or as a credential to promote your next film). There are different levels of prestige that go along with these awards. Receiving the Golden Bear from the Berlin Film Festival ranks higher up the scale than getting a Golden Gate award from the San Francisco Film Festival. Some non-competitive festivals will still have audience awards that are based on ballots filled out by filmgoers. In others the reward is simply in being selected.

Markets are always competitive. Winning at a market is not a matter of trophies, but rather a subjective judgment that is measured by what deals, contacts, and invitations you come away with.

There is a certain amount of overlap between festivals and markets, and some festivals hold their own markets. But there are some fundamental differences. Markets are for selling films, and festivals are for showing films. Markets are restricted to industry professionals (I use the word "professional" here in the loosest possible meaning of the term—sometimes all it means is that you have paid for your credentials); and festivals are open to the public (though I will leave aside the issue of exactly how open to the public a festival is when it caters its advertising to industry insiders, charges hundreds of dollars for a ticket, and is held in such a remote location that transportation and accommodation costs alone can amount to several thousand dollars).

Market screenings are not covered by the press, while your first festival screening will usually be reviewed, at least by *Variety*. In reality the boundaries can get a little fuzzy. Market screenings can sometimes become public events that are covered in the press and festival screenings are often used to sell films to distributors. For independent filmmakers, however, the most important distinction is how you get in. Markets are not curated. If your film meets the general criteria of the market, and your check is good and you have beat the deadline, you are in. On the other hand, acceptance into a festival usually means that someone has selected your film from among a number of entries.

WHICH ONES ARE MOST IMPORTANT?

Every year there are literally hundreds of film and video festivals and markets held in more that fifty countries around the world. Not all festivals and markets are created equal. The order of importance can vary depending on what kind of film you have made; what you want (I know I keep harping on this, but it is important); what time of year your film is completed (or at least at a stage where you can throw a scratch mix on a fine-cut and show it to a festival director); and, frankly, how well-known you are as a filmmaker.

That said, there is a certain ranking that can be applied to festivals. For American independent features, the top rank of festivals and markets are, in chronological order, Sundance, Berlin, Cannes, Toronto, Independent Feature Film Market, and New York.

The Sundance Film Festival takes place in Park City, Utah in mid-January and has a Fall deadline. Over the last six or seven years Sundance has become the most important festival for American independent filmmakers. Despite grumbling about how the festival is being taken over by industry suits and their cellular phones, this highly selective and very competitive festival gives attending filmmakers international exposure. The Sundance imprimatur definitely imparts a certain cachet. Sundance is notoriously difficult to get into (only eighteen dramatic features and sixteen documentaries were selected in '95). This difficulty spawned a rival festival, Slamdance, a Salon de Refusés-esque event in Salt Lake City that presented films that had been rejected by Sundance. Beginning in 1996, Sundance will address this concern by opening up a non-competitive sidebar for first features.

The Berlin International Film Festival presents more than 400 films and videos in a number of sections to nearly 7,500 industry and press representatives during February. The most important sections are the International Competition, the Forum, the Panorama, and the European Film Market. For American independents, and particularly for documentaries and gay films, Berlin has become known as the European festival of choice. The support offered to filmmakers by the American Independents and Features Abroad (AIFA) organization is one of the for most reasons for this.

Held in mid-May on the Riviera, the Cannes International Film Festival is the world's largest and most famous. Being one of the few American independents selected for either the Official Competition, Un Certain Regard, Director's Fortnight, or International Critics Week is a prestigious honor that instantly attracts major meeting attention. Entering the Market at Cannes on your own, however, is something that I would recommend only to the toughest and most experienced makers. Cannes is also not the place for documentaries.

The Toronto International Film Festival (formerly Festival of Festivals) shows hundreds of films to large, enthusiastic, and knowledgeable audiences. Despite the apocryphal statement by an American distributor that he "... devalues the currency twenty percent and the audience reaction thirty percent," Toronto is one of the most important venues for American independents. It runs in mid-September.

In between Toronto and the New York Film Festival in early October more than 2,500 filmmakers, distributors, buyers, programmers, agents, reps, critics, and assorted confederates of the American independent film world convene in New York to attend the Independent Feature Film Market. Now in its seventeenth year, and sponsored by the Independent Feature Project, this is the largest and most important film market specifically dedicated to American independent film. The IFFM presents more than four hundred features, documentaries, works-in-progress, shorts, and scripts. At its best, it offers exposure and opportunity to unknown film-makers while fostering the sense of a common vision and purpose that transcends competing economic agendas, and unites the American independent film community. At its worst, IFFM is a massive and impersonal endurance test with a strict hierarchy of badges and privileges, that effectively, if not intentionally, pits film-makers against each other in desperate competition for the momentary attention of beleaguered distributors and programmers and that elusive industry buzz that can elevate a film out of obscurity. For unknown filmmakers, the IFFM is still the place to go, especially for shorts and works-in-progress. For more established makers who are not going to have trouble getting festivals to look at their work, there is a definite downside in being overshadowed by the quirky-film-out-of-nowhere (i.e., *Clerks*). The result is that while the market has more and more first features, it has fewer and fewer second or third features.

The New York Film Festival is the most prestigious American festival. Put on by the Film Society of Lincoln Center (which also cosponsors the New Directors/New Films Festival in March), the festival shows relatively few films, and usually only a few of these are American indies. Fewer still are independent films made outside of New York—but it does happen. A New York Film Festival screening gives a film international attention and visibility (not the least part of which is a *New York Times* review).

Other important festivals include Rotterdam (which has one of the very best reputations among filmmakers for friendliness), Montreal (both the World Film Festival and the Festival of New Cinema and Video), New Directors/New Films in New York, Locarno, London, San Francisco (both the International Film Fest and, if the film is gay-themed, the S.F. International Lesbian & Gay Fest), Telluride, Munich, Mannheim, Seattle, Deauville, and Mill Valley. For shorts, add Oberhausen, and Clermont-Ferrand. For documentaries, add the National Educational Media Network (formerly the National Educational Film & Video Festival) that takes place in May in Oakland, California.

Internationally, Venice is the oldest and still considered one of the top festivals, but has never been well known as a haven for American indies. A key reason for this is their requirement that films not have played outside of their country of origin. As this condition is shared by Berlin and Cannes, filmmakers are faced with having to choose only one of these big festivals. This problem also comes up when filmmakers are caught between Berlin and Cannes and other festivals with competing deadlines. Every year a number of filmmakers have the unenviable decision of whether or not to accept an invite from Rotterdam while hoping that their invitation to Berlin is on its way. Venice also happens in early September, which is right around the time of Telluride (Labor Day Weekend) and right before Toronto and the Independent Feature Film Market.

I WANT MY FEATURE TO BE A BIG SUCCESS. HOW DO I START?

First you have to realize that you need more than one strategy. You might as well dream big dreams and start at the top. You apply to Telluride, Toronto, New York, and Sundance. Telluride turns you down but you get into the other three. You get an incredible reception, distributors start a bidding war for your film, and you open wide across the country. It could happen. It did for Terry Zwigoff and Lynn O'Donnell with their film *Crumb*. But the odds are about a hundred-to-one against this happening to you.

So now you have to figure out Plan B. If it is your first feature, you might start at the IFFM. Your 9:00 a.m. Sunday screening is not very well attended but one of the people there is independent distribution dynamo Bob Hawk who sings your praises to John Pierson (the man who put "reputable" into the term producer's rep) who takes your film on and gets you a deal with Miramax at Sundance. It could happen. It did for Kevin Smith and Scott Mosier with *Clerks*.

But, if you are not so fortunate, you have to be ready with Plan C. You could miss out on Sundance and premiere your film in Berlin to enthusiastic audiences and then play the London International Lesbian and Gay Festival, the Seattle

International Film Festival, the New York Lesbian & Gay Experimental Festival, the Chicago Film Festival, and the Denver Film Festival. Working with the festival staffs, you get a lot of interviews and reviews to hold for the commercial run in these cities a month or two later. This worked for Lawrence Helman and Marc Huestis on their self-distributed *Sex Is...*

Or you go on to Plan D, and then Plan E and F, and so on, until you finally step back, accept the realization that you cannot get what you want, and figure out what it is that you can get.

What you can get may be no more than some constructive critiques from programmers, distributors, and screening committee members. (Festivals with competitive sections will sometimes pass on the comments of the juries.) But, you should not underestimate the importance of making connections. People do not hold it against you that they did not like your film. Plus they will be able to put a face with the name when considering your next project.

While it is true that with enough perseverance (and money for entry fees) almost any film can eventually garner a festival screening, you will have to decide for yourself how much rejection you are willing to endure in order to get that screening.

The sad truth is that less than five percent of completed features will find theatrical distribution and less than twenty five percent will even get festival exposure. Ideally you have started thinking about strategies before you finish the film (and I am talking about more than rehearsing that acceptance speech again) but odds are that you haven't. If every filmmaker rationally considered the odds of success before they started shooting, no films would ever get made.

SHOULD I RUSH TO MEET A FESTIVAL DEADLINE?

It may be true that no work of art is ever completed, merely abandoned. Ultimately, however, if your film will be better if you do not rush, then don't. You are not going to have more than one premiere. If the *Variety* reviewer cannot make out the dialogue because you went with a scratch mix and the color is bad cause you are showing the first answer print, that is what everyone is going to see in the review and reviewers are not likely to do re-reviews. Because festivals like to have world premieres, most festival staffs are willing to look at films that are close to done. But no festival deadline is worth the risk of showing your film before it is ready.

HOW MANY FESTIVALS SHOULD I ENTER, AND SHOULD I GO?

You cannot enter them all. Aside from logistical problems, you would end up spending more on entry fees than you did on the film. Even if you submitted your film to a generous fraction of the possible venues, getting in is another thing altogether. The qualifications for getting into one festival might be as simple as returning an application, while another festival's selection process may rival the arcane drama of being tapped to join a secret society. In addition you have to consider the issues of overexposure and compensation. Exposure is good and is often the only compensation that a festival will initially offer. Though it is true that very few festivals pay film rental—transportation and accommodations are negotiable and achievable considerations. This is particularly true when you're at smaller fests. It is very gratifying to have the screening of your film before a sold-out house. But you want to be very stingy about added screenings. Bear in mind that every ticket that the festival sells represents a person who will not be buying a ticket later when your film plays at a local theater and you are getting thirty five percent.

The answer to whether you attend a festival will most often hinge on the simple question of who is paying for it. This is never an issue with markets because they never pay your way. If you do not attend the market then someone else who represents you must go. There is no point in sending a film to market if no one is there to sell it.

WHAT SHOULD I EXPECT OUT OF A FESTIVAL?

I spoke with two filmmakers who presented their works at the Independent Feature Film Market. The first made a three-minute short film that, as a direct result of a well-attended and well-received market screening, was invited to a number of festivals including Sundance. The other filmmaker showed a completed feature that was received with a response most charitably described as profound indifference. That filmmaker had to come to terms with the brutal and expensive reality that very few independent features get even minimal festival exposure, much less theatrical distribution, and that his film was not going to be one of those.

Ironically, the first filmmaker talked about what a painfully unpleasant experience the market had been, even though by any reasonable standard he had achieved more than he could have hoped for. The other maker went on about what a great time he'd had at the market and how valuable an experience it had been to meet other filmmakers and see their work, and make some personal connections with distributors and festival programmers. As clearly divergent as these outcomes might seem, both makers got something out of the market, and at least one of them had a good time!

GOD IS IN THE DETAILS:
FIVE PRACTICAL RULES FOR SURVIVING A FESTIVAL

1. *Wear Comfortable Shoes.* You are going to be on your feet all day long—this is no time to wear spike heels or break in a new pair of shoes.

2. *Do Not Dress in Costume.* I do not care how great an idea it seems to dress up, nobody talks deal points with Elvis—the man is legally dead.

3. *Carry Breath Mints.* You are going to be chugging espressos, chain smoking, and yapping all day; do the world a favor and freshen your breath. (Rule 3a: Don't Try to Quit Smoking at a Film Festival).

4. *Be Nice to the Help.* Film festivals are stressful, chaotic, and frantic enterprises. Many of the staff are likely to be volunteers, and as with any enterprise that depends on the kindness of strangers, the competence level is going to vary. For the most part they are trying their best. If something does go horribly wrong at your screening, you are going to get a much better response from the staff if you have not been abusing them for a week.

5. *Don't Panic When That Special Distributor or Festival Director Walks Out After 15 Minutes.* Festivals and, most especially, markets commonly show a number of films simultaneously. Distributors and programmers are there to check out as many films as they can. So, bolting the theater can often just mean that they liked your film well enough to want to see more later and meanwhile they have to catch a bit of that experimental feature that everyone is talking about. Despite protestations that it is arbitrary and unfair to judge a film on the basis of such a brief sample—"Sure, it's kinda stiff in the beginning, but it gets better as it goes on"—first impressions do count. If it takes a half-hour to get to the good part, you will have lost your audience.

6. *Filmmakers: Even Though Your Film Can Really Only Be Properly Appreciated on the Big Screen, Accept That Some People Will Want to See It On Tape.* This does not mean that you bring a bag of dubs to hand out. If distributors and programmers wanted to lug a bag of videotapes around with them all day, they would wear brown uniforms and drive big shiny trucks. Instead you should get their addresses and FedEx the tape after the festival.

7. *No Matter How Vitally Important It Is for You To Be There All The Time—Take a Break.* Do not spend your whole time at the festival scurrying to screenings and networking in cafes. There's a world outside of movies. Take at least an aftenoon off and have an adventure. A streetcar ride to some weird neighborhood will give you something interesting to talk about—hell, there might even be a script in it.

8. *Keep in Touch.* After you decompress a bit, dive back in and drop a line to the programmers and distributors who attended your screening. Thank them for looking at your work and ask them if they need a tape or a pressbook. Go through the stack of business cards you collected and add the names to your address book. Rehearse that acceptance speech again, and start working on your next film.

CHAPTER 15

DISTRIBUTION CONTRACTS

Robert I. Freedman

distribution contract is a memorialization of the agreement between the owner of distribution rights in a film or video (usually a production company or individual producer) and a company engaged in the business of marketing such works to users and purchasers (a distributor). What makes these agreements somewhat unique is that the product for sale is not a physical property, but rather intangible rights.

For simplicity, I will refer to film and video interchangeably as "audiovisual work." In its intangible form, an audiovisual work should be viewed as a collection of rights that may be sold or licensed in its entirety or piece by piece.

Since audiovisual works have been distributed for three-quarters of a century, and substantial precedent for these deals has been developed, a producer would be well advised to have a knowledgeable entertainment lawyer assist in the negotiation and contract review process.

The role of the entertainment lawyer is to represent a client in negotiating the terms of the distribution agreement; reviewing the distributor's contract; and counseling the producer on the entire contract process. Experienced lawyers are familiar with precedents in these matters and rely on favorable precedents to achieve a reasonable contract. However, the lawyer cannot assure that all of the producer's points will be won as the negotiation is an adversary process in which compromise generally prevails.

The negotiation of terms is usually based on precedent and payments distributors have paid for rights in comparable audiovisual works. Producers may obtain the knowledge by asking the distributor, asking other filmmakers who may have deals with that distributor, or asking an experienced lawyer.

Usually the distributor furnishes the producer with a distribution contract containing the terms and conditions of the deal. Producers should be fully aware that these contracts are written on paper and not etched in stone. Since the terms of the distribution contract will have an important role in the financial returns of the audiovisual work, the producer should understand all terms of the agreement and negotiate those terms that are not to the producer's advantage. The key word is "negotiate," for it is unlikely that the producer will be able to get all of the terms changed to his or her advantage.

The most important terms of a distribution contract are the definition of rights being granted, and the consideration to be paid for the grant of rights.

The rights granted to the distributor should be specific as to territory, license period, and media. In most deals, the distributor will require exclusive rights. The territory may be worldwide; limited to the United States, its territories and possessions; or include several countries. The license period may be as short as one or two years, or as long as ten to fifteen years. The media are usually divided among theatrical, home video, broadcast and cablecast, non-theatrical, and interactive multimedia.

Since some of these media overlap, the contract should contain a definition of the scope of the media being granted. Distributors often seek rights in all media. The producer should be aware of the rapidly changing world of new technologies (computer-based, interactive, etc.) and should structure the agreement so new media are not granted to a distributor that is not actively engaged in those areas since the distributor is likely to either warehouse those rights or sublicense them to a company that the producer could otherwise deal with directly.

It is essential for the producer to have a "reservation of rights" provision in the distribution contract. This provides that all rights not specifically granted to the distributor are reserved by the producer. By way of example, if the producer grants television and home video rights, but reserves all other rights, the producer will have retained, among other rights, the educational audiovisual rights, which the producer may exploit directly or license to a third party.

The consideration paid by the distributor for the rights may be in the form of advances, guarantees, or royalties, or a combination of the foregoing. An "advance" is a payment made to the producer on signing a contract or, more commonly, upon the delivery of materials. The advance is a prepayment of the producer's royalties, which is recouped by the distributor out of the producer's royalties. Although this guarantees front money to the producer, it will correspondingly defer payment of royalties.

A "guarantee" is an assurance by the distributor that the producer will receive a specified payment at a specified time, and, if royalties fall short, the distributor must advance monies so that the royalties and advance equal the amount of the guarantee. The guarantee may be recoupable by the distributor from subsequent royalties.

Royalties may be payable from the distributor's gross receipts, from adjusted gross receipts (i.e., total gross receipts less limited deductions) or net profits (i.e., total gross receipts less all costs and expenses). In each case, the terms "gross" and "net" must be clearly defined since there is no single industry standard.

Producers must analyze the kind of distribution deal that will maximize their bottom line. Most television distribution deals are gross deals where the distributor's fee comes off the top; then distribution expenses are paid and the gross balance is paid to the producer. In net deals the distributor is usually a co-financier of the project and after distribution fees and expenses are paid to the distributor, an agreed-upon proportion of the balance is shared with the distributor (usually fifty-fifty).

Distribution fees for television distribution range from twenty to forty percent (before expenses). Non-theatrical and home video deals are usually gross deals with fifteen to twenty percent of gross to the producer. Multimedia interactive deals are usually gross deals as well, with royalties at a slightly lower level of ten to fifteen percent of gross. Theatrical distributors may retain thirty to eighty percent of the gross to cover distribution fees and costs of prints and advertising, or deduct the cost of prints and advertising off the top (in which case, it is possible that the producer will derive no revenue from theatrical distribution). To determine the best type of deal the producer must make certain assumptions about income and expenses and compute whether a gross or net deal is better.

Contracts must specify when payments are to be made. Most agreements provide for semi-annual payments, but some are quarterly and some are annual. Payments will be due thirty to ninety days after the close of the accounting period. At the time of payment, the producer is entitled to an accounting as to how the distributor arrived at the amount to be paid. The contract should assure the producer that the accounting will be in sufficient detail to permit a full understanding of how the payment was determined.

A producer should insist on a right to audit the books and records of the distributor. If there are questions about the completeness or correctness of an accounting, the producer should have the right to have a representative examine the distributor's books and records. The producer should realize that the audit will be conducted at the producer's expense. Some contracts provide that if the audit discloses errors of more than five to ten percent in the producer's favor, the distributor must pay the cost of the audit and interest on the unpaid balance.

The distribution contract will contain a list of materials the producer is required to provide. These consist of technical materials (film and/or videotape), publicity materials, and a music cue sheet. Some contracts may also require delivery of a Certificate of Errors and Omissions insurance, a script, and copies of releases and production contracts. The producer must also assess the costs of providing the delivery materials. Distributors will want access to the producer's original materials, but the producer should insist that the original materials remain at the producer's laboratory.

Producers will want a clause preventing any alteration of the audiovisual work without the producer's consent. The distributor may want the right to edit for purposes of time and censorship, and the right to include its distribution credit at the head and tail. The producer might be able to negotiate for certain approval or consultation rights regarding the editing of the work and the advertising and promotion of the audiovisual work, including the jacket design for any home video sales. However, it is unlikely that the producer will obtain such rights with respect to foreign distribution.

The distributor will insist that the producer give certain "warranties and representations." These include that the rights granted to the distributor are free from encumbrances and that the exercise of the distributor's rights will not violate the rights of others. This means that the producer must assure that all rights have been obtained including releases and permissions from persons performing on or appearing in the audiovisual work; all music, film footage, artworks, and photographs have been cleared; and all underlying literary and dramatic rights have been obtained. The warranty will also include a statement that the audiovisual work does not contain defamatory material.

The producer indemnification usually states that in the event a claim or legal action is brought against the distributor because the producer has failed to obtain all necessary rights or because the distribution of the audiovisual work is otherwise violating a third party's rights, the producer shall make the distributor whole by paying the judgment or settlement and the distributor's legal fees and expenses. Since many independent producers cannot realistically be expected to cover such costs, the distributor may require the producer to obtain Errors and Omissions insurance. This insurance protects the producer and distributor against claims of copyright infringement, trademark infringement, violation of rights of privacy and publicity and defamation. However, the cost of obtaining and maintaining such insurance is substantial (anywhere from $1,000 to $5,000 per year), and the producer should limit the obligation to pay for this insurance to no more than three years.

The producer should insist on a provision in the contract that would allow the producer to terminate the agreement if the distributor defaults in its obligation. The distributor's obligation is usually limited to paying monetary damages to the producer. Agreements should also provide for a "notice and cure" period whereby if one party is in default the other party must send written notice of the default and the defaulting party has a period of time—usually ten to thirty days—to cure the default.

Agreements also provide for resolution of disputes. Since litigation is expensive, and the distributor may be able to afford the expense better than the independent producer, the producer should insist on an arbitration provision requiring the parties to arbitrate disputes. Since binding arbitration usually brings a faster resolution of disputes than litigation, this might be in the interest of both parties. It should be understood, however, that arbitration is not necessarily very fast or very inexpensive either. However, the producer will want an exception to this provision that would allow the producer to go straight to court in the event the distributor fails to pay or account. The distributor will always ask that disputes be resolved in the distributor's jurisdiction, but the producer may negotiate for the jurisdiction of the party bringing the lawsuit to prevail.

The producer should also seek to include a bankruptcy clause in the contract. This provides that in the event the distributor becomes insolvent or bankrupt, the rights to distribute the audiovisual work revert to the producer. This is important because if the distributor becomes insolvent or bankrupt, it will not be able to maintain its business and the audiovisual work may not be promoted or distributed.

One provision that rarely finds its way into distribution contracts is an affirmative obligation of the distributor to use its best efforts to maximize the distribution of the audiovisual work. A distributor interested in such work will tell the producer all of the things it will do to promote and market the work. However, when it comes time to sign the contract, those wonderful points might not be found within the four corners of the actual document. The producer may negotiate to have a general provision that the distributor will use its best efforts; or, even better, attach as an exhibit to the contract the distributor's marketing plan and make that exhibit an obligation of the distributor. If the distributor fails to conduct the promotion and marketing plan, it becomes a breach of the agreement and can be possible grounds for the producer to get rights back from the distributor.

Some distributors use very brief deal memos that summarize the important substantive terms of the distribution deal. These are fine to highlight the major points of the deal, but are inadequate in fully protecting the rights of either party in the event of a dispute during the term of the contract. The producer should insist on a complete contract spelling out all of the terms of the distribution deal (substantive and procedural), and that the contract should be in plain English with all words clearly understandable or defined.

The final consideration is that all of the issues discussed in this chapter should take place in the context of a deal with a good distributor. A good distributor is one who is enthusiastic about the audiovisual work, has suggested a credible marketing plan, can afford the expense of adequate promotion, and, most importantly, has a good track record with other producers. We have appended a sample distribution contract at the end of this book. It should be emphasized that all deals and contracts are somewhat unique; and the attached form is intended as a model, but all of its terms and conditions might not be applicable to any specific agreement.

CHAPTER 16

THE FUTURE
OF DISTRIBUTION

Lawrence Sapadin

I n 1957, the French film historian Georges Sadoul published a small volume called *The Marvels of Cinema* that ended with a chapter called "The Cinema of the Future." For anyone asked to write publicly about the future, it is humbling to refer back to such a startlingly accurate vision.

Sadoul recognized the profound significance of the shift from film to video, and foresaw the miniaturization of video equipment that would—almost forty years later—give individuals the means to create their own motion pictures, and open up new distribution opportunities.

"The day will come when the studio camera... will be reduced to a lens and a tube... that will be able to be held in the palm of one's hand, like the microphone of a radio reporter."

Citizen filmmakers would soon be carrying around these "micro-cameras" almost invisibly through the streets and in crowds, revolutionizing documentary practice, news gathering, and the art of direction.

With respect to distribution, Sadoul described with remarkable clarity what we now know as home video.

"We will see a new industry arise involving the sale of spools of magnetic film, costing less than a book and containing two hours of cinema. The art of film and its masterpieces will no longer be the sole province of museums, film societies and commercial theaters. Everyone will be able to watch film classics and new releases on a television set equipped to translate these magnetic tapes into image, color and sound."

Finally, Sadoul foresaw the possibility that a television set could bring more than movies into the home. He imagined the distribution of an electronic newspaper to the home where a device would permit the television to record a "filmed newspaper" each morning on tape that could be played back at any time of day or night, as often as one pleased.

It is only a small step from Sadoul's vision to the video-on-demand future that is being written about and tested today around the country.

If the principal technological shift from Sadoul's time to ours has been from the physical and chemical properties of film to the electronic technology of video, then the new era is one in which moving images, and their transmission, are shifting from electronic technology to digital form, opening again new realms of possibility for the creation and distribution of moving images.

HOME IS WHERE THE TELEVISION IS

The focus of new media development is the home. With Americans already spending a large portion of their waking, non-working hours sitting in front of the television set, big business is betting billions of dollars that we want to have more and different programming and greater control over how and when we watch it. The three main ways this new (and old, you can be sure) programming is expected to come into our homes is through video-on-demand delivery to our televisions, via online services to our computers, and by way of CD-ROMs and other packaged software.

1. *Video-on-Demand (or Wake Me When We Get There)*. In recent years, just about every telephone company (AT&T and the regional Bell companies) and all the major cable companies have been experimenting with the delivery of television and other kinds of information and entertainment programming direct to the home at an individual's request. Think of it as having the best video store in your area— right in your living room. You get a printed or on-screen catalog of hundreds or thousands of movies, television shows, and other informational programs (stock quotes, airline schedules, etc.); you punch up some numbers on a set-top box; and the program appears on your screen. There are about twenty tests going on in cities around the country to try out the technology or the public's appetite for à la carte program choices, or both.

Video-on-demand is an extraordinarily appealing idea. It's also an incredibly complex and technologically costly one. In late 1993, cable television giant Tele-Communications, Inc. (TCI), and the Bell Atlantic Corporation announced a proposed $33 billion merger motivated in large measure by this vision of on-demand video delivery. The cable industry is already in the business of delivering moving pictures to the home, but lacks the advanced switching technology that would enable a company to route a specific program to a specific household. The telephone industry, on the other hand, has the switching technology, but its wiring is unable, at least for now, to accommodate the heavy demands of video transmission. A Bell Atlantic/TCI merger would have combined the unique technological strengths of each industry and reached forty percent of U.S. households—enough to establish de facto technical standards for the new industry.

A few months later, however, the deal collapsed. Today, the most ambitious VOD trials have either changed their focus or been put on hold. A major Time Warner test in Florida has shifted emphasis from providing a full service video network to delivering—guess what—*telephone* service, in competition with the local Bell operating system. A Bell Atlantic test in the mid-Atlantic states, which Bell Atlantic pursued on its own, has (after well over a year of delays) shelved its initial technological approach and gone back to the drawing board.

Although video-on-demand may be suffering from an excess of hype (prompted by a combination of marketing euphoria and wishful thinking), the reality is that, despite the delays and unexpected costs, these systems *are* slowly being constructed in prototype, tested, and planned for the future.

How do they work? What do they hold in store for independent producers and distributors? Programming, rather than being transmitted according to a schedule by a central program service (like HBO), cable company (like Time Warner), or broadcaster (like NBC), will be converted to computer code (digitized, or digitalized, according to the new jargon) and stored on massive computer hard drives by your local video-on-demand company. When you want to see a program, or retrieve some other information stored on your local VOD system, you will push some buttons and the program will appear on your television set, much as you would retrieve a document from the hard drive of your personal computer. You will be charged for actual use, the way you are charged for gas, electricity, and current pay-per-view television programming.

Today, to reach their audience, independent producers must first convince a distributor to acquire their film or video. Then the distributor has to manufacture cassettes and send review copies to potential educational buyers, and finished goods to educators, retailers, and home purchasers. In a VOD environment, the producer or distributor would never need to have copies of the film manufactured. A master would be digitized and placed on a hard drive (or server) that educational or home users could access directly, on demand.

In the short term, there will be significant barriers for independent producers and distributors, principally the high cost of digitization (more than $50 a minute), and the limited server capacity of first-generation VOD systems. In the trials, space on the VOD systems is going as a priority to first-run Hollywood block-busters. Even as capacity expands, VOD systems—being commercial businesses—will naturally favor the more profitable titles. However, as in the home video market, there will eventually be a segment of "specialized product," including the work of independent filmmakers.

National Video Resources, an initiative of The Rockefeller Foundation, retained me to work with several video-on-demand trials to introduce one or more packages of independently produced programs on to their systems. Some of the programmers for these trials were interested in offering a diverse array of programming to their subscribers—including educational, documentary and children's programming. However, the programs have to sell. So there is a strong interest in brand recognition (i.e., children's television based on well-known books) and subject matter with a built-in audience (i.e., the Civil War).

An additional barrier will be the promotional and marketing effort required to let the public know the film is sitting there. Here, the grassroots promotion that is a hallmark of independent distribution will be essential. For example, a producer or distributor with a program or series on the environment might send a flyer (or e-mail) to national and local environmental organizations alerting them to the presence of the film on one or more VOD servers, instead of advertising, for example, a one-time public television broadcast. In a sense, television programs—including independent works—will end up being posted like a piece of e-mail, able to be retrieved by anyone on the VOD system.

2. *Taking it Online.* The main competition with VOD for becoming the information superhighway into our homes, schools, libraries, and businesses are the new computer online services that provide access to databases of news and information and to the vast resources of the Internet. The Internet developed in recent years primarily as a way for academics and scientists throughout the world to communicate and work together, sending data to each other over the phone lines, and gaining access to remote libraries and information databases. More recently, a number of companies—like America Online, Compuserve, and Prodigy—have begun providing their own information and e-mail services over private networks, as well as developing software to help their subscribers navigate the Internet.

For media producers, the most significant development has been the creation of the World Wide Web, a network within the Internet, which permits the transmission of sound and moving pictures as well as text. In addition, the Web permits a single document or screen to contain hypertext links that enable the viewer to click on highlighted words or phrases and be transported to another screen, image, or database anywhere in the world. The new screen may also have hyperlinks, and so on, taking a viewer on a global trip through various related documents, images, resources, and databases.

Media and visual artists are using home pages (the starting screen) on the Web to create a new kind of multimedia art form that can involve the collaboration of different artists worldwide. In one experimental effort, a media artist created an interactive, multi-authored Website that permits other artists to freely introduce their own hypertext links, creating a growing and expanding collaboration that includes the work of a multitude of electronic works.

For now, the technology by which most individual users get on the Web is impractical for retrieving full-motion video. However, in the future, one can easily imagine film and video artists (or distributors) posting clips of television programs on their own home pages for promotional purposes, and downloading completed works to individuals and educational organizations for a fee.

Like video-on-demand, the distribution of audiovisual works is moving rapidly toward an e-mail model of posting and retrieval. It will be like a home video store, but without the cassettes ... and without the store.

3. *CD-ROMs, DVDs, and Other Packaged Software.* Although video-on-demand is still a long way from being a practical reality, CD-ROM distribution, like online service, is an exploding reality. Almost all computers sold today include CD-ROM drives, and although the market is still not profitable for most titles, it seems that everyone has a CD-ROM project in development.

CD-ROMs (which stands for Compact Disc–Read Only Memory) are laser discs that look like audio CDs, but which can combine and store text, sound, and moving images. With a capacity of more than six hundred megabytes of computer data, these little discs can hold an astonishing amount of text and graphics, making them particularly appropriate for encyclopedias and other reference works, which—not surprisingly—are the most popular titles to date. They hold considerably less audio and much less video because those media demand huge quantities of storage capacity. In time, however, capacity will expand and these discs will store full-motion video along with audio, graphics, and lots of additional information.

Some cutting edge independent producers are using CD-ROM technology to build upon existing films, and to create entirely new works of art. Jayne Loader, one of the producers of the award-winning documentary *Atomic Cafe*, has produced a CD-ROM entitled *Public Shelter* that expands upon the research and archival material gathered for the production of that landmark independent feature. For *Atomic Cafe*, the producers unearthed vast amounts of early Cold War archival footage, including material from educational and government films, creating one of the most scalding (and hilarious) critiques of U.S. policy of all time. The CD-ROM will update the film, photos, text, and commentary on the Atomic Age. Users will be able to access original documents from the White House, Capitol Hill, the Pentagon, the Nuclear Regulatory Commission, and the CIA, to name just a few sources of archival material included in the disc. The entire program is a simulated World Wide Web experience, with twenty different home pages, each with attached browsers. The home pages are either real places (Los Alamos, Hanford, etc.), concepts, or issues. Each home page contains audio, video, and links to other home pages. Users can watch some of the propaganda footage featured in *Atomic Cafe*, or read brochures on how to wash fallout off vegetables. On a more somber note, recently declassified documents about radiation experiments on human subjects are also included.

At the more surreal end of the spectrum is a game called *Duellin' Firemen!* by a Chicago-based company, Runandgun, Inc. Founding partners and Rhode Island School of Design graduates Tony Grossman and Grady Sain have combined live film and computer graphics to create an allegory about making it in the music business. The premise is that a collision of Air Force One and the space shuttle Columbia has triggered the Great Chicago Fire of 1995. The game player controls one of two teams of firefighters, who are actually a rock band in disguise. The firefighters move through the city from fire-protected safe house to safe house, dealing with subplots in each house, and trying to put on the performance of a lifetime for the trapped guests. *Duellin' Firemen!* was created for the 3DO game format, a newcomer rival to the immensely profitable Sega and Nintendo formats.

In the area of children's media, author, sculptor, and computer artist Rodney Alan Greenblat is creating CD-ROM storybooks for kids. A recent title, *Dazzeloids* (published by Voyager), includes two interactive branching stories, animation, a dream sequence, and more than ninety minutes of dialogue, sound effects, and original music and songs.

For activist producers, the CD-ROM format could well emerge as the grassroots medium of choice. Although you would not know it from your last audio CD purchase, CD-ROM discs only cost about $1 per disc to produce, far less than VHS cassettes. At that price (and once CD-ROM technology permits full-motion video) a social-issue documentary could easily be distributed as a premium by an organization to its members, combined with documents (such as a Congressional contact sheet), archival materials, and even a video commentary from the organization's leader.

Finally, producers and distributors seeking to distribute existing work in non-interactive form may soon be turning to Digital Video Discs (DVD), which are being developed to replace VHS cassettes—much as audio CDs replaced vinyl records. CDs eliminated the clicks and pops of long-playing records; similarly, DVDs will provide a superior and longer-lasting image than 1/2" videotape. Also, like CD-ROMs, DVDs will be inexpensive to duplicate, making them a viable alternative distribution format.

Over time, the particularities of each of these packaged software media will dictate their most appropriate use. For example, since CD-ROMs permit random access to vast amounts of multimedia information, they are an ideal resource and reference medium. However, they are viewed on a computer screen, which, at least for now, makes them primarily a personal viewing experience. DVDs, on the other hand, may have limited interactivity, but—once the technical standards are worked out—will provide a low-cost distribution medium for independent producers and distributors that is aimed at television playback, the traditional method of viewing films and video programs in the home.

Some industry watchers consider CD-ROM and other packaged software products to be just a "bridge technology" until all software is delivered over telephone or cable wires via video-on-demand or online systems.

INDEPENDENT MEDIA, NEW TECHNOLOGY AND PUBLIC POLICY

Independent producers are a diverse group. Those working on more commercial projects will—if sufficiently talented—be able to create their own opportunities in the digital future. But whether we find social-issue documentaries, experimental works, or non-mainstream children's programming in new media formats (especially the video-on-demand and online environments) will depend at least in part on whether there are any regulatory requirements to provide space for noncommercial work.

Public television and cable access channels exist today because of successful public advocacy for the reservation of space for noncommercial programming on the then-new media of broadcast and cable television. However, the 1990s appear to be continuing the deregulatory emphasis of the 80s, which will make it more difficult for independent producers and distributors to gain full access to the new media. The threatened elimination of public funding for the arts and public television will only compound the problem, reducing or eliminating already scarce resources for independent production and experimentation with the new media.

Only successful public advocacy for the reservation of space for non-mainstream media in the new media landscape will assure the public access to a broad range of diverse audiovisual work; and only such advocacy will assure independent producers and distributors the opportunity to create and bring that work to the public.

RESOURCE LIST

[Editor's Note: The following list compiles many of the resources recommended by the authors in *The Next Step*.For more extensive information on festivals and distributors mentioned in *The Next Step*, please refer to *The AIVF/FIVF Guide to International Film and Video Festivals*, and *The AIVF/FIVF Guide to Film and Video Distributors*.]

ORGANIZATIONS

AMERICAN FILM INSTITUTE, 2021 Northwestern Ave., Los Angeles, CA 90027. (213) 856-7600; FAX (213) 467-4578.

AMERICAN HOSPITAL ASSOCIATION, 325 7th St., NW, Washington, DC 20004. (202) 638-7368; FAX (202) 626-2345.

AMERICAN LIBRARY ASSOCIATION, 50 East Huron St., Chicago, IL 60611. (312) 944-6780; FAX (312) 440-9374.

AMERICAN SOCIETY FOR TRAINING AND DEVELOPMENT, 1640 King Street, Box 1443, Alexandria, VA 22313-2043. (703) 683-8183.

ASSOCIATION OF INDEPENDENT VIDEO AND FILMMAKERS/FOUNDATION FOR INDEPENDENT VIDEO AND FILM (AIVF/FIVF), 304 Hudson Street, 6th Floor, New York, NY 10013. (212) 807-1400; FAX (212) 463-8519.

ELECTRONIC ARTS INTERMIX, 536 Broadway, 9th Floor, New York, NY 10012. (212) 966-4605, FAX (212) 941-6118.

INDEPENDENT FEATURE PROJECT (IFP), 104 W. 29th St., 12th Floor, New York, NY 10001. (212) 465-8200; FAX (212) 465-8525.

THE KITCHEN, 512 W. 19th St., New York, NY 10011. (212) 255-5793; FAX (212) 645-4258.

NATIONAL ALLIANCE FOR MEDIA ARTS AND CULTURE (NAMAC), Preservation Park, 655 13th St., Suite 201, Oakland, CA 94612-1222. (510) 451-2717; FAX (510) 834-3741.

NATIONAL EDUCATIONAL MEDIA NETWORK, Preservation Park, 655 13th St., Oakland, CA 94612-1222. (510) 465-6885; Fax: (510) 465-2835.

NATIONAL VIDEO RESOURCES, 73 Spring St., Suite 606, New York, NY 10012. (212) 274-8080. FAX (212) 274-8081.

PRAXIS, 345 Union St., San Francisco, CA 94133. (415) 834-1852; FAX (415) 834-1853.

REED MIDEM ORGANIZATION. 475 Park Ave. So., 2nd Floor, New York, New York 10016. (212) 689-4220, FAX (212) 689-4348. Registration information for MIP-TV, MIPCOM, MIPIM, MIP-Asia, MIDEM-Asia, MAPIC, MILIA.

SOUTHWEST ALTERNATE MEDIA PROJECT (SWAMP), 1519 W. Main St., Houston, TX 77006. (713) 522-8592; FAX (713) 522-0953.

STATE DEPARTMENTS OF EDUCATION. For curriculum frameworks: California (916) 445-1260; Florida (904) 488-6547; Texas (512) 463-9581.

U.S. DEPARTMENT OF EDUCATION, 400 Maryland Ave, SW, Room 2089, Washington, DC 20202. (202) 401-1576; FAX (202) 401-3130.

VIDEO DATABANK, School of the Art Institute, 112 S. Michigan Ave., Chicago, IL 60603. (312) 443-3793; FAX (312) 541-8063.

VIDEO SOFTWARE DEALERS ASSOCIATION, 16530 Ventura Blvd., Suite 400, Encino CA 91436. (818) 385-1500. Holds an annual convention that includes exhibits by manufacturers and distributors.

WOMEN MAKE MOVIES, 462 Broadway, 5th Floor, New York, NY 10013. (212) 925-0606; FAX (212) 925-2052.

TELEVISION BROADCAST-RELATED RESOURCES

ABC-AUSTRALIA, GPO Box 9994, Sydney, NSW 2001, Australia. (011) 612 437 8000.

ALIVE TV c/o KTCA TV, 172 E. 4th St., St. Paul, MN 55101. (612) 229-1356; FAX (612) 229-1283.

AMERICAN PROGRAM SERVICE/EASTERN EDUCATION TELEVISION NETWORK, 120 Boylston St., 5th Fl., Boston, MA 02116. (617) 338-4455; FAX: (617) 338-5369.

JANE BALFOUR FILMS, Burghley House, 35 Fortress Rd., London, NW5 1AD, UK. (011) 44 171 267 5392; FAX (011) 44 171 267 4241. Producer's rep for international markets.

BBC-TV, TV-Centre, Wood Lane, London W12 7RJ, UK. (011) 44 181 743 8000.

BRAVO/INDEPENDENT FILM CHANNEL, 150 Crossways Park West, Woodbury, NY 11797. (516) 364-2222; FAX (516) 364-7638.

CENTRAL EDUCATION NETWORK, 1400 E. Touhy Ave., Des Plaines, IL 60018. (708) 390-8700; FAX (708) 390-9435.

CHANNEL FOUR, 124 Horseferry Road, London SW1P 2TX, UK. (011) 44 171 396 4444.

HBO/CINEMAX, 1100 Avenue of the Americas, New York, NY 10036. (212) 512-1000; FAX (212) 512-8051.

IMAGE UNION, c/o WTTW, 5400 N. St. Louis Ave., Chicago, IL 60625. (312) 583-5000; FAX (312) 509-5301.

INDEPENDENT TELEVISION SERVICE (ITVS), 190 East Fifth St., Suite 200, St. Paul, MN 55101. (612) 225-9035; FAX (612) 225-9102.

LA SEPT/ARTE, 50, ave. Théophile Gautier, 75016 Paris, France. (011) 33 1 4414 7700.

LIVING ROOM FESTIVAL, c/o KQED, 2601 Mariposa St., San Francisco, CA 94110. (415) 553-2458.

NATIONAL ASIAN AMERICAN TELECOMMUNICATIONS ASSOCIATION (NAATA), 346 9th St., 2nd Floor, San Francisco, CA 94103. (415) 863-0814; FAX (415) 863-7428.

NATIONAL BLACK PROGRAMMING CONSORTIUM, 929 Harrison Ave. #101, Columbus, OH 43215. (614) 299-5355; FAX (614) 299-4761.

NATIONAL LATINO COMMUNICATIONS CENTER, 3171 Los Feliz Blvd., Suite 200, Los Angeles, CA 90039. (213) 663-8294; FAX (213) 663-5606.

NATIVE AMERICAN PUBLIC BROADCASTING CONSORTIUM, Box 83111, Lincoln, NE 68501. (402) 472-3522; FAX (402) 472-8675.

NEW TELEVISION/WGBH, 240 New Britain, Hartford, CT 06106. (617) 492-8455.

NHK-JAPAN, 2-2-1 Jinnan, Shibuya-ku, Tokyo 150-01, Japan. (011) 81 3 54 78 2085.

PACIFIC ISLANDERS IN COMMUNICATIONS, 1221 Kapiolani Blvd. #6A-4, Honolulu, HI 96814. (808) 591-0059; FAX (808) 591-1114.

PACIFIC MOUNTAIN NETWORK, 1550 Park Ave., Denver, CO 80218-1661. (303) 837-8000; FAX (303) 837-0857.

P.O.V., 220 W. 19th St., 11th Fl., New York, NY 10011. (212) 989-8121; FAX (212) 989-8230.

SHOWTIME NETWORKS INC., 1633 Broadway, New York, NY 10019. (212) 708-1600; FAX (212) 708-1217.

SOUTHERN EDUCATIONAL COMMUNICATIONS ASSOCIATION, P.O. Box 50008, Columbia, SC 29250. (803) 799-5517; FAX (803) 771-4831.

SUNDANCE FILM CHANNEL, see Showtime Networks.

WDR, Appellhofplatz 1, D-50600 Cologne, Germany. (011) 49 221 220 4970.

ZDF, D-55127 Mainz, Germany. (011) 49 61 31 701.

FUNDERS

JOHN D. AND CATHERINE T. MACARTHUR FOUNDATION, 140 S. Dearborn St., Chicago, IL 60603. (312) 726-8000.

NATIONAL ENDOWMENT FOR THE ARTS, 1100 Pennsylvania Ave., NW, Washington, DC 20506. (202) 682-5452.

NATIONAL ENDOWMENT FOR THE HUMANITIES, 1100 Pennsylvania Ave., NW, Washington, DC 20506. Phone: (202) 606-8278.

PAUL ROBESON FUND FOR INDEPENDENT MEDIA, 666 Broadway, Suite 500, New York, NY 10012. (212) 529-5300, FAX (212) 982-9272.

INFORMATION SERVICES/MAILING LISTS

ART ON FILM DATABASE, 2875 Broadway, 2nd Floor, NYC 10025-7805. (212) 854-9570. Inventory of film/video productions on the visual arts.

BASELINE ONLINE SERVICES, New York (212) 254-8235, or Los Angeles (310) 789-2030. An "entertainment industry" database.

CMG INFORMATION SERVICES, 187 Ballardvale Street, Suite B110, P.O. Box 7000, Wilmington, MA 01887-7000. (800) 677-7959, FAX (508) 988-0046. Large supplier of general mailing lists.

COPYRIGHT HOTLINE, ASSOCIATION FOR INFORMATION MEDIA AND EQUIPMENT (AIME), (800) 444-4203. Free service answering questions about copyright.

DIALOG INFORMATION SERVICES, (800) 334-2564. Online database accessible by individuals and institutions. Used by many libraries and universities. Contains the Foundation Center databases (Files 26 & 27) and NICEM's A-V Online (File 46).

MARKET DATA RETRIEVAL, 16 Progress Dr., P.O. Box 2117, Shelton, CT 06484-1117. (203) 926-4800, FAX (203) 926-0784. Large supplier of general mailing lists.

NICEM EZ CUSTOM SEARCH, (800) 926-8328. Customized computer searches of vast databases on films, videos, producers, distributors, filmstrips, etc.

PBS VIDEOFINDERS. (900) 860-9301. Computer search for film/video programs (by title, subject, filmmaker, etc.) for works on PBS or in R.R. Bowker's guide.

Note: Lists for specific curriculum and subject areas can usually be acquired from professional associations such as the American Anthropological Association, the Modern Languages Association, etc. Addresses for these groups can be found in the reference sections of most libraries.

NEW TECHNOLOGIES/COMPUTER SOFTWARE

FILMPROFIT, Big Horse Inc., 1536 18th St., San Francisco, CA 94107. (415) 431-5149.

THE VINE. (213) 957-1990. Online entertainment industry service (e-mail, bulletin boards, etc.).

WORLD WIDE WEB. Netscape's research site is called Lycos and can be found at http://home.mcom.com. Mosaic's research site is at http://gnn.com/wic/index.html. There are also a number of other sites whose primary function is to compile information and linkages, including the Yahoo pages (http://akebono.stanford.edu/Yahoo) and the Institute for Global Communications (IGC) at http://www.igc.apc.org.

PERIODICALS

ABC-Clio Video Rating Guide for Libraries, 130 Cremona Dr., Santa Barbara, CA 93117. (805) 968-1911; FAX (805) 685-9685.

Afterimage, Visual Studies Workshop, 31 Prince St., Rochester, NY 14607. (716) 442-8676.

American Journal of Nursing, 555 W. 57th St., New York, NY 10019. (212) 582-8820; FAX (212) 586-5462.

Angles: Women Working in Film & Video, P.O. Box 11916, Milwaukee, WI 53211. (414) 963-8951.

Animation Magazine, 28024 Dorothy Dr., Agoura Hills, CA 91301. (818) 991-2884.

AV Marketplace, R. R. Bowker, 121 Chanlon Rd., New Providence, NJ 07974. (800) 521-8110.

B&T's Little Film Notebook, IC8FV, P.O. Box 335, Rowley, MA 01969. (508) 948-7985. For super 8 fans.

Black Film Review, 2025 Eye St., NW, Suite 213, Washington, DC 20003. (202) 466-2753.

BOOKLIST, American Library Association, 50 East Huron St., Chicago, IL 60611. (312) 944-6780.

BUZZWORDS, ITVS, 190 Fifth St. East, St. Paul, MN 55101. (612) 225-9035.

Cineaste, 200 Park Ave. So., #1320, New York, NY 10003. (212) 982-1241.

Current: The Public Telecommunications Newsletter, 1612 K St., N.W., Suite 704, Washington, D.C. 20006. (202) 463-7055.

Curriculum Administrator, 992 High Ridge Rd., Stamford, CT 06905. (203) 322-1300; FAX (203) 329-9177.

Educational Marketer, 213 Danbury Rd., Wilton, CT 06897. (203) 834-0033.

Education Week, P.O. Box 2083, Marion, OH 43305. (800) 347-6969.

Film Comment, The Film Society of Lincoln Center, 165 W. 65th St., New York, New York 10023. (212) 875-5610; FAX (212) 875-5632.

Film Threat, 9171 Wilshire Blvd., Suite 300, Beverly Hills, CA 90210.

FILMMAKER: The Magazine of Independent Film, 132 W. 21st St., 6th Floor, New York, NY 10011-3203. (212) 243-3882.

Foundation News, Council on Foundations, 1828 L St., NW, Washington, DC 20036. (202) 466-6512.

Hollywood Reporter, 5055 Wilshire Blvd., 6th & 7th Fls., Los Angeles, CA 90036. (213) 525-2000; FAX (213) 525-2377.

THE INDEPENDENT Film and Video Monthly, AIVF/FIVF, 304 Hudson St., 6th Fl., New York, NY 10013. (212) 807-1400; FAX (212) 463-8519.

International Documentary: The Journal of the International Documentary Association, 1551 So. Robertson, Ste. 201, Los Angeles, CA 90035-4257. (310) 284-8422.

Library Journal, 249 W. 17th St., New York, NY 10011. (212) 463-6802.

Media Arts Information Network (MAIN), NAMAC, Preservation Park, 655 13th St., Oakland, CA 94612. (510) 451-2717.

Media and Methods, 1429 Walnut St., 10th Fl., Philadelphia, PA 19102. (215) 241-9201; FAX (215) 587-9607.

Media Matters, Media Alliance, c/o WNET Television, 356 West 58th Street, New York, NY 10019. (212) 560-2919.

NVR Reports, National Video Resources, 73 Spring St., Suite 606, New York, NY 10012. (212) 274-8080, FAX (212) 274-8081.

Release Print, Film Arts Foundation, 346 9th St., 2nd Fl., San Francisco, CA 94103. (415) 552-8760.

Television Business International (TBI), 531-533 Kings Road, London SW10 OTZ, UK. (011) 44 171 352 3211; FAX (011) 44 171 352 4883.

The Telco Report: International Television Program Magazine. 2730 Wilshire Blvd., Suite 200, Santa Monica, CA 90403. (310) 828-4003.

T.H.E. Journal, 150 El Camino Real, Suite 112, Tustin, CA 92680-3670. (714) 730-4011; FAX (714) 730-3739.

Training Magazine, Lakewood Publications, 50 S. 9th St., Minneapolis, MN 55402. (800) 328-4329.

TV World, 33-39 Bowling Green Lane, London EC1R ODA, UK. (011) 44 171 837 9204.

Variety, 5700 Wilshire Blvd., #120, Los Angeles, CA 90036. (213) 857-6600; FAX (213) 932-0874.

Video Business, 825 Seventh Ave., New York, NY 10019. (212) 887-8400.

Video Librarian, 3672 N.E. Liverpool Dr., Bremerton, WA 98311. (360) 377-2231.

Video Networks, Bay Area Video Coalition (BAVC), 1111 17th St., San Francisco, CA 94107. (415) 861-3282.

Video Software Magazine, 825 Seventh Ave., New York, NY 10019. (212) 887-8400.

Video Store Magazine, 201 E. Sandpointe Ave., Suite 600, Santa Ana, CA 92707. (714) 513-8400.

ARTICLES, PAMPHLETS, AND BOOKS

The Activist's Almanac, David Walls. Fireside, Simon & Schuster, New York, 1993.

AIVF/FIVF Guide to Film and Video Distributors and *AIVF/FIVF Guide to International Film and Video Festivals*, Kathryn Bowser. AIVF/FIVF, 304 Hudson Street, 6th Floor, New York, NY 10013. (212) 807-1400.

Alternative Visions: Distributing Independent Media in a Home Video World, Debra Franco. AFI Press. Order from AIVF/FIVF, (212) 807-1400.

The Beginning Filmmaker's Business Guide, Renee Harmon. Walker and Company. (800) 289-2553.

Bowker's Complete Video Directory, ed. M.K. Reed. R.R. Bowker, New York. (800) 521-8110.

Contracts for the Film and Television Industry and Dealmaking in the Film and Television Industry, Mark Litwak. Silman-James Press. Order from Samuel French, (800) 822-8669.

Electronic Media for the School Market Report: 1994-95 Review, Trends and Forecasts, SIMBA Information, Inc., 213 Danbury Rd., Wilton, CT 06897. (203) 834-0033.

Fields of Vision, eds. Leslie Devereaux and Roger Hillman. University of California/Berkeley Press, 1995.

Film and Video Marketing and *Home Video: Producing for the Home Market*, Michael Wiese Productions, 11288 Ventura Blvd., Suite 821, Studio City, CA 91604. (800) 379-8808, fax (818) 986-3408.

The Film Industries: Practical Business/Legal Problems in Production, Distribution, and Exhibition, Michael Mayer. Hastings House.

Guide to Information Access, ed. Sandy Whiteley. American Library Association, New York, 1994.

Hypertext, George P. Landow. Johns Hopkins University Press, Baltimore, 1992.

The Independent Film Industry Directory, Independent Feature Project, NY, (212) 465-8200. Lists domestic and foreign buyers attending the Independent Feature Film Market.

Index to AV Producers and Distributors, Plexus, 143 Old Marlton Pl., Medford, NJ 08055. (609) 654-6500.

International Film Financing Conference 1995; transcripts available from Film Arts Foundation, San Francisco, CA. (415) 552-8760.

International Guide of Documentary Buyers, Yoland Robeveille, regic 3i, 5 passage Montgallet, 75012 Paris, France. (011) 33 1 434 2068.

Keeping Pace With the New Television, Sheila Mahony, Nick DeMartino, and Robert Stengel. VNU Books International, 1980.

Mediating Culture, eds. William Anselmi and Kosta Gouliamos. Guernica, Toronto, 1994.

Money for Film and Video Artists and *Money for International Exchange in the Arts*, American Council for the Arts, One East 53rd St., New York, NY 10022. (212) 223-ARTS.

The Movie Business Book, Jason E Squire, ed., Fireside, Simon & Schuster.

Networks of Power, Dennis W. Mazzocco. South End Press, Boston, 1994.

NICEM's Film and Video Finder, Plexus, 143 Old Marlton Pl., Medford, NJ 08055. (609) 654-6500.

Off-Hollywood: The Making and Marketing of American Specialty Films, David Rosen and Peter Hamilton. Grove Press, NY.

"Plugged In Producers: A Guide for Working with Cable Networks," Larry Jaffee. *The Independent*, June 1991. FIVF, NY. (212) 807-1400.

Producer's Guide to Nontheatrical Distribution, Kate Spohr, National Educational Media Network, Oakland, CA. (510) 465-6885.

Producer's Source Book: A Guide to Cable TV Program Buyers, National Academy of Cable Programming/National Cable Television Association. (202) 775-3611.

Producing, Financing and Distributing Film, Baumgarten, Farber & Fleischer. Limelight Editions, NYC.

Public Broadcasting Directory, CPB, 901 E St., N.W., Washington, D.C. 20004-2037. (202) 879-9600.

The Red Book: PBS Packaging & Technical Guidelines, PBS, 1320 Braddock Pl., Alexandria, VA 22314-1698. (703) 739-5450.

Resisting the Virtual Life, eds. James Brook and Iain A. Bosl. City Lights, San Francisco, CA, 1995.

"Selling Documentaries to Cable," Thomas Gianakopoulos, *International Documentary*, April and May 1994. IDA, Los Angeles. (310) 284-8422.

Shaking the Money Tree: How to Get Grants and Donations for Film and Video, Morrie Warshawski. Wiese Books, 11288 Ventura Blvd., #821, Studio City, CA 91604. (800) 379-8808. Also available from AIVF/FIVF.

Something Pressing: A Guide to Public Relations for the Video and Filmmaker. Media Alliance, NY. (212) 560-2919.

Super 8 in the Video Age, Brodsky & Treadway. (508) 948-7985.

Taking it to the Theaters: The Empowerment Project's Guide to Theatrical and Video Self-Distribution of Issue-Oriented Films and Videos, Trent, Peale and Doroshow. The Empowerment Project, Chapel Hill, NC. (919) 967-1963.

They Must be Represented: The Politics of Documentary, Paula Rabinowitz. Verso, London, 1994.

Understanding Media, Marshall McLuhan. MIT Press, Cambridge, MA, 1994.

User's Guide to Film Distribution Deals, Jeffrey Hardy. Filmprofit, San Francisco, CA. (415) 431-5149.

Video Hound (manufacturers) and *Video Source Book* (home video and non-theatrical video titles), Gale Research, Detroit, MI. (313) 961-2242.

SAMPLE DISTRIBUTION AGREEMENT

AGREEMENT made the * day of * 19__, by and between _____, with offices at _____ (hereinafter "Distributor") and _____ (hereinafter "Producer").

It is agreed between the parties as follows:

1.   DEFINITIONS

a)   The Program refers to the film(s) and/or videotapes as more fully described in Exhibit A, appended hereto and made a part hereof.

b)   The "Territory" shall be _____.

c)   The "Term" of agreement shall be for a period of * (*) years from the date hereof, provided
Producer delivers the materials to be delivered within sixty (60) days of the date hereof. The Term
shall be extended for such period in excess of sixty (60) days in which Producer delays furnishing
all materials to Distributor.

d)   Distributor may notify Producer in writing at least sixty (60) days, but no more than one hundred
twenty (120) days prior to the expiration of the Term, of its intent to renew this Agreement for an
additional consecutive period of three (3) years (the "Renewal Term"). Producer shall notify Distributor in writing within thirty (30) days of receipt of such notice if Producer agrees to the
Renewal Term.

2.   GRANT OF RIGHTS

a)   Producer hereby grants to Distributor the sole and exclusive right to license the Program for
exhi bition and/or transmission in the Territory for theatrical and non-theatrical release in all
applicable gauges, all forms of television including, without limitation, cable television, pay-cable
television, satellite television and all forms of home-videocassette and disc entertainment ("Rights")
during the Term.

b)   Producer grants to Distributor the exclusive right to execute in its own name, during the Term, all
contracts for the exploitation of the Rights.

3.   DISTRIBUTOR'S OBLIGATIONS

a)   Distributor agrees to use prudent business efforts during the Term of the Agreement to effect
distribution of the Program throughout the Territory. Notwithstanding the foregoing, Distributor
makes no representations with respect to the level of sales or licenses that may be obtained for the
Program.

b)   To effect the distribution of the Program, Distributor may enter into agreements with subdistributors with respect to all or some of the Rights in all or part of the Territory. All subdistribution
agreements shall be subject to the terms and conditions of this Agreement. In territories where
subdistributors are used, Distributor will add a 5% surcharge to the fee set forth in this Agreement.
The territories where subdistributors are used are _____ speaking territories. Producer will be
informed in advance of any such subdistribution agreement.

4.   MATERIALS

Promptly upon execution of this Agreement, Producer shall deliver to Distributor's office, at
Producer's sole expense, the following materials:

a.   One new and unused original media master. Said master must be a one-inch videotape copied from the original videotape master.

b.   If one-inch videotape is supplied, tape must have international audio track with the following elements:

Channel 1-   Full mix audio track
Channel 2-   Music and effects only if Program has synch-sound on-camera dialogue
Channel 3-   Time code; EBU for PAL videotapes, SEMPTE for NTSC videotapes

c.   Access to original laboratory materials, evidenced by a laboratory letter in the form appended hereto as Exhibit B.

d.   Four videocassettes for screening and promotional purposes.

e.   A music cue sheet.

f.   A transcript of the completed Program in the English language.

g.   Ten black-and-white copies of a still photograph representative of the Program, available color transparencies and other publicity materials in Producer's possession.

All materials and information to be delivered pursuant to this paragraph shall be of professional quality, and Distributor may return any materials to Producer which are not of such quality and demand that Producer furnish substitute materials. In such event Producer will use its best efforts to promptly furnish such substitute materials.

5.   FEES, EXPENSES AND ROYALTIES

a)   In consideration of Distributor's services hereunder, Distributor shall retain the following fees (the "Distribution Fee"):

(i)   United States - _____ %
(ii)   Worldwide exclusive of United States - _____ %

The foregoing fees shall pertain to all forms of television (standard broadcast, cable, pay TV and pay cable, STV, and satellite television services) and home video use.

b)   Distributor shall deduct the following expenses ("Distribution Expenses") from revenue earned from the sale, license and rental of the Program: customs; shipping; costs of film prints and/or video tapes, cassettes and discs used for sale, license or promotional purposes; direct costs of any paid advertising; and costs of promotion not to exceed the sum of _____ per annum without Producer's prior written consent.

All other costs of doing business, including market entrance fees, travel and entertainment, postage, insurance, long distance telephone and telexes, shall be paid for by Distributor and shall not be deemed Distribution expenses.

c)   From all revenue received by Distributor in U.S. dollars in the United States from all uses of the Program, (less any withholding tax, duty or imposition) Distributor shall first deduct the Distribution Fees and then the Distribution Expenses. The balance remaining shall be "Producer's Royalties."

6.   CONTRACTS AND ACCOUNTING

a)   Distributor shall notify Producer of all contracts entered into by Distributor in the format appended hereto as Exhibit C. Distributor retains the right to change or revise said form at any time during the Term.

b)   Distributor shall send to Producer a quarterly statement of all monies actually received by Distributor from the exploitation of the Program, and the deductions of Distribution Fees and Distribution Expenses, and shall send with such statement such sum as may be shown to be due thereon to Producer. Such statements and payments shall be made within sixty (60) days of the close of each quarterly period.

c)   Distributor shall preserve for a period of two years records of all transactions effected and monies received and expenses deducted pursuant to this Agreement and Producer shall be entitled at its expense, to inspect or cause to be inspected such records upon giving reasonable notice to Distributor of its intention to do so.

d)   If Producer shall not have made any objections to any statement given by Distributor within two years of the date of such statement, Producer shall be deemed to have conclusively accepted the correctness thereof.

7.   SPECIAL SERVICES

If Producer requires Distributor to perform services other than those normally performed by Distributor in connection with the exploitation of the Program, then Producer shall compensate Distributor for the cost of such services at Distributor's prevailing rates for the performance thereof.

8.   DISTRIBUTOR'S RIGHTS

Distributor shall have the following rights in and to the Program to:

a)   Add Distributor's logo to the front and/or end of the Program.

b)   To make such cuts and edits in the Program, or to authorize others to make such cuts and edits, as may be required for exhibition time periods or by local censorship laws. Distributor shall not make or authorize others to make any deletions of credits, titles or copyright notices, nor shall Distributor make or permit others to make such changes in the Program as would misrepresent the Program or diminish the Program's editorial integrity.

c)   Advertise and promote and authorize others to advertise and promote the Program. In this regard Producer grants to Distributor the right to use the name, voice and likeness of all persons appearing on or rendering services to the Program, provided such use does not constitute an implied or expressed endorsement of any product or service. Distributor may use and authorize others to use excerpts from the Program not to exceed three (3) minutes in the aggregate only for advertising and promoting the Program.

d)   Translate the Program into other languages by dubbing or subtitling.

9.   PRODUCER'S WARRANTIES, REPRESENTATIONS AND INDEMNITIES

a)   Producer hereby warrants and represents that:
(i)   Producer has the sole and exclusive right and title to the Program absolutely and not jointly with any other person, firm or corporation.
(ii)   Producer has the sole and exclusive right to grant the Rights to the Program herein granted, and is free to enter into this Agreement without reference to any other person, firm or corporation.
(iii) The statements in connection with the Rights contained in this clause shall remain true for the term of this Agreement and the term of all licenses entered into hereunder.
(iv) The Program does not contain any material of whatsoever nature that is defamatory of any person, firm or corporation.
(v)   Producer has obtained all rights, permissions, consents and releases necessary for the exercise of such rights, and the exercise of such rights shall not infringe upon the rights of any person, firm or corporation, nor shall it give rise to the payment of any sums to any third party by Distributor or Distributor's licensees. Furthermore, Producer has paid or will pay, any residual, royalty or reuse fees that are payable or may become payable by Distributor's exercise of its rights thereunder.
(vi) Producer has not, nor will it, enter into any Agreement in conflict with the rights granted to Distributor hereunder.

b) Producer undertakes to indemnify Distributor and keep Distributor indemnified against all costs, claims and expenses including, without limitation, reasonable legal expenses, arising out of any of Producer's warranties and representations.

10. TERMINATION

In the event that either party is in default pursuant to this Agreement, the other party may give said defaulting party fifteen (15) days written notice to cure such default. If such default is not cured within that period by the defaulting party, the other party may terminate this Agreement by written notice to the defaulting party after the expiration of the period to cure.

In the event of termination pursuant to this paragraph or expiration of the Term of this Agreement, if Producer (or its duly authorized Agent) extends or renews any grant of the rights or any part thereof made by Distributor hereunder, Producer shall pay to Distributor such Distribution fee as Distributor would have been entitled to receive had Distributor made such grant under the provisions of this Agreement.

Producer shall pay the commission due Distributor forthwith upon payment for any such extension or renewal of the Program falling due and shall allow Distributor, at Distributor's expense, reasonable access to Producer's records for the purpose of investigating whether Producer has complied with its obligations under this paragraph.

11. RELATIONSHIP BETWEEN PARTIES

Nothing herein contained shall constitute or be deemed to constitute a joint venture or partnership between the parties hereto and neither party shall hold itself out in any manner contrary to the terms of this Agreement.

12. GENERAL

a) Producer shall not be entitled to make any assignment of the benefit of this Agreement except with the express prior written consent of the Distributor, such consent not to be unreasonably witheld. However, Producer may assign its right to receive income upon notice to Distributor and without Distributor's consent.

b) No express or implied waiver by either party of any provision of this Agreement or of any breach or default of either party that constitutes a continuing waiver or a waiver of any other provision shall prevent either party from acting upon the same or any subsequent breach or default.

c) This Agreement constitutes the entire agreement between the parties in connection with the exploitation of the Program and shall not be modified except in written documents signed by both parties. Any notice sent by pre-paid post shall be sent by registered post and shall be deemed to have been delivered within 3 days of sending thereof, any notice to be sent by telefax to compatible equipment shall be deemed to have been served when sent and any notice sent by cable shall be deemed to have been served within 48 hours of the dispatch thereof.

d) This Agreement shall be governed by and construed in accordance with the law of   , which is designated as the venue and jurisdiction for the settlement of all disputes arising hereunder.

Producer and Distributor hereby acknowledge their agreement and consent to all of the terms and conditions contained herein.

DISTRIBUTOR:
By:

PRODUCER:
By:

EXHIBIT A
PROGRAMS, LENGTH AND DESCRIPTION

EXHIBIT B
LABORATORY ACCESS LETTER

Gentlemen:

We have on deposit with you certain preprint material concerning the film or video property entitled: (hereinafter referred to as the "Program").

You are hereby advised that (hereinafter referred to as "Licensee"), its successors, designates and assigns, has been granted the right to license, distribute, subdistribute, sublicense and exhibit the Program worldwide, for all media, for a term expiring years from date of this agreement.

You are hereby irrevocably authorized, directed and instructed, and you agree to fill all orders from Licensee, its subdistributors, sublicensees and designees, at their sole cost and expense, for preprint material and positive prints of, or such other laboratory services with respect to, the Program as Licensee, its subdistributors, sublicensees and designees from time to time may order.

All materials or services which you may supply or furnish to or on order of Licensee, are to be paid for solely by Licensee, and the undersigned shall not be liable to pay any of the charges which may be incurred by Licensee for any work, labor, material or services pertaining to the Program,

You agree that you will not refuse to process Licensee's orders, or the orders of Licensee's subdistributors, sublicensees and designees, for materials or services relating to the Program nor assert any lien on the Program or materials relating thereto as against Licensee or its subdistributors, sublicensees or designees by reason of the failure of the undersigned or any of its other licensees or designees to pay any charge which they may incur for services and materials relating to the Program.

You agree that you shall not, during the term of the Licensee's license, without written consent of the undersigned and Licensee, permit removal from your possession of such preprint materials as may be necessary to permit you to manufacture for Licensee, its subdistributors, sublicensees, to designees, additional preprint material or prints of the Program; provided, however, that such preprint materials may be transferred to another laboratory designated by the undersigned, to be held subject to a laboratory access letter similar to this letter.

You certify that you have or will make available to Licensee the following materials:

The instructions contained herein are irrevocable and they may not be modified or rescinded except in a writing signed by the Licensee and the undersigned.

Please signify your understanding and agreement of the foregoing by signing in the space provided below.

Very truly yours,

PRODUCER:_____   LABORATORY:_____

By:_____   AGREED:_____

                               By:_____

EXHIBIT C

CONTRACT MEMORANDUM

DATE:

PRODUCER:

TITLE:

LICENSEE:

TERRITORY:

TERM:

RIGHTS GRANTED:

LICENSE FEE:

MATERIALS TO BE FURNISHED:

COMMENTS:

MIP-TV 1995 PRICES MAP

The following is reprinted courtesy of *TV World*. For more information please contact: *Ms. Tina Murray, TV WORLD, 33-39 Bowling Green Lane, LONDON EC1R ODA, ENGLAND*

NORTH AMERICA

COUNTRY OR MARKET	LIGHT ENT. (US$ per half hour)	DRAMA (US$ per hour)	CHILDREN'S (US$ per half hour)	DOCUMENTARIES (US$ per hour)	FILMS (*US$ per film)	EVENTS (US$ per hour)
Commercial broadcast nets (1)	350,000 - 635,000	500,000 - 3.25m	50,000 - 205,000	100,000 - 410,000	2m - 10.2m	1m - 15.3m
Broadcast syndication (2)	250,00 - 1.12m	500,000 - 2.05m	100,000 - 615,000	200,000 - 510,000	100,000 - 2.25m	750,000 - 3.05m
Markets 1 - 10	50,000 - 102,000	50,000 - 102,000	5,000 - 10,200	5,000 - 25,500	5,000 - 205,000	15,000 - 205,000
Markets 11 - 90	40,000 - 82,00	40,000 - 82,000	5,000 - 10,200	5,000 - 25,500	5,000 - 102,000	10,000 - 102,000
Markets 91+	10,000 - 51,000	10,000 - 51,000	1,000 - 10,200	1,000 - 10,200	1,000 - 51,000	1,000 - 20,400
FBS Member Sales (3)	1,000 - 25,500	1,500 - 10,200	1,000 - 15,300	1,000 - 15,300	1,000 - 20,400	1,000 - 15,300
Weekly Pay cable (4)	100,000 - 615,000	20,000 - 1.73m	25,000 - 76,500	20,000 - 175,000	1m - 8.16m	1m - 5.1m
Basic Cable(5)						
Hotels-20m Rooms	5,000 - 306,000	10,000 - 153,000	10,000 - 76,500	5,000 - 76,500	5,000 - 1.15m	20,000 - 1.15m
Hotels - 40m Rooms	1,000 - 102,000	2,000 - 204,000	1,000 - 25,500	1,000 - 51,000	5,000 - 102,000	-
	1,000 - 51,000	1,000 - 102,000	1,000 - 10,200	1,000 - 20,400	1,000 - 51,000	-
	-	-	-	-	50,000 - 2.05M	1m - 15.3m
Canada (C$)						
English-speaking national nets	1,500 - 46,000	10,000 - 153,000	1,500 - 20,400	5,000 - 15,300	6,000 - 255,000	-
English-speaking regional nets	500 - 10,200	12,000 - 15,300	3,000 - 8,160	1,000 - 10,200	3,000 - 30,600	
English-speaking pay-TV/cable	5,000 - 6,120	10,000 - 30,600	3,000 - 6,100	3,000 - 6,120	16,000 - 61,200	
English-speaking educational nets	600 - 2,000	2,000 - 5,000	800 - 1,500	1,000 - 5,000	see notes	
French-speaking networks	30,000 - 35,500	10,000 - 30,600	4,000 - 15,300	5,000 - 10,200	10,000 - 102,000	
French-speaking cable	-	8,000 - 9,460	1,50 - 3,060	-	1,000 - 30,600	

LATIN AMERICA

COUNTRY		DRAMA (US$ per hour)	CHILDRENS (US$ per half hour)	DOCUMENTARIES (US$ per hour)	MOVIES (US$ per film)
Argentina	a	3,920 - 7,850	580 - 4,900	1,960 - 3,920	4,900 - 14,700
	b	490 - 5,880	490 - 2,940	980 - 3,920	2,940 - 9,800
	c	100 - 490	100 - 490	100 - 490	980 - 1,960
Bolivia		200 - 820	200 - 410	200 - 410	510 - 1,020
Brazil	a	4,000 - 15,000	2,000 - 3,000	3,000 - 7,000	20,000 - 60,000
	b	500 - 5,000		3,000 - 7,000	10,000 - 50,000
	c	2,000 - 6,000	1,000 - 1,400	1,000 - 1,500	5,000 - 12,000
Chile	a & b	2,000 - 5,000	700 - 1,300	2,000 - 3,000	8,000 - 20,000
	c	1,500 - 2,500	400 - 1,000	800 - 2,000	1,000 - 3,000
Colombia	a	2,000 - 7,000	800 - 1,000	1,400 - 3,000	10,000 - 15,000
	c	500 - 800	50 - 90	50 - 1,000	800 - 1,200
Costa Rica		200 - 1,000	100 - 400	500 - 1,000	1,500 - 2,500
Dominican Rep.		200 - 900	200 - 600	200 - 400	2,000 - 4,000
Ecuador	a	900 - 2,800	500 - 1,000	1,000 - 1,500	2,000 - 4,000
	c	500 - 1,000	400 - 700	750 - 1,000	1,000 - 2,000
El Salvador		250 - 700	100 - 300	500 - 500	500 - 1,000
Guatemala		200 - 400		150 - 300	500 - 1,000
Honduras		200 - 500		200 - 350	700 - 900
Mexico	a	800 - 10,000	900 - 2,200	2,200 - 4,200	20,000 - 80,000
	b	800 - 4,000	800 - 2,200	1,200 - 3,000	12,000 - 30,000
	c	200 - 400			2,000 - 4,000
Nicaragua		150 - 350	150 - 350	150 - 350	1,000 - 500
Panama		450 - 1,100	100 - 200	500 - 900	1,000 - 900
Paraguay		200 - 600	200 - 600	200 - 400	600 - 1,400
Peru		1,000 - 2,000	500 - 1,000	500 - 1,000	1,000 - 3,000
Puerto Rico[a]		1,530 - 4,100	510 - 1,020	2,050 - 4,100	5,100 - 25,500
Uruguay		1,000 - 1,650	300 - 800	300 - 800	1,500 - 2,500
Venezuela	a	2,000 - 7,000	300 - 1,000	1,000 - 3,000	5,000 - 25,000
	b	1,000 - 2,000	300 - 1,000	800 - 1,600	1,000 - 40,000
	c	50 - 150	50 - 150	50 - 150	200 - 500

EUROPE

COUNTRY	LIGHT ENTERTAINMENT (US$ per half hour)	DRAMA (US$ per hour)	TV MOVIES (US$ per movie)	CHILDREN'S (US$ per half hour)	DOCUMENTARIES (US$ per hour)	FEATURE FILM (US$ per film)
	100 - 150	350 - 300	200 - 300	100 - 200	100 - 300	200 - 300
Albania	2,300 - 2,600	3,500 - 6,200	11,000 - 12,000	2,300 - 2,600	3,500 - 4,600	10,000 - 15,000
Austria	1,000 - 4,000	5,000 - 4,000	5,000 - 7,000	1,000 - 2,500	2,000 - 4,000	5,000 - 20,000
Belgium	100 - 200	250 - 600	500 - 750	100 - 300	200 - 400	600 - 1,000
Bulgaria	240 - 350	500 - 1,000	700 - 1,785	240 - 350	650 - 725	1,200 - 2,500
Croatia	175 - 1,000	500 - 3,000	200 - 4,000	175 - 1,500	360 - 2,000	800 - 3,000
Czech Republic	350	500 - 600	700 - 1,000	300	400 - 600	800 - 1,100
CIS / Russia	110 - 450	300 - 450	400 - 800	150 - 180	400 - 320	450 - 90
Cyprus	2,300 - 4,500	2,000 - 5,000	3,000 - 5,000	1,200 - 1,400	1,800 - 4,000	4,000 - 6,000
Denmark	7,000 - 10,000	25,000 - 70,000	25,000 - 65,000	6,000 - 20,000	13,000 - 40,000	40,000 - 3m
Finland	1,200 - 1,800	2,000 - 5,000	3,800 - 7,000	1,100 - 1,500	2,300 - 2,700	4,400 - 10,000
France	1,200 - 13,000	30,000 - 100,000	50,000 - 150,000	6,000 - 25,000	12,000 - 25,000	50,000 - 3m
Germany	800 - 1,500	2,000 - 4,000	4,000 - 4,500	900 - 1,500	1,000 - 1,900	6,000 - 10,000
Greece	400 - 600	600 - 800	700 - 1,000	300 - 600	600 - 720	1,500 - 1,800
Hungary	450 - 760	800 - 1,500	1,200 - 1,800	380 - 450	600 - 720	1,050 - 1,400
Italy	600 - 800	800 - 1,800	1,500 - 2,500	600 - 800	1,200 - 1,600	2,000 - 3,000
Luxembourg	800 - 10,000	5,000 - 65,000	20,000 - 75,000	4,000 - 13,000	8,000 - 25,000	30,000 - 3m
Malta	75 - 100	130 - 300	150 - 400	75 - 150	150 - 200	5,000 - 6,000
Netherlands	2,000 - 3,000	6,000 - 7,000	2,500 - 5,000	1,000 - 1,500	3,000 - 5,000	5,000 - 100,000
Norway	500 - 700	2,500 - 5,000	3,000 - 4,000	500 - 600	1,000 - 3,000	4,000 - 5,000
Poland	1,200 - 2,400	2,500 - 3,000	700 - 1,500	200 - 500	500 - 2,500	1,500 - 1,200
Portugal	300 - 400	500 - 700	900 - 1,200	150 - 300	480 - 600	8,000 - 15,000
Romania	1,500 - 2,500	1,500 - 5,000	15,000 - 46,000	3,000 - 10,000	5,000 - 15,000	1,000 - 1,800
Slovakia	1,400 - 4,000	2,500 - 5,000	6,500 - 12,000	1,000 - 2,500	500 - 4,500	1,000 - 1,500
Spain	1,500 - 2,400	2,500 - 5,000	8,000 - 10,000	1,000 - 2,500	2,000 - 4,000	4,000 - 20,000
Sweden			5,000 - 7,000	1,500 - 2,000	1,500 - 4,000	5,000 - 10,000
Turkey	10,000 - 25,000	20,000 - 20,000	20,000 - 120,000	3,000 - 20,000	15,000 - 35,000	10,000 - 3m
United Kingdom						

ASIA AND AUSTRALASIA

COUNTRY	LIGHT ENTERTAINMENT (US$ per half hour)	DRAMA (US$ per hour)	TV MOVIES (US$ per film)	CHILDREN'S (US$ per half hour)	DOCUMENTARIES (US$ per hour)	FEATURE FILM (US$ per film)
Australia (ABC)	7,000 - 11,000	15,000 - 38,000	23,000 - 35,000	2,300 - 5,000	5,000 - 11,000	15,000 - 50,000
Australia (commercial)	6,000 - 9,000	15,000 - 38,000	40,000 - 100,000	2,300 - 4,000	5,000 - 19,000	100,000 - 350,000
Australia (SBS)	1,850	3,285	5,475	1,643	3,285	5,475
Bangladesh	75 - 100	200 - 350	350	70 - 130	220 - 270	400 - 900
Brunei	163	500	600 - 800	230	500	1,000 - 2,000
Burma	150 - 300	250 - 350	300 - 350	150 - 300	300 - 800	350 - 800
China (national)	750 - 1,000	1,500 - 2,000	2,000 - 3,000	500 - 1,000	1,000 - 3,000	3,000 - 5,000
Hong Kong	500 - 700	1,500 - 2,400	3,000 - 5,000	500 - 1,000	1,400 - 4,000	10,000 - 100,000
India	1,500 - 2,000	3,000 - 4,000	3,000 - 4,000	1,000 - 1,500	1,200 - 2,000	1,000 - 10,000
Indonesia	600 - 1,000	1,000 - 1,600	1,500 - 3,000	500 - 700	170 - 1,500	500 - 2,500
Japan (NHK)	10,000 - 25,000	10,000 - 50,000	20,000 - 100,000	10,000 - 15,000	10,000 - 40,000	10,000 - 2m
Japan (commercial)	10,000 - 25,000	10,000 - 50,000	35,000 - 170,000	5,000 - 20,000	10,000 - 70,000	4,000 - 6,000
Malaysia	150 - 175	300 - 350	700 - 900	100 - 150	125 - 200	900 - 1,500
Nepal	500 - 1,000	1,500 - 2,600	1,800 - 4,000	700 - 1,200	400 - 2,500	4,000 - 6,000
New Zealand	750 - 1,500	1,600 - 4,000	1,000 - 5,000	400 - 750	1,150 - 3,000	4,500 - 22,000
Pakistan	350 - 500	750 - 1,000	750 - 1,200	200 - 375	375 - 870	500 - 1,500
Philippines	700 - 1,000	2,500 - 5,000	2,500 - 6,000	500 - 1,100	500 - 1,500	3,000 - 10,000
Singapore	800 - 1,000	800 - 1,200	1,500 - 2,400	400 - 1,000	750 - 1,000	2,000 - 3,000
South Korea	800 - 1,500	2,000 - 4,000	3,000 - 8,000	800 - 1,200	1,000 - 5,000	10,000 - 60,000
Sri Lanka	150 - 300	300 - 850	500 - 750	200 - 300	280 - 300	450 - 1,000
Taiwan	500 - 2,000	2,500 - 5,000	2,000 - 3,000	500 - 600	500 - 3,000	3,000 - 30,000
Thailand	300 - 600	600 - 2,000	1,200 - 2,400	350 - 800	500 - 2,000	2,000 - 15,000

AFRICA

COUNTRY	NON-FEATURE (US $ per hour)	FEATURE (US $ per film)
Algeria	250 - 830	750 - 1,300
Angola	650	750 - 1,300
Bophuthatswana	600	1,200
Ethiopia	200 - 400	200 - 400
Kenya	200 - 450	400
Gabon	300 - 800	300 - 1,500
Mauritius	200 - 220	200 - 400
Morocco	400 - 830	500 - 1,000
Namibia	300 - 500	600 - 1,000
Nigeria	1,000 - 2,000	1,000 - 4,000
Seychelles	150 - 200	200 - 350
South Africa	4,000 - 10,000	4,000 - 10,000
Swaziland	200 - 250	300 - 600
Tunisia	500 - 700	800 - 1,200
Zambia	200 - 350	250 - 600
Zimbabwe	250 - 300	250 - 500

MIDDLE EAST

COUNTRY	NON-FEATURE (US $ per hour)	FEATURE (US $ per film)
Bahrain	450 - 600	1,000 - 1,200
Dubai	600 - 1,000	1,000 - 1,500
Egypt	700 - 1,300	1,750 - 2,500
Iran	600 - 1,500	2,000 - 2,500
Iraq	500 - 1,000	1,200 - 2,000
Israel	1,000 - 2,000	1,200 - 4,000
Jordan	650 - 750	1,000 - 2,000
Kuwait	900 - 1,000	1,750 - 2,000
Lebanon	300 - 900	800 - 900
Oman	600 - 700	1,400 - 1,600
Qatar	700 - 750	1,400 - 1,600
Saudi Arabia	1,000 - 1,400	2,000 - 3,500
Syria	350 - 650	250 - 1,250
Abu Dhabi	550 - 750	1,400 - 1,600

CARIBBEAN

COUNTRY	NON-FEATURE (US $ per hour)	FEATURE (US $ per film)
Bahamas	200 - 240	280 - 300
Barbados	220 - 230	200 - 500
Bermuda	70 - 85	180
Cuba	30 - 80	50 - 100
Haiti	160 - 200	50 - 200
Jamaica	200 - 240	350 - 450
Netherlands Antilles	110 - 200	150 - 300
Trinidad and Tobago	250 - 325	200 - 500
St. Lucia	75 - 100	100 - 150
Dominica	40 - 80	80 - 100

SAMPLE MUSIC CUE SHEET

Page:_____ of _____
Date:_____
Series:_____ Program Length:_____ Contract Number:_____
Program Title:_____
Contact Name:_____
Phone Number:_____
Address:_____
_____

	Music Title	Usage/Length	Composer	Publisher	Lyricist	Copyright Proprietor	Performance Rights Society
1							
2							
3							
4							
5							
6							

CODES:	**USAGE**	**PERFORMANCE RIGHTS**
	1 Background	1 ASCAP
	2 Feature	2 BMI
	3 Theme	3 SESAC
	4 Concert	4 Public Domain
		5 Other *(please specify)*

JOE BERLINGER

Filmmaker Joe Berlinger is the president and executive producer of Creative Thinking International, Ltd., the nonfiction film company that he and partner Bruce Sinofsky started in 1991. The filmmaking team's first collaboration was *Outrageous Taxi Stories*, a cult favorite on the international festival circuit, which Berlinger directed and produced and Sinofsky edited. Their next major collaboration was *Brother's Keeper*, which they jointly produced, directed, and edited. The film was self-distributed theatrically by the filmmaking team, earning more than $1.5 million at the box office. *Brother's Keeper* was named 1992's Best Documentary by the Director's Guild of America, the New York Film Critics Circle, and the National Board of Review. Other major awards include the 1992 Sundance Film Festival Audience Award. Later the film was broadcast on PBS's *American Playhouse* series, as well as in seventeen countries worldwide. Most recently, Berlinger and Sinofsky completed *The Begging Game*, an hour-long film about the lives of New York City panhandlers. The film was broadcast on PBS's *Frontline* series. They are currently in post-production on a feature-length nonfiction film for HBO, to be broadcast in late 1995, followed by a theatrical release in early 1996. The pair has also directed numerous television commercials for such clients as Kodak, Wal-Mart, Nuprin, and the Partnership for a Drug-Free America.

CHRISTINA CRATON AND TIM SCHWAB

Christina Craton and Tim Schwab are independent media moguls based in rural South Dakota, where they share a home and studio with Buddy the Wonder Dog and two spoiled cats. Their films have won more than a dozen national and international awards, been featured at screenings throughout North America and Europe, and broadcast nationally on PBS and the Discovery Channel. They are active in free-speech and environmental causes, the New Day Films Co-op, and are currently working on a half-hour film, *The Burning Barrel*, for the Independent Television Service (ITVS).

MICHAEL FOX

Michael Fox is based in San Francisco and writes about film and television for *The Independent*, the *San Francisco Chronicle*, *SF Weekly*, *Film/Tape World,* and numerous other publications.

ROBERT I. FREEDMAN

Bob Freedman has been practicing entertainment law in New York City since 1967. He is a senior partner at Leavy Rosensweig & Hyman with an emphasis on film and television. He has authored the leading legal text on television contracts, *Entertainment Industry Contracts—Television*, published by Matthew Bender, and has lectured extensively on legal and business matters in film and television. He represents independent producers, institutional clients, and individual producers, directors, writers, composers, and performers. Bob has represented AIVF/FIVF since 1978.

SUZANNE STENSON HARMON

Suzanne Stenson Harmon is outreach coordinator at the Independent Television Service (ITVS), where she has worked since 1992. In this capacity, she has created or implemented innovative broadcast outreach strategies in print or online for many ITVS programs including *Stolen Moments: Red Hot + Cool* (with the AIDS service community), *The Ride* (with teen and family service providers), *The Uprising Of '34* (with history and labor activists), *Positive: Life With HIV* (with people living with HIV/AIDS), *When Billy Broke His Head...* (with the disability community) and *The United States of Poetry* (with poets, performance organizations, adult and youth literacy specialists, and arts advocates). A native of Iowa, Suzanne was initiated into activism and advocacy in Boston and Minneapolis as a contractor or staffer for more than sixty issue-based campaigns and candidates for office. She is also the mother of a media-savvy five year old.

KATE HORSFIELD

Kate Horsfield was a founding director and is currently the executive director of the Video Data Bank at the School of the Art Institute of Chicago. She is also on the board of the Independent Television Service and is president of the Lyn Blumenthal Fund for Independent Video. Horsfield has produced more than 120 video interviews with artists such as Louise Bourgeois, Sol LeWitt, Lee Krasner, and Joseph Beuys. She produced *Video Against AIDS*, a collection of videotapes that challenged the mainstream media's coverage of AIDS, and she is currently producing a fourteen-hour collection of video called *A Survey of Video Art: The First Decade*. Horsfield collaborated with Nereyda Garcia Ferraz and Branda Miller on the hour-long documentary, *Ana Mendieta: Fuego de Tierra*.

KAREN LARSEN

Karen Larsen has her own public relations firm in San Francisco specializing in publicizing independent feature and documentary films, film festivals, and special events. She is currently publicist for the Mill Valley Film Festival, the San Francisco International Lesbian & Gay Film Festival, the Asian American Film Festival, the Film Arts Festival, and *The Living Room Festival* on KQED television. She serves as a consultant to the National Educational Media Network and to many independent filmmakers. She handles local publicity campaigns for Sony Pictures Classics, Kino, First Run Features, Zeitgeist, and other distributors. She has taught classes at Media Alliance, Film Arts Foundation, and the National Educational Media Network.

JULIE MACKAMAN

Julie Mackaman is a freelance writer and consultant to independent producers and non-profit organizations. For twelve years, Mackaman was co-director and development director of the San Francisco-based Film Arts Foundation, a regional organization of more than three thousand independent producers. She was a founding member of both the National Coalition of Independent Public Broadcasting Producers and the Association of California Independent Public Television Producers.

ERICKA MARKMAN

Ericka Markman is president of Markman Media, a Washington, D.C.-based consulting firm that specializes in non-theatrical video marketing. Her clients include Time-Life Video, Pyramid Film & Video, and National Video Resources. She currently manages National Geographic Television's educational video business. Formerly she served as director of marketing and distribution for the Annenberg/CPB Video Collection and as development director for the PBS American poetry series *Voices & Visions*. Ms. Markman holds an MBA and a masters degree in education from Stanford University.

MARC MAUCERI

Originally from Oregon, Marc Mauceri attended New York University's Tisch School of the Arts, and received an undergraduate degree in film/television. He worked as an assistant producer and assistant editor on a few documentaries, notably *Blood In The Face*, a controversial look at the militant right wing in America. In 1988 he joined First Run Features, an independent distributor, and since 1990 has headed their theatrical division. He also coordinates marketing and acquisitions for the company. Mauceri lives and works in New York City.

PETER MOORE

Peter Moore is a Berkeley, California-based film person and cook who has been involved in the exhibition and distribution of American independent film for twenty years. He currently performs a variety of tasks for the Castro Theater, the Film Arts Foundation, and the Pacific Film Archive.

DAVID ROSEN

David Rosen is managing director of Praxis, a new-business development firm specializing in CD-ROM multimedia, online service, and interactive television. Praxis clients include Home Box Office, Fujitsu, Bell South, KQED/San Francisco, Consumers Union, and the Benton Foundation. He was previously Commodore International's marketing director, responsible for the worldwide introduction of the first consumer CD-ROM system of players, titles, and accessories. He is also author of *Off-Hollywood: The Making & Marketing of Independent Films* (Grove), sponsored by the Sundance Institute and Independent Feature Project.

LAWRENCE SAPADIN

Lawrence Sapadin, an attorney and media consultant, is currently vice president for business affairs at Unapix Entertainment, Inc., a home video and television distribution company based in New York City. Sapadin has served as managing director of the public television series *P.O.V.*, executive director of the Association of Independent Video and Filmmakers (AIVF), and was founding president and chairman of the Independent Television Service (ITVS).

MILOS STEHLIK

Milos Stehlik is the director of Facets Multimedia, a Chicago-based media arts center he co-founded in 1975. In addition to an active exhibition program that includes screenings of independent and foreign films and producing the Chicago International Children's Film Festival, Facets is a pioneer in the distribution of foreign and independent film and video to home video markets. The Facets Video catalog includes more than 24,000 videos, laser discs, and CD-ROMs, distributed to both stores and directly to consumers. Facets Video is also a video label that has released 150 exclusively licensed titles including the work of many American independents, ranging from features to documentaries and experimental work.

NANCY WALZOG

Nancy Walzog is the founder and president of Tapestry International, Ltd., a New York-based production and distribution company specializing in quality programming for the foreign and domestic television, video, and multimedia markets. Tapestry distributes independently produced films as well as signature series on PBS such as *Nova*, *The American Experience*, and *Great Performances*. Her clients include the BBC, ZDF, Channel 4, HBO, Showtime, Swedish TV, NHK, and La Sept/ARTE. Walzog holds a film degree from NYU's Tisch School of the Arts as well as an MBA in Management from Pace University's Executive Program.

MORRIE WARSHAWSKI

Morrie Warshawski is a writer and a holistic arts consultant. He is the former executive director of both Bay Area Video Coalition (San Francisco) and The Media Project, Inc. (Portland, Oregon). In more than twenty years in the arts he has advised dozens of individual media artists on career development and fundraising issues; served on many grantmaking panels; and consulted with numerous agencies on topics ranging from long range planning to board development. His clients have included The MacArthur Foundation, The National Endowment for the Arts, New Orleans Video Access Center, South Carolina Arts Council, and many others. He is the author of a popular book on fundraising, *Shaking the Money Tree: How to Get Grants and Donations for Film and Video* (Wiese Books, Los Angeles). His feature articles and poems have appeared in magazines and newspapers throughout the US.

DEBRA ZIMMERMAN

Debra Zimmerman has been executive director of Women Make Movies since 1983. During her tenure, Women Make Make Movies has grown into the largest distributor of media by and about women in North America, with a collection of more than 350 internationally recognized films and videotapes. She has curated and organized video and film exhibitions for numerous organizations, including the American Film Institute and the International Center for Contemporary Arts in London. Zimmerman has lectured on women's media and the distribution of independent film and video throughout the world, most recently in Japan, Finland, and Brazil. She is also the associate producer of *Why Women Stay*, a video documentary on battered women, and is currently president of the board of directors of the Association of Independent Video and Filmmakers.

THE ASSOCIATION OF
INDEPENDENT VIDEO & FILMMAKERS

Diverse, committed, opinionated, and fiercely independent—these are the video and filmmakers who are members of AIVF. Documentary and feature filmmakers, animators, experimentalists, distributors, educators, students, curators—all concerned that their work make a difference—find the Association of Independent Video and Filmmakers, the national service organization for independent producers, vital to their professional lives. Whether it's our magazine, *The Independent Film & Video Monthly,* or the organization raising its collective voice to advocate for important issues, AIVF preserves your independence while letting you know you're not alone.

AIVF helps you save time and money as well. You'll find you can spend more of your time (and less of your money) on what you do best—getting your work made and seen. To succeed as an independent today, you need a wealth of resources, strong connections, and the best information available. So join with more than 5,000 other independents who rely on AIVF to help them succeed.

JOIN AIVF TODAY!
Here's what
membership offers:

THE INDEPENDENT FILM & VIDEO MONTHLY

Membership provides you with a year's subscription to *The Independent.* Thought-provoking features, news, and regular columns on business, technical, and legal matters. Plus festival listings, funding deadlines, exhibi-

tion venues, and announcements of member activities and new programs and services. Special issues highlight regional activity and focus on subjects including media education and the new technologies.

INSURANCE

Members are eligible to purchase discounted personal and production insurance plans through AIVF suppliers. A wide range of health insurance options are available, as well as special liability, E&O, and production plans tailored for the needs of low-budget mediamakers.

TRADE DISCOUNTS

A growing list of businesses across the country offer AIVF members discounts on equipment and auto rentals, film processing, transfers, editing, and other production necessities. Plus long-distance and overnight courier services are available at special rates for AIVF members from national companies. In New York, members receive discounted rates at two hotels to make attendance at our programs and other important events more convenient.

CONFERENCE/SCREENING ROOM

AIVF's new office has a low-cost facility for members to hold meetings and small private screenings of work for friends, distributors, programmers, funders, and producers.

INFORMATION

We distribute a series of publications on financing, funding, distribution, and production; members receive dis-

counts on selected titles. AIVF's staff also can provide information about distributors, festivals, and general information pertinent to your needs. Our library houses information on everything from distributors to sample contracts to budgets.

WORKSHOPS, PANELS, AND SEMINARS

Members get discounts on events covering the whole spectrum of current issues and concerns affecting the field, ranging from business and aesthetic to technical and political topics. Plus members-only evenings with festival directors, producers, distributors, cable programmers, and funders.

ADVOCACY

Members receive periodic advocacy alerts, with updates on important legislative issues affecting the independent field and mobilization for collective action.

COMMUNITY

AIVF sponsors monthly member gettogethers in cities across the country; call the office for the one nearest you. Plus members are carrying on active dialogue online—creating a "virtual community" for independents to share information, resources, and ideas. Another way to reach fellow independents to let them know about your screenings, business services, and other announcements is by renting our mailing list, available at a discount to members.

MEMBERSHIP CATEGORIES

Individual/Student Membership

Year's subscription to *The Independent* ● Access to all plans and discounts ●
Festival/ Distribution/Library services ● Information Services ● Discounted
admission to seminars ● Book discounts ● Advocacy action alerts ●
Eligibility to vote and run for board of directors

Supporting Membership

All the above for two individuals at one address, with 1 subscription to
The Independent

Non-profit Organizational/Business & Industry Membership

All the above benefits, except access to health insurance plans ● 2 copies of
The Independent ● 1 free FIVF-published book per year ● Complimentary bulk
shipments of *The Independent* to conferences, festivals, and other special events
● Special mention in *The Independent* ● Representative may vote and run for
board of directors

Library Subscription

Year's subscription to *The Independent* only

JOIN AIVF TODAY!

Membership Rates

- ❏ $25/student (enclose copy of student ID)
- ❏ $45/individual
- ❏ $75/supporting
- ❏ $75/library subscription
- ❏ $100/non-profit organization
- ❏ $150/business & industry
- ❏ Magazines are mailed Second-class;
  add $20 for First class mailing

Foreign Mailing Rates

- ❏ *Surface mail*
  (incl. Canada & Mexico) - Add $10
- ❏ *Air mail*
  —Canada, Mexico, Western Hemisphere-
    Add $20
  —Europe - Add $40
  —Asia, Pacific Rim, Africa - Add $50

Name(s) _____

Organization _____

Address _____

City _____

State _____ ZIP _____

Country _____

Weekday tel. _____

Fax _____

$_____ Membership cost
$_____ Mailing costs (if applicable)
$_____ Contribution to FIVF
(make separate tax-deductible check payable to FIVF)

$_____ Total amount enclosed (check or money order)

Or please bill my ❏ Visa ❏ MC

Acct # _____

Exp. date ❏❏ ❏❏

Signature _____

AIVF, 304 Hudson Street, New York, NY 10013 ● tel: 212.807.1400; fax: 212.463.8519